Thomas Wharton Collens

**Humanics**

Thomas Wharton Collens

**Humanics**

ISBN/EAN: 9783337368173

Printed in Europe, USA, Canada, Australia, Japan

Cover: Foto ©Andreas Hilbeck / pixelio.de

More available books at **www.hansebooks.com**

BY

# T. WHARTON COLLINS, ESQ.,

PROFESSOR OF "POLITICAL PHILOSOPHY," UNIVERSITY OF LOUISIANA, EX-PRESIDING
JUDGE CITY COURT OF NEW ORLEANS, ETC.

"The proper study of mankind is Man."

NEW YORK:
D. APPLETON AND COMPANY,
346 & 348 BROADWAY.
LONDON: 16 LITTLE BRITAIN.
1860.

# CONTENTS.

|  | PAGE |
|---|---|
| PROLOGUE, | 1 |
| VITALITY, | 15 |
| SENSATION, | 69 |
| EMOTION, | 110 |
| THOUGHT, | 173 |
| ACTION, | 328 |
| RETROSPECT, | 353 |

$$
\text{MAN IS} \begin{cases}
\text{Vegetality or} \begin{cases}
\begin{rcases}
\text{Existence} \\
\text{Alimentiveness} \\
\text{Approbativeness} \\
\text{Cautiousness} \\
\text{Combativeness} \\
\text{Secretiveness} \\
\text{Acquisitiveness} \\
\text{Destructiveness} \\
\text{Philoprogenitiveness} \\
\text{Inhabitiveness} \\
\text{Adhesiveness} \\
\text{Constancy} \\
\text{Amativeness} \\
\text{Constructiveness}
\end{rcases} \text{Vitativeness or Selfishness} \\
\end{cases} \\
\text{Animality or} \begin{cases}
\begin{rcases}
\text{Motion} \\
\text{Weight} \\
\text{Resistance} \\
\text{Change} \\
\text{Connection}
\end{rcases} \text{Causality, Eventuality} \\
\begin{rcases}
\text{Substance} \\
\text{Extension} \\
\text{Locality} \\
\text{Form} \\
\text{Severalty}
\end{rcases} \text{Comparison} \\
\begin{rcases}
\text{Quality} \\
\text{Density} \\
\text{Savor} \\
\text{Color, \&c.} \\
\text{Sound and Tune} \\
\text{Odor}
\end{rcases} \text{Individuality}
\end{cases} \\
\text{Humanality or} \begin{cases}
\begin{rcases}
\text{Hope} \\
\text{Watchfulness} \\
\text{Conscientiousness} \\
\text{Firmness} \\
\text{Intent}
\end{rcases} \text{Truth} \\
\begin{rcases}
\text{Faith} \\
\text{Veneration} \\
\text{Marvellousness} \\
\text{Sublimity} \\
\text{Ideality}
\end{rcases} \text{Beauty} \\
\begin{rcases}
\text{Charity} \\
\text{Imitation} \\
\text{Sympathy} \\
\text{Joyousness} \\
\text{Language}
\end{rcases} \text{Morality} \\
\begin{rcases}
\text{Quantity} \\
\text{Relation} \\
\text{Mode} \\
\text{Order} \\
\text{Progress}
\end{rcases} \text{Utility}
\end{cases}
\end{cases}
$$

displaying **LIBERTY AND NECESSITY**

$$
\begin{cases}
\text{Science} \begin{cases}
\text{of Nature} \\
\text{of Self} \\
\text{of Society} \\
\text{of the Soul} \\
\text{of God}
\end{cases} \\
\text{Action} \begin{cases}
\text{in Arts} \\
\text{in Economy} \\
\text{in Politics} \\
\text{in Morals} \\
\text{in Religion}
\end{cases}
\end{cases}
$$

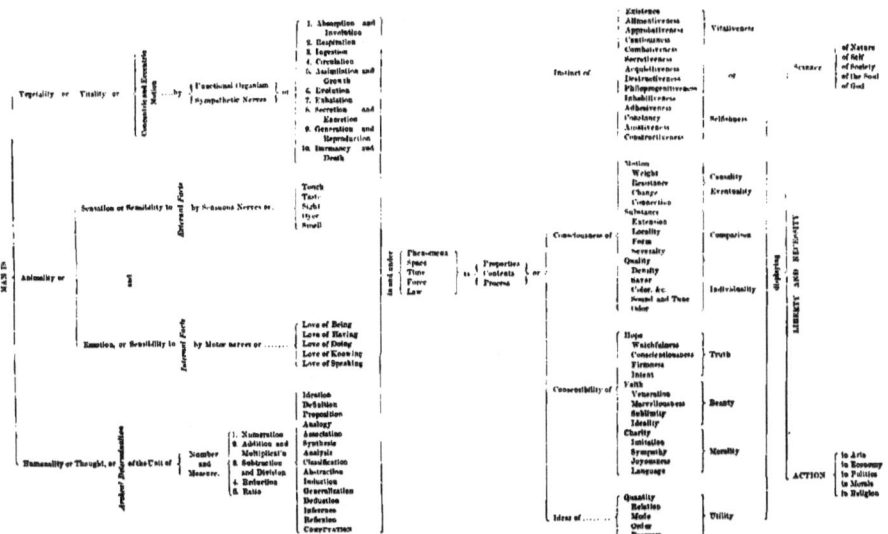

# HUMANICS.

## PROLOGUE.

*"The proper study of mankind is Man."*

At the beginning of European Philosophy, (whether we start from the seven sages, or from Pythagoras,) "Know thyself" was the precept first given in charge to man; and, from that day to this, the injunction has been ever reiterated, and its wisdom has always been admitted.

Has the precept been obeyed? In aspiration it has, if not in realization; for every struggle of philosophy has been to obtain a more distinct conception of human nature and destiny. Indeed, philosophy, from its origin to this day, has been but an effort to solve the problem of man's moral, intellectual, and social constitution—an attempt to make the ethical and rational elements of humanity, when once discovered, subservient to humanity's progress. In reading the books of the founders and expounders of the systems, theories, and schools of philosophy which have been before the world, we find them all devoted mainly to the discussion of man's sensation, sentiment, reason, and action. Every point is investigated: searching and deep analysis, encircling and archcasting synthesis, inventive and fanciful analogy, have been called to the aid of wisdom and genius seeking to know if man is the mere recipient of sensation and impression, or the glorious radiator of a light within. Wherever divergence or contradiction is possible, modified and opposite opinions break forth; and the products are the theories of the Presentationists and Representationists, Unitists and Dualists, Materialists and Idealists, Absolutists and Nihilists.

Thus far, philosophy has hardly dared to assume any other *name* than the one its founder modestly adopted to express a candid confession of incertitude, and a sincere desire of knowledge. The philosopher even at this day contents himself with being designated "a lover of wisdom;" and diffidently asserts the existence of the science of "*Humanics.*"

Yet Humanics should be permitted to erect a school in the field of knowledge; for, if no complete and permanent edifice can as yet be raised, sufficient materials are nevertheless on hand to begin the work of constructing a "Science of Human Nature."

But if we erect Humanics into a science, what would be left to Philosophy?

Much, very much; and indeed a concession of territory to Humanics, instead of injuring Philosophy would leave her in the clear and undisputed possession of her great and legitimate domain; and her true object and supreme scope, heretofore clouded, would plainly appear.

Literally, the word Philosophy means the love of wisdom; but, in its full sense, it means *the science of universal truths ;* and thus the philosopher, who is not too presumptuous, claims the merit of being, at least, *a searcher* of universal truths.

I use the word truth as synonymous with the word fact. If therefore any truth or fact is known which does not pervade all the sciences, it is not comprised within the purview of Philosophy. For instance, the proposition which enunciates that the three angles of a triangle are equal to two right angles, is a truth ranging only through certain sciences and arts, such as Geometry, Astronomy, Mechanics, &c.; but falling short of universality, it does not belong to Philosophy.

I do not mean to say that Philosophy never considers or investigates these limited facts. If it could dispense its adepts from obtaining this kind of knowledge, it would enjoy a privilege which no other science possesses. All the sciences and arts are connected with each other—relate to and run into each other; but when Philosophy examines and expounds limited facts, it does so collaterally and subsidiarily, by way of illustration or proof, to show a dependency upon some unlimited truth, or for the purpose of arriving by induction at some supreme principle.

So far, then, from being independent of all other sciences, Philosophy is the science of sciences; for in order to find the truths which are common to all sciences, it searches through every one of them.

Hence the domain of Philosophy is immense; but it does not absorb Humanics, Logic, Ethics, and Religion. These sciences remain perfectly distinct, so far as they apply facts, limited or universal, to one distinct subject or bearing. These sciences, like every other, deal with many universal truths, borrow many limited facts from kindred sciences; but have also particular facts exclusively their own. The collection of the whole into one synthetical body, forms a separate science which is not to be confounded with Philosophy; for Philosophy claims only such ingredients of Physics, Humanics, Theology, &c., as are applicable to all the sciences, and leaves the rest to its true owners in the ledger of human knowledge.

To give an example in a certain class of sciences: The proposition that "the whole includes a part," is a universal axiom, and belongs to Philosophy; but so far as it is used with one or more lesser facts in demonstrating the laws of number and extension it is a mathematical truth; and the mathematician, in this view, need not trouble himself with the consideration of its universality.

A converse example would be equally demonstrative. It is a fact that the power of water as a motor is in proportion to its height. Now if this fact were found in the case of water only, it would belong exclusively to the science of Hydraulics; but observation extends it to all liquids, also finds that it is a law of every falling body; then that it is the law of weight in general; and finally, that it is resolvable into the great laws of universal gravitation.

If Philosophy in general be viewed only from a single point, and that point be taken as a beginning or pivot of all knowledge, a system arises characterized by a distinctive idiosyncrasy which admits only such facts as adapt themselves to the initial idea. Thus we have Scholastic, Theistical, Skeptical, Sensational, Ideal, Mystical, Eclectical, Positive, and Metaphysical Philosophy; and thus too, each school defines the science to suit its own theory. Here it is the science of the soul, there the science of thought, elsewhere the knowledge of self or of man; with one it is the critique of pure reason, with others the science of the infinite and absolute, with many it is the knowledge of the cause, nature, and principle of things, existence, &c.; and with some it is the doctrine of the origin of ideas.

The definition with which I started, viz., that Philosophy is the science of universal truths, shows that I have attached myself to none of these systems, nor do I exclude any of them. My definition, I consider, escapes the fault which can be imputed to the others, viz., breadth without sufficient precision, or precision without sufficient breadth.

If, for instance, we say: "Philosophy is the science of the causes, principles, and nature of existences and things," we would make it embrace all sciences in their generalities and *in their details;* for, each science is an aggregation of harmonious principles and causes, more or less general, relating to a definite subject. If, on the contrary, we define Philosophy as the science of soul, or of thought, or of man, we confine it to a circle which would seem to be that of Psychology, &c.

On the one side we would invade and take exclusive possession of the dominions of every particular science—so that to write a complete philosophical treatise would be to compose an encyclopedia. On the other hand, if we adopt any one of the above less general definitions, we usurp the place of a few limited sciences and leave the rest out of view.

Thus Philosophy would have no ground of its own, no individual mission.

Now I would fain avoid all this confusion; yet far from starting any new and exclusive system, all I seek, by the definition proposed, is to classify for the sake of clearness, and by this classification to make a fundamental division of Philosophy into two parts. The first I assign to *Universal* Philosophy—the second to *Special* Philosophy, such as the Philosophy of Ethics, Physics, Law, &c.

By this division we may, in a degree, be better able

to know the ground we survey, and more readily know what to do with the materials we gather.

The division of Philosophy into universal and special, tends to induce a search for universal analogies, generalizations, and harmonies; and through the discovery and clear enunciation of general laws, to bring together facts which now appear isolated and disconnected, and thus perhaps reconciling ideas heretofore held to be contradictory.

For example, what two things could appear more disconnected than the fall of an apple and the revolutions of planets? Yet by the mighty grasp of Newton's mind, through a rigorous process of generalization, these two facts are shown to be identical in essence, and assignable to the same universal law.

Before then how many and how unsatisfactory were the theories invented to explain the movements of the planetary system; but the discovery and proof of a universal *fact*, or rather the well-grounded generalization of an infinite variety of apparently independent *facts* under one universal law, removed dissensions, cleared the rubbish of ages from the current of intellectual progress, and allowed it to flow into broader and deeper beds.

Our idea of Philosophy is therefore simply this: it is the searcher and enumerator of universal truths; and, as such, it attends to the classification of science in general.

So when universal truths are considered in themselves and independently of any particular science, or when facts (general or limited) are considered as with reference to any synthetical view of all science, or for the purposes of unlimited generalization, then we are within the purview of Philosophy *proper*, or as I would prefer to term it, " Universal Philosophy."

But should general ideas, or the general connection of all things, or the dependency of each thing upon all things, be considered with reference to any particular science, or should we syncretize the facts of that science so as to reduce them to one or a few primary principles, then we have its especial philosophy. Hence the expressions Philosophy of Language, Mind, Morals, Government, Law, &c.

Now that we have defined Philosophy, and ascertained what really belongs to it, in the apportionment of science, let us resume the subject of Humanics.

Humanics is the science of man.

As with regard to Philosophy, let us be careful not to give greater extension to Humanics than properly belongs to it.

We are apt to look into nature only so far as it concerns or affects us; or, considering all things, from the weed and worm to the stars and sun, as made for man alone, we are prone to view all distinct sciences as mere details of the science of man; but the immensity of creation soon crushes our presumption, and we must dwindle into a limited sphere, contenting ourselves with being—what we really are—a small, but wonderful portion of God's work: high, no doubt, in the scale, yet only a single term of an infinite series.

Hence, recalling the fact that all sciences are connected and dependent upon each other, let us endeavor to mark the place of Humanics. To do this, let us find, if possible, the traits which it does not borrow from any other science or from Universal Philosophy.

Every science bears the impress of our nature; for no science can be framed without calling into service the powers of our physical, moral, and intellectual constitution.

VITALITY and the love of *Self*, or egotism, assert the claims of life and liberty developed in Jurisprudence, Government, &c.

SENSATION and the love of *Truth*, or of reality, gather the concrete and abstract contents of all knowledge.

EMOTION and the love of *Society*, or social feelings, furnish the moral and spiritual motives which prevail in Ethics, Political Economy, &c.

THOUGHT and the sense of *Utility*, give the processes and the forms disclosed by Mathematics, Logic, Æsthetics, &c.

ACTION and the love of *Evolution*, impel to the practical uses of our bodily organization, and to the concrete formation of the Arts, Language, &c.

Every science involves in itself our physical and moral constitution—every art is the work of that constitution. Hence, sciences and arts necessarily conform to human nature itself, and are moulded agreeably to it as their matrix and author; but it is not the province of any science, *except* HUMANICS, to study man in the aggregate, and in every particular, as a distinct or pivotal subject of knowledge.

Indeed, in teaching Mathematics, Logic, Physic, Ethics, Art, &c., the essential elements of humanity from which they arise are only incidentally noted: sometimes all mention of them is entirely omitted.

Thus, it is clear, a place in the classification of knowledge is necessarily marked for the science of *Humanics*. While, without its contributions, the other sciences would be imperfect; and while they all appeal to it for grounds and rationale, they do not singly or together profess to embrace its contents. Hence, Humanics is not only a specific science, but of great dignity and value.

It singles out man from among the Zoological reign, and makes him the subject of especial study. While it analyzes every detail of his organization and essence, it attaches itself principally to his distinguishing characteristics, and seeks to find their synthesis.

Zoology herself sanctions the concession of a distinct place to Humanics; for zoology has found it necessary, even when studying man as a mere animal, to set him apart from all others in a class by himself.

If we considered any science to include, as a part of itself, all that is necessary to its proof or elucidation, then each science would comprise every science. All things are blended, interlinked, seriated, and reciprocal in the scheme of nature. Nothing can be absolutely isolated. Every atom relates to all atoms. Any fact belongs and relates to every other fact. For example, a vein of the body belongs to and depends upon the aggregate circulation of the blood. To explain a vein, the whole of anatomy, &c., must be studied.

Hence, if other sciences must appeal to Humanics for proofs and landmarks, Humanics in turn must, for the same purpose, resort to them all.

How then are we to know what properly belongs to Humanics, and what is merely collateral?

Simply by keeping in view *our design*, which is to know *man* as distinguishable from all the rest of animate and inanimate nature.

Every fact, every relation which enables us to do this, must be considered; but the differentia and generalizations, as applicable to man's nature, are alone the property of Humanics.

With this delineation of the scope of our subject, and with this index to the object of our work, it will be impossible to confound Humanics with Philosophy. On the contrary, it seems to me that the distinction drawn, in another part of this prologue, between Special and Universal Philosophy, renders it useless to argue any further to show that the special philosophy of Humanics does not disturb the functions or diminish the sphere of Universal Philosophy. Hence, without further discussion, I refer to what I have already said above, merely adding:

Humanics brings all truth to bear upon man; seeks to prove his title to all that is peculiarly his own; makes him the focus of intellectual vision.

Philosophy, on the contrary, gathers all truth to generalize, independently, upon all existing things; seeks to find the common property of all existences and phenomena; displays the light of an intelligence all over the Universe.

Humanics brings many truths to converge upon man.

Philosophy views all truth as radiating from some grand principle, which man and every thing else must rely.

Hence, Humanics must look into the whole nature of man.

Zoology describes him only so far as he belongs to the series of *sensational* organisms.

Psychology contemplates him only as an *intellectual* being.

Ethics regards him only in his *emotional* character.

Physiology observes him only as the vehicle of *vital* functions.

History depicts him as performing *action*.

But man is not merely sentimental, moral, vital *or* automatic: he is all of these together. Hence it is necessary, in order to know him, to bring back these elements to their common centre, and to reconstitute the human unit.

Let us therefore study each of the constituents: their co-ordination with the whole—their points of connection as a body—their respective reaction as parts of the totality—their combination into a single man.

And thus taking man as sensation, thought, emotion, vitality, and action forming together *one* organism, we proceed to our investigation. This division into—

        1. Vitality,
        2. Sensation,
        3. Emotion,
        4. Thought,
        5. Action,

is the most radical, and withal the most adequate I can find, in the least number of general terms, to comprise all the *phenomena* exhibited by man as an organic entity.

A lesser number would exclude many facts—many realities; so that a portion of the whole truth being omitted, we would often fail to make a just estimate or explanation of whatever we may be striving to solve or expound.

A greater number of parts, we find upon trial, would only give *sub*-divisions of the elements we have stated, obliterate clear marks of distinction, and thus create confusion.

*Vitally* man embodies the conditions and processes of *vegetative* life: he has organs of generation, respiration, secretion, nutrition; and so have plants, and like them he grows, lives, reproduces himself, decays, and dies.

*Sensationally*, man embodies the conditions and processes of *animal* life. Man feels, tastes, smells, hears, and sees; and so do brutes. Like them, he has bones, muscles, nerves, blood, &c. Like them, he is locomotive, &c.

*Emotionally*, man embodies not only the animal propensities, but also human sentiments. On the one side, he is the creature of instinct; on the other, a moral agent. Thus, there is in emotion a link which connects with brute feeling, and another which unites with intelligence.

*Intellectually*, man embodies distinct elements, and becomes essentially himself, finding ground to hope for a total severance of the thread which ties him to matter.

*Actively*, man combines all the elements of organic evolution, Life, Sensation, Emotion, and Thought, for the purposes of Truth, Beauty, Art, and Progress, and constantly vindicates on earth his claims to a Divine Parentage.

Before proceeding, I submit the following table of the view I have taken of man, in this volume:

# I.

## VITALITY.

I BEGIN with this proposition:

The distinction between Vegetable and Animal organization is, that Vegetation *does not*, while Animality *does*, embody SENSATION: their common attribute being VITALITY.

Plants have Vitality.

Animals have Vitality and Sensation.

Man (we note it here in advance) has Vitality, Sensation, and Thought.

This differentia is conceded, tacitly or expressly, by all physiologists, and is *a* primary law of their classification. The moment they detect in any organism, however simple, an apparatus of sensation however embryonic, they give the organism a place in the animal kingdom; but if it is devoid of any medium of sensation, it is conceded to vegetable nature.

The difficulty they meet with, and which I will strive to overcome, is to draw the true demarcation between vital and sensational *acts*. They are embarrassed by some of the active phenomena that seemingly obliterate their line of distinction. In the lower grades of animal life there are organisms which naturalists have hesitated to rank above plants, so incomplete and dull is their sensibility; while some plants are so vital, they seem to exhibit sensation.

Hence they have, in doubtful cases, resorted to a more minute investigation. In the lower varieties of Radiata and Mollusca, Infusoria and Polypi, a number of other conditions proper only to animal life, are found; while in the highest development of sensitive plants—the Mimosa, Venus-Fly-Trap, and others showing tokens of sensibility—every analogy of form and process serves to identify them with vegetable life.

Thus one plurality of signs belongs to vegetation, and another to animality. Each reign has indicia peculiarly its own; and wherever a single phenomenon is *apparently* inconstant, a reference to the multiple index, and to the assemblage of analogies, dispels every doubt. Every item of the index is not, however, found in every individual, yet there are always a sufficient number to make the test conclusive.

The great number of these indicia, and the imperfection of the words used to describe them, make it difficult to frame a summary definition of either class of organisms. *Practically*, however, our knowledge of the marks which belong to one kingdom or to the other, precludes any error. We know from constant experience the peculiar forms and modes of each; and, thus looking upon nature, we never fail to distinguish a plant from an animal.

The certainty and ease with which this is done by means of the multiple index and the sum or assemblage of types found in each individual, has dispensed Philosophers from a strict allotment of the attributes of Vitality, Sensation, and Thought; and they are not clearly separated from one another.

Hence great confusion and doubt arises when we seek to assign certain acts either to life, instinct, or reason.

In a psychological, ethical, religious, humanic point of view, it is important that this confusion and doubt should be made to disappear.

To do this my method is very simple. I will take man as a sum total, subtract from this totality all the phenomena exhibited by vegetation; and these I will class as the attributes of Vitality. Then subtracting all the phenomena exhibited by sub-human animals, I will class their attributes as Sensational; and will assign the clear remainder, if any I find, to Thought—to Humanity.

When this operation is performed, we will then see that we have been too prone to consider *all acts* performed by man as dictated by thought—that when we see a sub-human animal do *any act* that man does, we have been too prone to regard it as the work of intelligence—*that we have not raised instinct in man sufficiently high, whilst we have drawn the inferior limit of* THOUGHT *too low;* thus refusing to life and instinct due credit for much they do for us, and charging thought with deeds to which it never degrades itself.

The certainty with which we can fix the limits of vegetable, animal, and human life *physically*, will enable us to fix the same limits *psychologically*. The physical circle will serve us to ascertain the metaphysical boundaries; and though yielding (to *matter* or to vitality and instinct) all and every act and deed ever done by plant or sub-human animal, there will still remain *a mind* for man alone—a pure and glorious mind which may claim a child-to-father-relationship with God.

Why accept this physical boundary between Vitality, Sensation, and Thought? Why accord to Vitality all and every phenomenon exhibited by Vegetation—to Sensation every *other* phenomenon exhibited by sub-human animals—and leave to man, as his own essential property, the residue only? We answer, simply because the distinction is visible, is dictated by the real and direct state of the case, and has the merit of being the work of Nature's God himself. We have no right to obliterate or disturb the lines drawn in nature. Philosophers profess to base their systems on nature itself—to find in nature the proof of their ideations. Hence they ought not to allow the vagueness and imperfection of language to confuse them; and hence, after once affixing the term "Vitality" or "Life," as entering into the definition of a plant, as being the essential content which distinguishes a plant from inorganic matter, they cannot, when they behold in man any phenomenon, force, process, or act previously observed in plants, attribute these phenomena to any other force or law than that of Vitality. The consistency and plainness of language requires this. If what is merely vital in plants ceases to be so when discovered in man, an insoluble contradiction arises: language no longer enunciates any distinct conception: one thing receives several names, and these names become expressive of ideas suggested by the other terms "Sensation" or "Thought;" and thus the things themselves become confounded or irreconcilable. When we admit, once for all, that every organic action seen in plants *is vital*, no matter how complex and wonderful it may be, we will not be embarrassed to distinguish vital from sensational forces in the acts of animals; and the boundary between vegetable and animal kingdoms, between Vitality and Sensation, will be as plain in philosophy as it is in physiology. Is the shrinking of the mimosa, the motion of the sun-flower, a vital or a sensational phenomena? Philosophy by her definitions of terms has left this doubtful. To solve the doubt, let us try the effect of a positive determination of the extent of each term—let vitality and vegetation embrace the same purview; and, allowing nature to speak for herself, let us hope that she will, in her admirable consistency, enable us to understand man better than we do.

As between Sensation and Thought let us adopt the same rule—let all acts of sub-human animals be yielded to Vitality and Sensation; and let these be the purview of instinct and consciousness in man as well as beast. Is the act of the "Dog of Montargis" wholly sensational, or is it intelligent? If the latter, then where does instinct end and thought begin—then what distinct and exclusive claim can man assert to the immortality of the soul? Is it not plain, that if we do not give away to vitality and sensation, (to their forces and laws,) all that the Dog of Montargis did, the line between Animality and Human nature is effaced, or becomes doubtful, so that instinct and thought could hardly be distinguished.

It is well settled that if we wish to understand ourselves, reason clearly, and be understood by others, we should as much as possible avoid using words in an ambiguous or equivocal sense. Hence, if we sanction the term "intelligent" as applicable to the actions of a Dog, we must be at a loss to find some other term to express the peculiar nature of the superinstinctive acts of man. Even the word rational would not do: for rationality and intelligence import one another. Thus, if we wish to avoid in Humanics, the fallacies of ambiguous middle, &c., so often denounced by scholastic logic, we must cease to designate the actions of sub-human animals, dogs, &c., as "intelligent;" or must restrict the term to the faculty of direct perceptions—to immediate sensation alone. If the term must embrace the tricks of a Fox, as well as the manifestations of God's mind in the Universe, the sooner it is discarded, for obscurity and uncertainty, the better. Rather than cheat ourselves and others by the use of such terms, new terms of exact and limited meaning should be invented. We might, for instance:

  Instead of *Vitality*, say VEGETALITY;
  instead of *Sensation*, &c., say ANIMALITY;
  instead of *Intelligence*, &c., say HUMANALITY;

and place in each of these terms the phenomena peculiar to itself: that is to say, from Humanality exclude all that man has in common with the other animals, and from Animality all that the animals have in common with Plants.

Thus, in the conformity of language with reality, we may harmonize philosophy with nature.

Is it not absurd to attribute to the intelligence of man any of the processes or acts which plants accomplish as thoroughly as he does? Is it not plain that *none* of the evolutions of a plant can be attributed to an intelligence or will of its own?—that a plant's evolutions are involuntary and mechanical?—that the *same* evolutions in man must be also unintelligent and instinctive? It seems very idle to ask such a question; yet it is too true that the neglect to ask it gives place to continual and manifold error, and even to great systems of philosophy. It is because we habitually refer all human action, however involuntary it may appear, to our rational faculty and voluntary powers, that Locke, and Hume, and Condillac, and their successors, have succeeded in establishing their school of "Sensationalism."

For instance, finding that man prefers to eat the fruit of the trees, and never thinks of pasturing on the grass of the fields, they are prone to attribute his choice to reasoned experience, rather than to the instinct which clings the infant to his mother's breast; and thus, having confounded our thought with our instinct, the sensationalist cannot discern any attribute in man which beasts do not also possess.

All the internal or external movements of which plants are capable are phenomena of Vegetality. Every thing a plant does is vital—and nothing else—nothing more.

None will dispute this proposition; but the consequences which it produces are of the greatest importance, and require the close attention of every philosopher.

What are these *movements* of plants? Can plants *do* any thing? Can they do any thing which we are in the habit of attributing to Sensation and Thought?

How much of what we usually accord to Animality or Humanality must we restore to Vegetality? How much of the constitution of man must we set apart as belonging to mere Vegetation? What forces, organs, processes, and acts are common to plants, animals, and men? In fact, when we shall have performed the operation of subtracting these from the sum of man's constituent elements, may it not appear that we have heretofore been confounding the workings of our vegetative organism with the higher display of sensation and thought?

Let us see.

Plants are capable of:
    1st. Absorption and involution of heat, light, and electricity;
    2d. Respiration of aërial gases;
    3d. Ingestion and preparation of aliment;
    4th. Circulation of nutritive elements;
    5th. Assimilation and growth;
    6th. Evolution and radiation of heat, light, and electricity;
    7th. Exhalation of aërial gases;
    8th. Secretion and excretion;
    9th. Generation and reproduction;
    10th. Dormancy and death.

Plants have functions common also to animals, as if a plant were, to that extent, an animal; or, as if an animal were, to that extent, a plant. The plant—1, gathers warmth, &c.; 2, breathes; 3, eats and drinks; 4, bleeds; 5, digests and assimilates; 6, radiates; 7, exhales; 8, sweats; 9, copulates and breeds; 10, sleeps and dies; and, in these respects, plants are alike to animals.

The fact that the plant *eats* and *respires* the very things which animals excrete and exhale, not only furnishes a beautiful example of the economy, equipoise, and co-ordination of nature, but also makes proof of a correspondence of functions in the two kingdoms of the organic world.

On this point, I call attention to the following parallel, which I find at page 141 of Professor Allen's admirable work, "The Philosophy of the Mechanics of Nature:"

"*Antagonistic forces and functions developed by the oppositely modified propagation of the electro-dynamic action of the sun, through the mechanisms of the organs of plants and of the organs of animals.*

"The electro-dynamic action of the sun when propagated through the modifying agency of the organs of—

| PLANTS, | | ANIMALS, | |
|---|---|---|---|
| *Reduces* groupings of atoms of,............. | { Carbon, Oxygen, Hydrogen, Nitrogen, | *Restores* the same atoms of............. | { Carbon, Hydrogen, Oxygen, Nitrogen, |
| *From* their natural fluid inorganic static conditions of............. | { Water, Carb. Acid Gas, Nitrog'n of Air, | *To* their natural fluid inorganic static conditions of............. | { Water, Carb. Acid Gas, Nitrogen, |
| *To* the constrained solid organic static conditions of............. | { Vegetable organic formations; | *From* their constrained solid static conditions of............. | { Vegetable organic formations; |
| and continually sustains these groupings of atoms of vegetable formations in the variously modified conditions of | | and continually sustains these groupings of atoms of animal formations in the variously modified conditions of | |
| Cohesion, as exhibited in................ | { Hemp, Flax, Cotton, &c.; | Cohesion, as exhibited in................ | { Silk, Wool, &c.; |
| Elasticity, do., do., | { India Rubber, Wooden Springs, &c.; | Elasticity, do., do., | { Whalebone, Horn, &c.; |
| Acids, do., do., | { Lemons, Sorrel, &c.; | Acids, do., do., | { Oils, Fat, &c.; |
| Alkalies, do., do., | { Morphine, Strychnine; | Alkalies, do., do., | { Saliva, Gastric Juice; |
| Food, do., do., | { Cereals, Fruits, and Grasses; | Food, do., do., | { Meats, Fishes, &c.; |
| Fuel, do., do., | { Wood, Peat, &c.; | Fuel, do., do., | { Oil, Fats, &c. |

*Developing,*
during the recoil of all these groupings of atoms of both vegetable and animal organic formations to their natural static condition of carbonic acid gas and water, the inorganic reaction popularly recognized as the phenomena of

>   FERMENTATION,
>   COMBUSTION
>   HEAT,
>   LIGHT,
>   ELECTRICITY,
>   STEAM POWER,
>   ANIMAL MOTIVE POWER."

And he should have added, *vegetable* motive power; for we shall show that plants have also MOTION.

The forces which the professor mentions as "antagonistic," are, doubtless, identical, for he describes them under a single term, "the electro-dynamic *action of the sun.*" At any rate, they are harmonic, and reciprocating in their work; and there is a parity in the mechanism of their instruments of production.

I will not extend the limits of this work to repeat what may be found in any work of comparative physiology, in order to show how nature has framed the first germ-cells, or embryonic net-work, for nutrition, respiration, generation, &c., in the plant; and how, by specializations more and more complex and definite, it becomes possible for individual organisms to live without having roots in the ground, and to move from place to place. It may be noted, however, *en passant*, that at the boundary between vegetation and animality, among the zoophytes, for instance, the animal is attached to a root; while, among the zoospores, for instance, the vegetable moves freely in space.

In fact, I may safely assume, on the authority of the best physiologists, that plants have throats, lungs, ducts, pores, intestines, seminal parts, &c.; all the *apparatus* necessary for their rudimentary process of nutrition, respiration, and reproduction; else how could they perform these functions?

Hence, a portion of man's nature is *vegetal*.

On this point there can be no doubt, and discussion would serve to make it more and more evident; for natural history and natural science abound with facts —analogies, seriations, and equations—to exemplify and demonstrate it.

But what of MOTION? Does vegetality import *motion?* Is the force which sustains vegetality productive of *motion?* If it does so, then to what extent are the motions of animals attributable to the principle of vegetality?

These are questions which it is necessary to solve with clearness, in order to disentangle the science of man. Yet these questions have been much neglected; and to this neglect must we assign much of the obscurity and uncertainty of Psychology. While we have been constantly comparing man with the lower animals;

while we do not hesitate to find analogies between him and the insect, the reptile, the fish, the bird, and the beast, we too often omit, and even seem to dread, to extend our comparisons to the herbage and trees which live around us, and which, perpetually for our use, elaborate the breath and bread of organic life. Surely, many a debate upon instinct and volition, voluntary and involuntary action, would have been saved, had the functional *motions* of plants been studied, and had their connatural identity with the functional motions of animals been, at the same time, ascertained.

We should have remembered, that if we move at all, we owe our power of doing so to the *vital* forces within us. The vital forces are, in animals, the *motors* of every functional process; but they work in plants as well as in animals. Plants have the vital force—plants have *life*—they contain *no other* principle of functional, physiological, or organic motion. Hence, if plants exhibit any movement, it must be attributed to the automatic forces of vitality only; and hence, too, the same forces must be capable of producing the same movements in animals as in plants. Hence, all the acts of man of which plants are capable, are the evolutions of his *vegetality;* and, *to that extent*, man's nature is identical with that of vegetation.

*Plants seek the light.*—By an instinct of self-preservation, they always direct their stems towards the points from which they may best obtain the luminous ray necessary to their vitality. They strive to expose the surface of their leaves to the greatest light; that is to say, towards the southern sky. The sun-flower greets the rising orb of day, and follows him in his course. The hedysarum gyrans has movements which vary according to light and shade; for, in the sun light, the central leaflet of its petioles is erect, and, in the shade, or in the night, it is depressed; while, on the other hand, the two lateral leaflets of the petioles have an oscillating motion, which, incessant during both day and night, increases or diminishes in rapidity with the degree of heat, being slower in cold, and quicker in warm weather.

If, in a cellar, we place tuberculous roots, such as potatoes, they will sprout on the side opposite the trap door or window.

Mustel, the naturalist, planted a jessamine vine in a flower-pot; placed the flower-pot in a high box; pierced loop-holes in the sides of the box; carried it into a cellar, which had only one opening to admit the light, and left the vine to grow. It grew TOWARDS *the light;* and came out through the loop-holes on that side. Then he turned the box, so that the loop-holes which had been on the dark side, became exposed to the light, and so that those which had been opposite the window were thrown into darkness. Thereupon, the vine turned its stem, changed the direction of its growth, re-entered the box, then grew across it, and came out again through the loop-holes of the recently illuminated side. Mustel repeated this alternation of light and darkness several times, making a series of loop-holes at each change of position; and the effect continued till the interior of the box became filled with a mat-work of vine.

Was there not an instinctive power in that vine, to thus pursue that light?

*Plants extract (from Water, Air, &c.) the Heat necessary to their preservation and growth.*—The obvious fact that snow at the foot of a tree melts sooner than snow at a distance, proves that plants possess a temperature higher in winter than in summer. That the temperature is lower in summer is equally well proved by the coldness of the fluid which is discharged from many vines and vine-like plants when cut across. These phenomena have been examined with great care by many celebrated naturalists; and the result has been the universal admission that the heat of plants in winter is several degrees higher, and in summer several degrees lower, than that of the external air.

In winter, the temperature of the earth and of the water below its surface, is higher than that of the atmosphere; and, therefore, pump or suck up only the water, &c., they can obtain from the ground below. In summer, the water in the earth is cooler than the air; and the plants, having absorbed it by their roots, evolve it through their stems and leaves, dispensing freshness around us.

To germinate, plants concentrate heat in their seeds and germ-cells—to generate, they collect it in their pistils, stamens, and sperm-cells. During both these processes in plants, the heat is greatest in those parts which perform the function in progress.

"May we not therefore conclude that nature has given to plants the power of *extricating for themselves* an additional supply of caloric, at the important periods of hybernation, germination, and impregnation?"

Let us note, *en passant*, that the organisms of plants (as well as of animals) are varied with, and adapted to, the temperature of the localities in which they are found.

Thus geographers are able to divide the world into regions of altitude, of latitude, and of surface, to which certain plants, animals, and races of men are aboriginal: they class the Proteacea, the Kangaroo, and the Australian in one group—the Banian, the Elephant, and Hindoo in another, &c. Different plants, like different races of men, have their appropriate climates; but climate, as a cause, is not sufficient to explain the varieties; so that the design of God, and the intervention of *his* Wisdom and Will in the distribution of the laws of organic motion and formation must be proclaimed.

*Plants are actually sensible to Electricity.*—It has long been known that Electricity influences the growth of plants. Pouillet's experiments demonstrate that during the process of vegetation, electricity is constantly generated; and this, also, during the process of decomposition. "If a wire be placed in apposition with the bark of a growing plant, and another be passed into the pith, contrary electrical states are indicated, when tested by an electrometer. If platinum wires be passed into the two extremities of a fruit, they will be found to present opposite conditions. In some fruits, as the apple or pear, the stalk is negative and the eye positive, whilst in such as the peach or apricot, the contrary state exists. If a prune be divided equatorially, and the juice be squeezed into two vessels, the portions will in like manner indicate opposite electrical states, although no difference can be perceived in their chemical qualities."

Now, the author from whom I have copied this passage, adds: "*All* that has been said of the effects of vegetation, in producing a disturbance of electric equilibrium, will manifestly apply to the nutritive processes of animals also; and there is no deficiency of indications that such is the case."[*]

Nor does he fail to recite them.

*The respiration* of carbonic acid gas, and the expiration of oxygen and carbon, by vegetation, is too well known to need any description here; but, let it be noted, that the breathing of animals is an *act* or movement as entirely *involuntary* and *automatic* as it is in plants.

[*] Carpenter's Com. Anatomy, p. 462.

Yet it is motion or action in both.

No volition or design of the individual has any thing whatever to do with it. It goes on passively, just as a machine does when supplied with the element of propulsion. Inside the organism, as in a steam engine, there is a chemical force or action which seizes and decomposes the fuel. The only difference is, that in one case the fuel is carried to the furnace by the act of man, and in the other it is supplied by the act of God.

In both cases the instrument, whether machine or organism, vegetable or man, is *unconscious* of its own movement in reducing the aërial gases to their elements. Man may know that he breathes, but his knowledge takes no part in the action. In fact, the breathing of animals goes on *during sleep;* and Buffon very forcibly says:

"A plant is an animal asleep."

Yet, with all this unconsciousness, the leaves (those bronches or lungs of plants) must, to fulfil their functions, be free to assume a suitable position, and *are capable of motion* to place themselves in that necessary position.

The upper surface of a leaf is provided with a tough and glossy cuticle, which serves as a protection to its delicate pores and cells. Now, if we try to change the relative position of the two sides of the leaf, if we place the upper side down, so as to expose the tender parts, soon will we see the leaf turn upon its axis to resume its original and proper attitude, and finally set its sheltering roof again towards the sky, so as to shed the rain and reflect the light. Like the sleeping man who "turns in his bed," the unconscious plant has an instinct to put the body in the best posture for the comfortable play of its organs.

*Plants procure their food.*—It is erroneous to suppose that when a plant is in want of nutriment, it remains passive. On the contrary, it *seeks* its proper food and *takes* it, if within its reach.

If a rose-tree is planted on the verge-line between two different soils, this fertile and that sterile, the roots, as soon as they adhere to the earth, will begin to spread in all directions; but soon those which have entered the sterile ground turn off from their course, as if they had found out that their mates enjoyed better fare. A bend is formed, and the roots grow in the direction of the richer ground. Now, if (to prevent these greedy travellers from interfering with their well-fed neighbors) a ditch is dug on the line of demarcation, the poorly-fed roots will grow first downwards, and then under the ditch, till they reach the more congenial juices they started to obtain.

*Plants drink.*—Who is not familiar with the effects exhibited when the dry ground around plants is moistened from the watering-pot, or by a shower of rain? The thirsty vegetation, with the tiny throats of its roots and epidermis, takes up the liquid boon, and becomes refreshed and invigorated. Call this absorption if you please; but remember that special organs are appropriated to the purpose. The "spongioles" are the organs specially destined for introducing the fluid nutriment into the system. These spongioles are located in the root of the plant, and are beautifully adapted to the object. Many of the lower animals are no better provided, and some (the Actiniform and Alegonian polypes, for instance) receive water by simple transudation. Man also has his *absorbent* vessels operating imperceptibly to him. But it is said the higher animals seek for, find and swallow the water they need. Yea; and so do the higher plants.

"Thus," says the Journal of the Royal Agricultural Society, "it was noticed that when the water of the New River was conveyed through wooden pipes, that if these pipes were carried within thirty yards of trees, the roots would *find the joints* of the pipes, and fill the interior with foxtails of fibres." "It is well known to the Agriculturalist," says the Gardener's Magazine, "that the course of large drains, even at a considerable depth in the ground, is liable to be interrupted by the extension of roots not only from trees, but also from apparently insignificant plants. Thus at Saucethorpe in Lincolnshire, a drain nine feet deep was filled up by the roots of an elm tree which was growing at upwards of fifty yards from the drain." The Magazine cites many other examples, and among the rest: " a lime tree which grew at a distance of about fifteen feet from the shaft of a well, SENT *a single root* through the soil *in a direct line towards a* POINT of the shaft at which there was a small aperture *left by the deficiency of a brick:* this aperture was at a height above the level of the water in the well, but the root having past through it, *divided* into a bush-like mass of fibres which *descended into the water*, and formed a large mass at the bottom of the well." Countless instances, fully as remarkable as this, might be adduced; but it is useless. Every cultivator and botanist knows full well, that plants can and do "go to drink." As the plant cannot remove itself to a new situation, it overcomes this difficulty by an elongation of its radial fibres.

Hundreds of instances parallel to the above might be selected from the natural history of *animals.*

Here is one extracted from a recent number of the "*Scientific American:*"

"FISHES TRAVELLING BY LAND:—Dr. Hancock, in the Zoological Journal, gives a description of a fish called the flat-head hassar, that travels to pools of water when that in which it has resided dries up. Bosc also describes another variety which is found in South Carolina, and, if our memory serves us well, also in Texas, which, like the flat-head, leaves the drying pools in search of others. These fishes, filled with water, travel by night, one with a lizard-like motion, and the other by leaps. The South Carolina and Texas varieties are furnished with a membrane over the mouth, in which they are enabled to carry with them a supply of water to keep their gills moist during their travel. These fishes, guided by some peculiar sense, always travel in a straight line to the nearest water. This they do without the aid of memory, for it has been found that if a tub filled with water is sunk in the ground near one of these pools, which they inhabit, they will, when the pool dries up, move directly toward the tub. Surely this is a wonderful and merciful provision for the preservation of these kind of fishes; for, inhabiting, as they do, only stagnant pools, and that too, in countries subject to long and periodical droughts, their races would, but for this provision, become extinct."

Now, if we attribute the action of the new-born child who instantly begins to suck his mother's breast—the action of the sick dog cropping the herb which makes him vomit—the action of the young duck resorting to the water—the action of the fox dodging and misleading the hunters—the action of the bee and beaver building their cell or dam, to intelligence of any kind, consistent reason would oblige us to confess that the action of plants, in seeking food and drink, is also intelligent; for the two courses of action are essentially alike. We would thus tacitly or expressly admit that plants possess a quantum of intelligence in themselves, sufficient for the uses of their organism; but knowing that such is not the case, that it would be doing violence to language and fact to apply the term "intelligent," to any act or motion of plants, we find it necessary, absolutely necessary *to reverse the case;* and to find in the " vegetative " functions and forces of animals the laws of their action in seeking, selecting, and consuming their food, etc. By this reversion, order at once appears; and the *impulses* of vitality and instinct (in man, as well as in other animals and vegetables) being once known, however complex they may be, as distinct from the *deliberations* of thought, they may then be comprehended.

*Plants copulate and breed.*—To fulfil this function they are capable of movements or acts of great complexity, similar to the movements and acts of animals in the process of fecundation and reproduction; and it is impossible to discover any *essential* difference, in this order of phenomena, between vegetable and animal organisms.

To show this—to show that there is nothing especially animal in the act of generation, but that it is with every functional and sensible motion connected with it, equally vegetative, it is only necessary to make a comparison between the two kingdoms—taking the animal as the pivot of the comparison.

1. Animals have two sexes.

Since more than a century the distinction of gender is known to exist in plants.

2. Some animals are hermaphrodites.

A great number of plants are in the same condition.

3. Some animals (the Helix and other univalves)

have both sexes distinct in each individual, but to be impregnated they require another individual having also this double sex, and the act of conjugation is done by the double pair.

The Mulberry and other Linnæan Monœcia are adapted to this mode of generation.

4. In many classes of animals, and indeed in the greatest number, the individuals are of different and separate sex.

All the Diœcia are in this state; the sexes in this class of plants being not only in separate flowers, but in different individuals.

5. Many animals fecundate by couples, and by *approach* and conjugation.

At the period of fecundation of certain species of confervæ, the two tubes which are the sexual organs of the plant, approach, meet, and intergroove; and then, the male tube ejects a thick, greenish liquid, which enters the female tube and there coagulates; but in time, it breaks the sheath, and comes forth a ready formed, though tiny, plant.

6. The fecundation of many birds, reptiles, &c., consists in mere contact.

So it is with some plants which are reproduced by the mere contact of "germ cells," and "sperm cells."

7. The male among fishes casts its spawn upon the waters; and the current or wave carries it to the eggs the female has left upon the sand.

Similar to this is the well-known fact, that there

are male flowers which cast their pollen into the air, and that the winds convey it to the distant female.

8. Many animals are viviparous, producing a live progeny.

The lilies and other such plants, produce little plants already formed at the moment of birth.

9. Many animals (birds, reptiles, &c.) are viviparous; that is to say, are reproduced by eggs.

The seeds of plants, are really vegetable eggs.

10. Animals in the act of generation evince signs of the most energetic sensibility.

So do plants: the Arum, for instance, evolves a burning heat, and changes color during the process of conjugation.

11. The polypus is multiplied by division.

Plants are reproduced from cuttings.

This parallel might be carried much further; and a volume of details might be adduced to show that the generation of animals and of vegetables should be recognized physiologically as identical phenomena. If the modus varies among animals, it also varies among vegetables; but an essential parity can always be pointed out.

At the same time, I call attention to the fact, that *vegetables move themselves*—perform visible movements to accomplish the generative function.

It is generally known:

That the "stamen" *bends* itself to kiss the "pistil," and impart the "pollen."

That the "spore" *detaches itself*—the "spiral-filiment" *whirls itself* out of its own cell to enter into the "germ cell," or female organ.

That a "capsule" when its seed is ripe, will suddenly *open itself*, curl its palms inwards, and as by a spring cast or *scatter its seeds* to a distance around.

Thus, among animals, when the male chases the female—when he courts her favor—when in heat she gladly yields—the act that takes place must, I contend, be considered as purely automatic, and to be determined by impulse, emotion, instinct. Though the animal may be conscious of these acts, they are none the less involuntary and vegetal; for if they were not due to vegetality alone, and if sensation were requisite, plants, not being possessed of sensation, could not perform them, with such complication as we find revealed by vegetable physiology.

*Plants sleep and die.*—They require sleep to recuperate their vital elements, and they use the forces thus collected to resist with energy the advent of death.

No fact is more fully conceded than the sleep of plants. When night sets in, vitality seems to retire from their periphery; and the greatest number indicate by the drooping position of their leaves, the closing of their flowers, and the suspension of their inhalation of carbonic acid, that they are resting in sleep. Nor is this merely the effect of the absence of light; for it has been ascertained that the leaves of plants kept constantly in the dark, open and close at regular intervals as during sleep. De Candolle tried the effect of artificial light upon them, and often failed to disturb the regularity of the alternation. Some plants, (like Bats, &c.,) sleep during the day and watch at night. Others have their accustomed hours—some go to sleep in the morning or at mid-day, some at midnight, &c. Thus naturalists, by selecting certain flowering plants, whose hours of sleep were different, have been able to compose the celebrated "*Dial of Flora*," which (by the opening and closing of the flowers of each plant in its turn) gives precise indication of the hour of the day or night.

This phenomenon was discovered by Linnæus, under the following circumstances: Having sown some Lotus seed, he watched the progress of the plants, and at last discovered upon one of them two flowers. When evening came he could not find the flowers again, and supposed that some one had plucked them. On the following morning, to his great surprise, he beheld them again, and they once more disappeared at evening. He then examined the plants with care, and saw that at evening the leaflets had approached each other, and thus concealed the flowers from view. Struck by this, he pursued the investigations it suggested; and the sleep of plants became a scientific fact.

The death of plants is, like that of animals, occasioned by every cause which disturbs their organs and functions; and like animals plants are able to resist, within certain limits, the attacks of disturbing agents.

The *calandala arvenisis* folds its leaves at the approach of a tempest. The *Mimosa eburina* lets its foliage hang down as soon as the shadow of a cloud threatens it with rain. Thus these, and other flowers, guard themselves against the weather. When the storm threatens, the movements of plants clearly indicate acts of self-preservation. The *Quinque folia* spreads its golden petals in the form of a tent so as to shed the water, but as soon as the rain ceases, she lifts her petals towards the sky,—the *Umbelliferæ* fold into the form of a cap,—the *Infundibulæ* reverse their funnels toward the ground,—the *Caryophylæ* hang their heads,—in short, every plant seems to foresee the danger, and to *use* the means which nature has provided them with to avoid it.

It is not only against the weather, but against many other accidents that plants are capable of self-protection.

Vine-like plants have *tendrils* which serve them to grasp and hold upon points of support, so that they cannot be thrown down.

The *Dionæa municipala* or Venus fly-trap, can destroy the insects that attack them. Their leaves are provided with double lamina fringed with slender hairs, and spread out like two wings, but which suddenly close as soon as touched by the aggressive insect, which is thus imprisoned and destroyed.

The Chinese *Pitcher Plant*, which grows in dry places, does not waste the water it extracts from the ground, but its leaves are formed in the shape of a pitcher, having a regular lid, and hanging by a tendril, so as to hold the water and preserve it from evaporation, for future use.

The *Mimosa pudica* is so vital, that it is commonly known as the "Sensitive plant," and has been cited as an example to show that plants are capable of sensation; while, on the contrary, it enables us to understand the muscular *contractility* of animals as a phenomena of their Vegetative nature distinct from their nervous or animal sensibility. The pinnated leaves of this plant shrink from the hand, or from any other substance or force which may touch them; and no explanation of this movement will bear examination except that which attributes it to the recoil (automatic though it be) of a self-preservative disposition in the organism.

The *Roots* and other organs of Plants suffer and die under the influence of poison and other uncongenial substances, such as arsenic, corrosive sublimate, opium, chrosine and the like, which produce upon them much the same effects as upon animals; but they are as capable of *rejecting* this injurious matter as they are of *selecting* their proper food. Bonnet and Dutochet proved this by many experiments, in which they used fluids and soils impregnated with a variety of solutions, such as acetate of lead, common salt, &c., and they found that the roots would refuse or throw back all substances unfit for their economy.

### VEGETALITY IN ANIMALITY.

The preceding facts are sufficient, I think, to authorize an attempt to make a more definite division between vegetal and animal nature conjoined, but distinguishable in animals themselves.

It has been contended that an animal is a *reversed* vegetable; that the central organs of the animal are found at the circumference of vegetables; that the intestines of animals have the functions of leaves and roots of animals; that the intestines which are placed *below* the diaphragm of animals to *absorb and deposit* CARBON and *excrete* OXYGEN, correspond with the leaves of plants which are *above* the earth; that the *lungs* of animals and the *roots* of plants, one at the *upper* and the other at the *lower* part, correspond in *absorption* of OXYGEN and *excretion of* CARBON; and so on. Whether this counter-similitude can be traced throughout, even to the process upon Hydrogen and Nitrogen, is unessential to our purpose; for certain it is that the vital organs of animals are *inside* the body, and that therefore they cannot be immediately moved into activity, as those of plants whose vital organs are on the *outside*, and in direct contact with the elements on which they depend for life and activity. Hence, for animals there must be a medium to enable their organs to take in, and inosculate with, those elements. Hence, in order to enable them to communicate with the external world, the organs of respiration, digestion, circulation, generation, &c., in animals are provided with *nerves* which impel those organs to the necessary *acts* of appropriation; but we find upon investigation:

1°. That these necessary motions for appropriation, &c., are not performed by the nerves, but are executed by the MUSCLES—uncontrolled by thought.

2°. That the *Nerves* are only the medium of communication; and so far as the vital functions are concerned, the nerves serving them perform their duty, *independently of the will*, and even of consciousness.

The MUSCULAR TISSUES of the human body are the instruments of its movements—the nervous threads convey the stimulus *to* or *from* the muscles; and this is done sometimes with and sometimes without the dictate of the will.

For all the operations of the vital organs—for all those operations which plants, as well as animals, are known to perform—*the will* (whether instinctive or rational) *has no control*—the whole movement *internally* is purely mechanical; and I hope to show hereafter that even the *external* movements of sub-human animals are only the evolutions of an instinctive-will, however complicated they may be.

The action of *muscle* is accomplished through its power of "*contractility.*" The muscular fibres, when irritated, draw themselves into a condensed form; and, when the stimulus is discontinued, they relax into their normal tonicity. This corresponds with the contraction and relaxation of certain vegetable tissues, (Dionæ, &c.,) of which the component cells, when irritated, produce a movement by means of a similar change of form.

"Contractility" is a property of the muscle itself— "a power belonging to it in virtue of its peculiar structure;"* for numerous experiments have been made upon fibres when separated from nervous connection; and it is well settled their isolation does *not* destroy their energy and mobility. Even a single fibre, when isolated, may (by the aid of a microscope) be seen to contract and relax; and when the severed leg of a Frog or Rabbit has been set in motion by galvanism, and has ceased to move though the galvanism is continued, it will recover its power if allowed *to rest*, and the movement will re-occur during several intermitted trials.

The fibres of each muscle are arranged in the direction in which *it* is destined to act; and while all the muscles exhibit this disposition, a difference in the complexity of threads, gives two kinds of muscle—1°, the *striated*, which act when stimulus is applied by the will through the nerves; and 2°, the *non-striated*, which the will cannot influence.

* Carpenter's Elements of Physiology.

When a single *striated* fibre is touched by any irritating substance, it contracts singly and alone, and does not communicate its motion to any other; but when the stimulus is applied by the will, through the nerves, all the striated fibres composing the muscle will contract simultaneously.

When a *non-striated* fibre is irritated, its contraction will communicate itself to the others successively, so that by a single touch a wave of contraction and relaxation is transmitted in the direction of the length of the muscle.

Thus, it seems, there are active muscles—muscles which move, and yet are purely vegetative; while there are others which, though retaining their vegetality, are modified so as to be roused into action by the signals of animal sensation or the dictates of animal will; and hence we might here draw a line to distinguish the striated fibres as *animalized* muscle, and the non-striated as *vegetative* muscle.

But let us pursue our inquiry into the *independent* ACTIVITY of muscular tissue.

Contractility persists for a time after death, particularly in the limbs of cold-blooded animals, whose respiration, like that of plants, is low. The heart of a Frog will continue to beat many hours after its removal from the body; and the Sturgeon's heart hung up to dry, has been seen to continue beating until the auricle had become so hard as to rustle during its movements.

Contractility exhibits itself when the fibre is touched by any strong chemical or even any solid inert substance. The same result is produced by heat, cold, and electricity.

Nor is contractility the only active power possessed by the unsentient tissues of the body. They have a *selecting* energy, which enables them to seize their appropriate materials in requisite proportion. Their differences of density and contexture—the variety in the proportions of their elements—render it necessary that they should be able to make a proper and measured extrication out of the current of circulation, or that circulation should give to each organ its exact and special due; yet the supply takes place from the common reservoir of chyle, &c., in precise accordance with the necessary quality and quantity.

"Selectility" is, therefore, another *active* and admirable property of the vegetative tissues. It exists, as we have already shown, in plants, and serves more thoroughly to identify the non-striated tissues with vegetation.

Nor is the choice of congenial elements the only evidence of the Selectility of fibrous tissues—the *local* effects and distribution of certain Medicines and Poisons are well known; and are forcible illustrations of this *unconscious discrimination* in the processes of Vitality.

THE NERVOUS SYSTEM, physiologically studied, sustains our views of vegetality in animality.

In fact, there are certain classes of nerves and modes of nervous activity purely mechanical, and entirely foreign to conscious sensibility.

"It is," says Carpenter's Physiology, "easily established by experiment, that the *active* powers of the nervous system reside in the ganglia; and that the *trunks* serve merely as conductors of the influence which is to be propagated towards or from them. If a nervous ganglion is destroyed, all the parts supplied by its nerves are paralyzed, but if a nervous trunk is divided, and then the portion still connected with the ganglion is pinched, sensations are felt; but it is not so when the severed portion of the trunk is irritated, for in this case nothing is felt, but a *motor* influence is communicated to the muscle." Indeed, it is now well settled, by the experiments of Sir C. Bell, that some nerves are purely *sympathetic*, transmitting the stimulus of vegetative functions; that other nerves are purely *motor*, distributing locomotive impulse; that others again are purely *sensitive*, conducting the influences of the external world.

THE SYMPATHETIC NERVES are those appertaining to the organs of absorption, respiration, ingestion, digestion, circulation, assimilation, exhalation, secretion, excretion, and generation, composed, as we have seen, of non-striated muscle, &c. This class of nerves do not belong to the sensorium proper, nor to the brain—they exhibit no sensibility; and thus in due and logical parity do we find the insensitive nerve connected with the insensitive viscera. We say insensitive so far as communication with the brain is concerned; for the feelings of pain or pleasure experienced by the viscera, &c., are only known to the sensorium through the irritation of tissue indirectly affecting the sensory nerves. Hence the term "*sympathetic.*" Under all circumstances these nerves convey no knowledge of the visceral *movements;* for their duty is only to impress the other tissues with feelings of sexual ardor, atmospheric pressure, impeded circulation, necessity of nutrition, &c.; and though they produce a reaction upon the sensitive nerves, they are positively independent of the *motor;* or, in other words, they are *not* controlled by the will.

Hence, in the veiled recesses of our body the wheels, cords, valves, pumps, furnaces, and regulators of heat, electricity, &c., move in harmonious evolutions, and are incessantly at their wonderful work without our help, and without our being able to know what they are doing.

Hence when, in the lower orders of animals, zoospores, mollusca, &c., we behold vital and visible action displayed, though the animal has *no nerves*, or if nerves exist *no senses*, we may at last understand that the movements of organism are the attribute of vitality and not of sensation, for movement takes place without sensation and even without nerves.

The office of sympathetic nerves merits our special attention.

The nerves of sensibility hold towards the sympathetic nerves the same relation as towards the external world.

The sensitive nerves are affected by *external phenomena*, but the senses do not in turn affect or influence outward things.

The sensitive nerves are affected by the *sympathetic nerves*, but the senses do not in turn affect or influence the sympathetic nerves.

The motor system transmits no stimulus or motion to the sympathetic.

Thus we find the circuit to be this: An original stimulus arises in the tissues of vegetative life;—the stomach, lungs, and other viscera, by their own irritation or relaxation: the sympathetic nerves call for nutriment; this call is distributed by the sympathetic nerves to their ganglia and to the spinal cord; here the feeling is at once conveyed to the motor nerves, which immediately impress the muscular fibre with notice to comply with the demands of the viscera; this stimulus imparted to the fibre is perceived by the nerves of sense, and these also join in carrying stimulus to the motors, and in enlightening them in their work. But neither the sensitive nor motor nerves act upon the viscera—they awake the limbs, &c., to *outward* action; to gathering food, or seeking an object of sexual desire.

The circuit passes to the *external world* before it re-enters the viscera in the shape of food, or is re-united in the form of sexual connection.

This leads us to infer that the nerves which appear first in lower orders of animals, are of the *sympathetic* kind. As long as the fibres are so vascular that they can be excited by immediate contact with the elements, they need no nerves—hence certain mollusca have in fact no nerves; but when the first envelope is thick enough to prevent immediate contact, the internal parts require nerves to carry their irritability to the circumference, and induce the contractility of the tunic. Hence we may, with the physiologists, consider a polypus as being *only a stomach*, having its sympathetic nerves to arouse the activity of its cortex for the ingestion of nutriment.

Like vegetality, animality progresses in series of greater and greater complexity of primary organs and the accession of new ones. Every order as it ramifies from its proximate stem presents some peculiar development or superaddition; but the original parts remain, and retain their initial properties. They retain their distinctness so as to afford us additional proof of the multiple nature of man. The vital nerves, for instance, are the only nerves found in the Hydra, an animal consisting only of a stomach; but when in higher animals we find sensitive nerves and members annexed, still the stomach and its nerves retain their distinctness. Its nerves remain so free that the sensitive do not command them. The sensitive nerves which are superadded in the progress of animality, indirectly receive impressions from the sympathetic system, but cannot impart any to it.

Hence, though a starving man may (through moral and intellectual conviction) resist the temptation to steal the food within his reach, yet his organs of nutrition will persist in their demands and provocation. So also with sexual desire, &c.

The natural and spiritual body contend against each other for supremacy over the motor nerves; and too often does the flesh prevail.

The Motor nerves now require our attention. They proceed from the Spinal-cord, Cerebellum, and Medulla Oblongata.

These nerves, though frequently under the direction of the thinking will of man or the instinctive will of animals, are as frequently the mere agents of *unconscious* reaction.

They may be directly influenced by the irritation (not sensation) of the tissues.

Of this fact the proofs are abundant; for many instances of *movement* due to the motor nerves independently of the sensitive, can be cited; and without further preamble I will adduce a few:

1. "If the spinal-cord of a Frog," says Carpenter's General Physiology, " be divided in its back, above

the crural plexus, so as entirely to cut off the nerves of the lower extremities from connection with the brain, the animal loses all voluntary control over these limbs, and no sign of pain is produced by any injury done to them; *but* they are not thereby rendered motionless; for various stimuli applied to the limbs themselves will cause movements in them. Thus, if the skin of the foot be pinched, or if a flame be applied to it, the leg will be violently retracted. Or, if the cloaca be irritated by a probe, the feet will endeavor to push away the instrument. Still, there is *no* reason to believe that the animal *feels* the irritation, or *intends* to execute these movements in order to escape from it; for motions of a similar kind are exhibited by men who have suffered injury of the lower part of the spinal cord, and who are utterly unconscious either of the irritation which their limbs receive or of the actions which they perform."

2. "If the head of a Centipede," says Carpenter, " be cut off whilst it is in motion, the body will continue to move onward by the regular and successive action of the legs as in the natural state; but its movements are always forwards, never backwards. They are carried on, as it were mechanically; and show no direction of object, no avoidance of danger. If the body be opposed in its progress by an obstacle of not more than half of its own height it mounts over it, and moves directly onwards as in its natural state; but if the obstacle be equal to its own height its progress is

arrested; and the cut extremity of the body remains forced up against the opposing substance, *the legs still continuing to move.*"

3. "If again the nervous cords of a Centipede be divided in the middle of the trunk so that the hinder legs are cut off from connection with the cephalic ganglia, they will continue to move, but not in harmony with those of the upper part of the body," &c. "They are still capable of performing reflex movements by the influence of their own ganglia, which may thus continue to propel the body, in opposition to the determination of the animal itself. The case is still more remarkable when a portion of the nervous cord is entirely removed *from the middle* of the trunk; for then 1st, the anterior legs will remain obedient to the animal's control; 2d, the legs of the segments from which the nervous cord is removed are *motionless;* whilst 3d, those of the posterior segments continue to act through the reflex powers of their own ganglia, in a manner which shows that the animal has no power of checking or directing them."

4. "If the head of a Centipede be cut off, and while it remains at rest, some irritating vapor (such as ammonia or muriatic acid) be caused to enter the air tubes on one side of the trunk, the body will be immediately bent in the opposite direction, so as to withdraw itself as much as possible from the influence of the vapor. If the same irritation be then applied on the other side the reverse movement will take place;

and the body may be caused to bend in two or three different curves by bringing the irritating vapor into the neighborhood of different parts of either side. This movement is evidently a reflex one," &c.

5. "Every one knows," says Carpenter, "that the adjustment of the size of the pupil to the amount of light, is effected *without any exertion of the will* on our part, and even without any consciousness that it is taking place. It is performed, too, during profound sleep; when the influence of light upon the retina excites no consciousness of its presence—when no sensation, therefore, is produced by it."

6. "A Dytiscus (a kind of water beetle) having had its cephalic ganglia (or brain) removed, remained motionless so long as it rested on a dry surface, but *when cast into* WATER it executed the usual swimming motions with great energy and rapidity, striking all its comrades to one side by its violence, and persisting in these for more than half an hour."

7. "That the Cerebro-Spinal-Axis is a distinct centre of automatic action, and does not derive its power (as formerly supposed) from the cerebrum, is made evident from a variety of crusiderations. Thus infants are sometimes born without any Cerebrum or Cerebellum; and such have existed for several hours or even days, breathing, crying, sucking, and performing various other movements. The Cerebrum and Cerebellum have been experimentally removed from birds and young mammalia, and all their vital operations have

nevertheless been so regularly performed as to enable them to live for weeks and even months. In the *Amphioxus* we have an example of a completely formed adult animal, in which no rudiment of a cerebrum or cerebellum can be detected."

Dr. Carpenter, with these and thousands of other such facts before him, concludes as follows:

"Hence, all the movements which are performed through the instrumentality of the Cerebro-spinal-system of ganglia and nerves are essentially *automatic;* and their character as Reflex, Instinctive, Emotional, or Voluntary, is entirely dependent upon the nature and seat of the IMPULSES *which respectively originate them.*"

THE SENSORY NERVES are those which convey special sensations of Touch, Taste, Sight, Sound, and Smell to their internal centres, the Sensory Ganglia and Cerebrum.

The sensory ganglia *receive* the influences of the external or objective world.

The cerebrum converges and radiates these influences, resolving them into the phenomena of *consciousness.*

CONSCIOUSNESS is the essential property of the Cerebrum. Hence, as we have seen, the *ablation* of the Cerebrum removes consciousness only; and leaves the sensory nerves and ganglia to their automatic action of receiving the influences of the objective world—resistance, sapidity, light, sound, and order.

In the absence of the cerebrum or of consciousness, the influences received by the sensory nerves and ganglia, act mechanically and directly upon the motor nerves, just as any stimulus acts upon the fibres of a plant or muscle—and the *movements* to which the motor nerves are adapted, are determined in harmony with the special nature of the external impulse. Under *these* circumstances, the animal (we repeat the fact) is not conscious of any feeling, evinces no knowledge of what occurs to or in his organism; yet he lives and moves, and his nerves of sensibility convey propelling forces to the motor nerves to which they are adapted.

The researches of Flourens have settled all this to a certainty.

From all the investigations of the best physiologists of the present time, it may be safely assumed as proved that—

The Cerebrum is the seat and radiator of consciousness, only.

The Cerebellum is the receptacle and distributor of the reactions of consciousness—so that the ablation of the cerebellum only destroys all harmony between consciousness and motion.

The Sensory nerves and ganglia are the receptacle and distributors of impulses from the external world.

The Motor system is the complex instrument of

motion, provoked either directly through the Sensory ganglia, or indirectly through the Cerebrum and Cerebellum.

The Sympathetic System is the mere auxiliary and distributor of vitality.

These fundamental parts being all within one body, and being interwoven, necessarily affect each other mediately or immediately, and it required careful analysis to distinguish their several portions, the links between them, and the course of action of one upon the other; but now that the lines of distinction are drawn, we find that the philosophers of old who thought that sensibility was everywhere, were misled by the universality of movement and of action and re-action. They confounded sensibility and movement, sensibility and consciousness; though the three are clearly distinct.

I have shown that movement takes place without sensibility or consciousness.

I now show that movement takes place through sensibility, but without consciousness.

The facts adduced above to show the results of an ablation of the whole brain, or of a severance of connections between the brain and nerves, are already sufficient to demonstrate the diverseness of sensibility and consciousness; but there are other facts still more direct.

Flourens, the great French physiologist, says, that

when the cerebrum is carefully removed so as not to disturb or injure the other nervous centres, all consciousness is obliterated; but nothing except consciousness ceases. The vital forces and special senses remain active.

Life, with its processes of nutrition, respiration, sleep, &c., continues. Thus, if a Bird be the animal deprived of its cerebrum,

— it maintains and *recovers* its equilibrium,

— it walks when pushed,

— it flies when thrown into the air,

— it sleeps at night, and for that purpose closes its eyes, and puts its head under a wing,

— it eats when food is put into its mouth, but does not go to seek it, &c.

But what is most to our purpose is the fact that the animal remains subjected to the performance of a variety of actions *through the nerves of* SPECIAL SENSE :

— it wakes and opens its eyes when *noise* is made,

— its pupils contract and dilate with the increase and decrease of light,

— it is attracted towards the light, for it moves itself to the illuminated parts of the room,

— it recoils from an offensive smell,

— it resists the ingestion of substances distasteful as food, or adverse to nutrition, &c.

Hence sensibility exists exclusively of consciousness.

Nor does the Cerebellum have any share of consciousness.

If the cerebellum is removed, and the cerebrum is maintained, motion is disturbed, but consciousness is unaffected. The movements consciousness suggests cannot be duly realized when the cerebellum is subtracted. It is then impossible for the animal, though he is perfectly aware of what he ought to do, to co-ordinate his motions, or make them harmonize with the dictates of his will: he loses his balance; his gestures and steps are irregular and imperfect. He moves, but it seems that the nerves of special sense suffer a reaction which disturbs even the direct action they might have upon locomotion, &c.

Hence motion itself is not dependent upon the cerebellum, but only that motion which the consciousness of the cerebrum suggests.

Hence the ablation of the cerebellum only severs and abates the indirect connection which consciousness and motion had with one another.

Hence consciousness subsists unaffected by the ablation of the cerebellum, as long as the cerebrum exists; and while the animal is aware of the disorder of motion caused by the ablation of the cerebellum, he regrets but cannot control that disorder.

Hence consciousness is restricted to the cerebrum alone; and the cerebellum belongs to the motor system, in which it is only the auxiliary servant of the cerebrum.

The phenomenon of an organic or locomotive movement resulting directly from the nerves of special sense and other sensitive ganglia, *without the intervention of the cerebrum,* takes place frequently even when the animal is in full and normal possession of all his cerebral organs, including the cerebrum itself.

Of this kind of motion the following examples are cited from physiologists:

The *start* upon a loud and unexpected sound;

The sudden *closure of the eyes* to the dazzle of light or at the approach of injurious bodies;

The *sneezing* excited by an irritation of the nostril;

The *convulsive laughter* induced by tickling;

The *vomiting* caused by the sight, smell, or taste of something loathsome;

The *yawning* occasioned by ennui, depression of spirits, or imitation;

The *scratching* and handling of self, and the thousand and one changes of position of the body and its members, hands, feet, lips, &c., taking place unattended to by ourselves, though we may be wide awake.

The body seems endowed with *instincts* (apart from any volition) to provide for its own preservation and *comfort.*

Certain it is that we are not simultaneously conscious of nine-tenths of the movements of our limbs; and the fact that consciousness, or its seat the cerebrum, is not necessarily concerned with them, is made perfectly apparent by their taking place during sleep.

Yet, they *do* also take place *while we are awake,*

and we are often perfectly conscious of their occurrence; but we are not thereby to infer that they depend upon, or are necessarily determined by consciousness. Consciousness may *interfere* with them, regulate or stop them; but their causation is not in consciousness: else, how could they occur during sleep, or when unattended to, or in animals having no trace whatever of a cerebrum or cerebellum?

We are conscious of them just as we are conscious of the movements, &c., of *another person, or of a machine* under our control. Their mutations, &c., go on without our intervention, &c.; but our consciousness, judgment, &c., might induce us to intermeddle, or we might choose to refrain.

The acts arising from the medulla oblongata come under this head; so also do those coming out of the spinal cord. Breathing and eating, and even walking, can hardly be considered as being in the direct charge of consciousness.

Hence, says Carpenter's Physiology, " the man who is walking through the streets in a complete revery, unravelling a knotty subject, or working out a mathematical problem, performs the movement of progression, &c., with great regularity. He will avoid obstacles in the line of his path, and he will follow the course he is accustomed to take, though he may have intended to pass along some very different route; and it is not until his attention is recalled to his situation that his train of thought suffers the least intermission, or that *his will* is brought to bear upon his motions."

Hence, a man about to pass along a narrow plank or tree placed across a chasm, *intuitively* throws out his arms to balance himself; and if he pays any attention to the action of his arms, their adaptation of position to the necessities of the case is thereby disturbed : he becomes giddy, and falls.

Hence, too, the *respiratory* movement goes on of itself, and regulates itself; becomes rapid while the body runs or strives, decreases when the body rests, continues while it sleeps—all independently of sensation; and, indeed, it is good that these movements do not depend upon consciousness and attention in us any more than in plants; for they did require our undivided and constant watchfulness; we would not have time for any thing else, not even for sleep, and a moment of forgetfulness, determent, or sleep, would be fatal to life itself.

Hence, too, the *mastication* and *swallowing* of food, though we may be conscious of it, is best accomplished without the interference of our will, or even of our attention. Where is the person who can assert that during his meals he watches and manages these movements intendingly? If any one does this, we simply suggest that he must be a very dull table companion to his family and friends, and that if he were to let automatic instinct chew for him, the work would be better done, and he would have more time to listen, think, and converse.

Now, reverting back to the millions of animals of the classes below the Vertebrata—to the Crustaceæ, Insecta, Archnæidæ, Annulata, Mollusca, Radiata, Entozoa, Acalepha, Polypi, and Infusoria, which have *no cerebrum*, we may safely conclude that they (with certain fishes and other vertebrata which resemble them in this respect) have *no power or gift of consciousness.*

There is no escaping this conclusion, for it is as certain as death that the cerebrum, and the cerebrum alone, is the seat or organ of consciousness.

And nevertheless let it be noted that, by the aid of *unconscious sensation*, they go and come, seek their food, avoid their enemies, and make their dwellings.

They are automatons, and their senses are the levers of mechanical movements performed by the body.

Thus we see that, from the beginning of all organization to its end, (through all the consecutive and branching series of vegetal and animal forms,) vegetative phenomena exhibit themselves with wonderful uniformity of action, and without essential change in the living tissues; so that, in vital properties, the animal is like unto the plant.

To the animal, the nervous systems are added one after the other, and become more and more intricate only to serve the progressive complexity in the evolutions of Vitality.

But Vitality ever retains its distinctive characteristics, answering in the plant and in the animal—in all organic nature, to this definition: Vitality is vegetative activity.

Hence Animality is vegetative activity, with its process of nutrition *reversed*, and a nervous system *inserted*.

The distinction between the two is therefore not in the phenomena of movement, locomotion, contractility, nutrition, respiration, reproduction, and other forms of motion; but it is in a change of the poles of adaptation to the external elements.

What else than this parallelism and agreement, or rather this unity in diversity, could we expect, when we know:

That plants and animals both spring from a germ, known in physiology as the organic germ cell.

They are made up, in toto, of these cells, and every plant or animal is derived from one organic germ cell, which multiples itself to form a complete individual. The cells which originate and make up the animal differ in no obvious particular from those which germinate, increase, and propagate the plant. The great Oak, or the tiny "Red-Snow," on the one hand, and the locomotive Man, or parasite Spongia on the other, are respectively derived from simple germs, identical in typical construction and properties.

In the course of organization these cells undergo a sort of *partial* transformation, whereby one set forms bone, another set forms muscle, and other sets form nerves, skin, hair, &c.; but so far as *motion* is concerned, all the vital functions and the movements of the body are mostly accomplished by tissues composed of cells which have undergone the least alteration from the primary type.

The microcosm of life is the organic germ cell.

### CONCLUSIONS.

I am perhaps too hasty in presenting any conclusion at this stage of our argument; yet I think it already sufficiently apparent:

That, in Zoonomy,

— the share of Vegetality is Life and Motion.

— the share of Animality is Sensation and Consciousness.

That the propelling forces of an organism come directly from the exterior, and impart their energy by immediate contact, or through the nerves of special sense, or they come indirectly from the exterior, and impart their energy by immediate contact with the viscera, or through the sympathetic nerves, to sensibility, &c.

That motion is not evidence of sensation or of consciousness in an organism.

That motion is the property of the fibrous or contractile tissues of an organism.

That locomotion is an evolution of vitality—sensation being only its Sentinel and Beacon.

That motion is *not* a property of the nervous system, which is only the vehicle, but not the *doer* of motion.

That motion is adapted to the ends of life, even without sensation or consciousness.

That motion in Vitality is the harmonization of chemical elements and physical forces, with organic arrangement.

That Life, Vitality, or Vegetality, is the enlarging *vortex*, or concentric motion and distribution, of chemical elements and physical forces upon a predetermined and re-engendering type.

*Inertion instead of Motion is Death;* and diminution instead of enlargement, eccentric instead of concentric motion, dispersion instead of distribution, are the ways of Death.

And I add:

That since the organic types in so many classes, orders, species, and varieties are specific, perpetual, and predetermined—those types must be due to the Grand Archeus of the Universe.

That since the plants and animals themselves do not design or think their vitative movements, that there is a Universal Mind that designs and thinks for them.

And here arises the question yet unanswered, whether, when movements of an organism are induced through *consciousness*, they are automatic or optional, necessary or free.

It is my hope that, in the next discourse, this problem will be solved: at this stage the answer would be premature, and is designedly omitted.

## II.

## SENSATION.

In philosophy, I hold that all questions are questions of fact, all theories are assertions of fact, and all science is knowledge of fact. The whole subject-matter, premises, evidences, and conclusions of science, whether physical, mental, or moral, consists of a series of facts made evident directly by, or through the sensational or the *innate* mind, or indirectly through deduction or induction. So true is this, that upon analyzing any course of reasoning, we will find that every alleged demonstration is a good or bad adaptation of *facts* to one another; and that an argument may be defined as the exhibition of a fact in such terms as to make it apparent that it agrees or disagrees with, belongs to, or is included in another.

Take the metaphysical abstractions of Hegel and his predecessors, the procrustean skepticism of Compte and his predecessors, or the blind mysticism of Jacobi and his predecessors, and you will see (upon close examination) that they profess to deal only with *facts*, to stand only upon facts, and to arrive only at a knowledge of facts. When one school contends that science is wholly mental, and that there is no objective reality, it makes an assertion of fact; when another school insists that all things are material, and that there is no spiritual reality, it makes an assertion of fact; and when a third school teaches that nothing can be proved, and that the creation of truth is instinctive faith alone, it makes an assertion of fact. All the details of these systems, and of those which occupy the ground between them, are assumptions or evidences of particular facts considered as concluding towards the main fact advanced. I fear that mere assertions predominate; and it would be well if the idea of science as containing nought but ascertained facts were applied to the study of philosophy, and particularly to the rationale of Humanics. Suppose that every proposition stated by philosophical writers were noted with the interrogation, *is this a fact?* How many of them upon examination of the proof would remain? Might we not then (endeavoring to achieve a practical result) make an inventory of the general truths, the universal facts, upon which they all agree or have left no doubt? and also might we not subjoin an inventory of the most important propositions upon which they disagree, or which they have left without clear demonstration? This inventory would be of supreme utility; for, by it we would know what were the real conquests of philosophy, and what work it has to do hereafter.

But let not the sense I attach to the word "fact," be misapprehended. We are told by logicians, that facts are the truths resulting from something *done*, and they distinguish facts from *events*, from the *realities of things*, from *ideas*, &c. Thus they say, the action which took place at the death of Cæsar was an *event*, while the death of Cæsar, as having actually taken place, is a *fact*. Thus also they say, a dot, a line, a man, a beast, &c., are not facts; *e. g.* we cannot say that Cæsar was a fact. Nor is "an idea" a fact; for we cannot call our thoughts facts. 'Tis well; let us take all this play upon words as valid discrimination, and what does it amount to? Nothing; for, we do not reason things or conclude things, but *of* things, events, ideas. All our reasoning involves the affirmation or negation of some circumstance, property, or law of matter, mind, action, &c. To do this we must use verbs; and all things are nought to intelligence till some assertion is made of them. Thus we may define fact to be a true assertion; and say that all true assertions are facts. The event *is* happening or *has* happened—God *exists*—nature *is* real—the spirit *liveth*—a point *is* a place in space—the idea *is* well conceived—are all statements of fact. In other words, the moment we put a verb and a noun together we declare a fact; and then, not till then, can any predicate be formed—then, and not till then, can any reasoning take place—then, and not till then, can any science exist. This is so plainly true, that no argument is needed to establish it, and it suffices to appeal to the consciousness of every one in order to demand immediate adhesion to our averment.

We cannot say we have a knowledge of any thing, whether it be matter or motion, idea or substance, body or spirit, till we assert something in relation to it—so that, after all, the whole of philosophy is in facts, and depends upon their correct ascertainment—the whole content of thought is fact, and all correct reasoning depends upon the freedom of that content from what may be called false facts.

Therefore, when we read any philosophical author, we should through all his verbal distinctions, his invention of arbitrary nonentities, his artifices of language, his phantoms of imagination, &c., look constantly to the question: What are the facts? Are they faithfully described with no more and no less than what they really contain? are they properly classed? are they proved or demonstrated? &c. These and similar questions, are the tests of all philosophy; and with such tests no man need be mystified either by the metaphysics of nihilism, the cosmogony of atheism, or the premature hypothesis of spiritualism.

But, to say that the contents of human knowledge consist of *facts*, is not a sufficient solution of the question we started to solve; for we have already found ourselves obliged to allude to facts *assumed* but ultimately disproved, as distinguishable from facts positive and *true;* so that we have not yet found the stand-place of reliance, the initial point of reason, which is to serve as our test between truth and error.

Philosophers have debated much to decide whether our knowledge of things perceived, be *mediate* or *immediate;* and they have made important consequences, one way or the other, depend upon the solution of the question.

Both parties admit the interposition or agency of the instruments of sensation, in the act of perception.

One party contends that this agency of the senses does not preclude us from considering that our knowledge of objects perceived is direct, immediate, or presentative. The other holds that the interposition of sense makes the knowledge indirect, mediate, or representative.

From this distinction they start the question, whether the things perceived are *real* or not; and whether we have evidence of the veracity of the senses. Hence the contest between idealism and realism. If the veracity of the senses can be reasonably denied, what proof, it is asked, have we of the reality of any thing—or even of our own existence?

It does not clearly appear how the distinction between representative and presentative knowledge doth materially help either side in deciding upon the reality or unreality of perception; for if we cavil with our senses, we may plead the general issue in one suit as well as the other, and we may impeach the witnesses, whether they make out the case directly or circumstantially.

Suppose that sense apprehends the " things out of itself and in their proper space ;" how does it follow, from this alone, that the perception is not entirely false? Does not the lunatic who sees a phantom before him, see it *out* of himself, and as in its proper space? Suppose, conversely, that what appears as a thing external to myself, be merely an *image* within my mind, can I assume, from the fact of its being an image or even an innate idea, that it is false?

No, neither argument will ever produce a conviction. No, the certitude of objective reality, is indifferent to these distinctions, and is supported by other evidence besides that which is brought to sustain the theory of immediate cognition.

As long as the agency of the instruments of sense, of the touch, of the nerves, of the brain, &c., must stand as an undeniable fact in the debate, the question between the presentationists and representationists, so far as the verbal distinction is concerned, must remain undecided.

Does my eye *throw out* filaments of light and push them into contact with outer objects, or does it simply *receive* images?

If it receive images, how is it that these images cannot be realized as existing within us? How can we shake off the consciousness, that it is not an image but the thing itself we behold? Yet how can we dispute the facts demonstrated by Anatomy and Optics, which show that the eye is constructed like a camera obscura which *receives* images?

If it does *not* receive images, how can any real difference between the hallucination of a spirit seer and the normal vision of everybody be accounted for? How could dreams be distinguished from ordinary perceptions? How could we recall scenes and events of our past experience? Yet it is perfectly certain that the evidence of Anatomy and Optics stops short at the retina, for beyond this no image was ever found, and nothing in the analysis of vision can account for the further transmission of the image, while nothing in the dissection of the brain enables us to follow the picture to any point within the nervous or cerebral organism.

The real question between the presentationists and representationists, is whether the data given us in consciousness, be true or false.

Hamilton, whose accurate and universal knowledge of the writings of philosophers, is perfectly reliable, says: "No philosopher has ever formally denied the truth or disclaimed the authority of consciousness; but few or none have been content implicitly to accept, and consistently follow out its dictates."

Barring any "inconsistency" they may have been guilty of, the philosophers are perfectly right—right in not denying the truth or authority of consciousness—right in not implicitly accepting its dictates.

This is only an *apparent* paradox, or contradiction. Why?

Because it is too true that our senses, perceptions or consciousness, let the name be either, often deceive us, and we are all on our guard against the data furnished; yet it is also true that it is by the evidence of sense, perception or consciousness, that it is itself corrected—it is by *its own* data that it corrects itself.

Practically, consciousness is a witness who is constantly contradicting himself, and yet is the *sole* witness on whose testimony we must act. We cannot simply dismiss the case, but are compelled, at our peril, to give judgment positively one way or the other.

So that we must admit the authority of the witness, though he prevaricates, and differs with himself, and our endless task is to find out wherein he belies or misapprehends himself; or rather what he really says or means.

The true view of the matter is to consider all the data furnished by consciousness as *facts;* but not to take any of these facts as presenting the whole truth. If, for instance, I *see* a ghost standing before me, following me everywhere, as Brutus when he saw the shade of Cæsar; must I take this as a *fact?* Undoubtedly I must; but I should ascertain whether the apparition is presented TO or FROM the mind. Behold, I see the sun, at dawn in the east, at noon at the zenith, at eve in the west. Must I take this as a fact? Undoubtedly

I must; but I should ascertain which of the two doth move, the sun or myself; and if I decide erroneously, I might be tempted to persecute a Galileo as a lunatic, a heretic, a wretch who denies both the evidence of his senses and the Word of God.

Thus, the authority of consciousness standing on its true merit, should be fully admitted, not as requiring implicit reliance upon any single data it furnishes; but as requiring reliance upon all the data taken together, accompanied by a warning, that the omission of any part of the existing data, whether known or not known, will leave us *practically* with a deluded consciousness.

The problem presents itself like a case to be tried before a judge and jury upon a mixed issue of law and fact. No single item of the evidence may be sufficient to determine the issue of fact, no single principle of law may be adequate to solve the legal difficulties, but the whole evidence and jurisprudence summed up, may present a clear result of premises established, circumstances reconciled, falsehood detected, and logical conclusions perfectly apparent.

We cannot ignore the fact that both perception and judgment are imperfect and irregular in their powers and action; and are constantly correcting their own selves and each other—so that their contents and decisions are constantly called in question, and undergoing revision and change. Where and what, then, is *reality?* I answer it is the what-is-felt at present. Any other definition is a lie; for reality is not speculative but practical; and every man acts upon his present feeling and conviction as reality, and no man knows any other reality; though every man also knows that his feelings and convictions are constantly undergoing transmutation and transformation.

Yet this is not so desperate and alarming as at first it would seem.

This mutability has a basis; and *is*, in fact, the movement of revision and correction carried on by our faculties. It is the march of intellectual humanity going on in each man's mind, rallied and encouraged by the following aids:

1°. Artificial helps to natural powers, through instruments, chemical analysis, &c.;

2°. Admonitions of sense to sense, whereby our senses check and rectify the impressions of each other;

3°. Repetition, or the reiterated observations of the same fact in different ways or at different times;

4°. Human testimony, or concurrent and precedent investigations by other men, communicated through language, signs, &c.;

5°. The laws by which thought or consciousness itself is governed, and which act as a rule and compass to all our judgments.

If we look back upon our own experience and hear the testimony of all men past and present, we find that there is a multitude of always-present realities, of which the human kind has never been divested, and in which it daily gains increasing confidence. Realities of existence, of self and not-self, of social intercourse, moral sentiment, bodily feeling, scientific order, natural law, mode of thought, &c. These being repeated over and over again in all time past, as well as in the present, and being asserted by all men, assume a character of certitude so great that we exnecessitate, feel we have a real foothold, and cannot give adhesion to the doctrines of idealism or nihilism.

Besides, as we have said, reality is not speculative but practical; and we find that in practising and acting upon these reiterated and re-verified realities, which vividly shine in consciousness, no mishap befalls us; and thus as we go, we acquire new confidence in the harmony of nature, and in the truth of her revelations.

What do we mean when we say that a thing, a quality, &c., is "*real*"? We simply declare that our perceptive powers have been impressed or moved in one way or the other. Whether this impression or movement is felt as arising within us or out of us, the first idea of it is, that it is felt. It must be felt or not felt: if not felt, no notion or idea of it could exist in our minds, and thus its negation would be determined; but, if felt, it *is*, and it must be affirmed—at least so far as the fact of being felt is considered. Whatever opinion, notion, conception, judgment we may form of the impression or movement, whether as trustworthy or deceptive, the idea of reality attaches itself to what is felt, as well as to the judgment conceived in relation to it. Indeed, the judgment itself is an impression or movement *felt*, BY and IN *the mind* or soul. Beyond what consciousness declares or testifies, there is for us nothing, zero, nought, negation; and therefore the opposite of negation, reality, must be on what this feeling doth testify and declare.

It is in consciousness that we feel the high operations of reflection and thought, which depend upon our immortal archeus; for, our rational soul works upon the data consciousness has obtained through sensation.

Every movement *to*, *in*, or *from* the mind, REVEALS itself to the mind itself, and it is this revelation which is taken as REALITY, *in presenti*. Yet there is a degree in the admission. A new phenomenon or idea is received with caution. Other beliefs in the mind may contest the genuineness of the new data; and a period of transition and investigation occurs. The new comer may be even rejected, in toto, as a deceit; but this rejection is always based upon the evidence given by the then present condition of the mind as to what is felt and real. Most frequently old and tried acquaintances present themselves; and are acknowledged in the proportion of their age and frequency. When their visits recur in a known and familiar garb, they are instantly accepted without distrust.

We thus find, that reality is in the testimony of consciousness—that outside of the what-is-felt there is no fact—and that truth is therein or nowhere; while, on the other hand, it is also certain we must and do regard our sensations, perceptions, &c., with doubt, suspicion, &c. So we necessarily oscillate between the admission and denial of reality. Indeed, we *simultaneously* trust and distrust therein, and this double feeling or conviction is founded on the very consciousness which relies upon itself to impeach itself. While we judge *of* it we judge *by* it. It unites the characters of justiciary, witness, and party, all three of whom are affected by every sentence pronounced. If the tribunal condemns the witness, as such,—it condemns and discards itself. This it cannot do; for it *subsists* in spite of itself. Thus it may rectify, not annihilate itself; and it lives to act according to its gifts, and to accept at every given point of time its own self, its own evidence, and its own judgment as valid—as exhibiting reality.

Let it not be assumed that, in what we have said, we have been confounding perception, consciousness, and judgment. They are really inseparable, though distinguishable. They are all revealed *to* feeling, *in* feeling, and *by* feeling. They constitute together the what-is-felt; and it is vain to attribute falsehood to one rather than to the other. Judgment rectifies perception, and perception rectifies judgment. What is it that compares, classifies, generalizes perceptions, and finally finds their harmony? Judgment. What is it that prevents judgment from making gratuitous assumptions and accrediting random theories? Perception. Where do we seek for the content of either or both? In consciousness, where they are one. Out of this circle we cannot go, nor can we confine ourselves at any time to any one point of the circle; for it is the circle of the what-is-felt, made up of all the elements of certainty and uncertainty, and of interfused judge, witness, and party.

How vain, then, is the dispute between the idealists and sensationalists—one party arguing that all knowledge is received, and the other that it is all produced, by the mind. All they know and all they can know is the what-is-felt, *as it is felt;* and as it exhibits itself *by, to,* and *in* consciousness, whether as sensation, perception, memory, reflection, judgment, or as any other content of self or phenomenon of not-self. The truth or falsehood of these, may be argued upon the premises of either doctrine. Either theory may furnish reasons to affirm or deny reality, as the realists and nihilists, in their respective works, have abundantly shown against one another. For myself I am content to take the what-is-felt as it is, with its combined certainty and uncertainty; for that is all God has given me, to deal with at my own peril.

Reader, permit me, before proceeding further, and merely by way of incidental and unessential remark, to suggest a thought. Its admission or rejection is not material to any proposition I desire to insist upon; yet it seems to me worthy of passing notation.

I have admitted that perception is subject to error; but to error which it is, itself, constantly correcting. This, in a certain school of philosophy, would be regarded as contradiction and heresy; for it qualifies or modifies their dogma of the absolute certitude and consistency of the contents of consciousness; and leaves us, they say, to doubt man's past, present, and future ability to attain a correct consciousness of THE REAL.

I might simply reply by an appeal to the facts which attest the imperfection of all things, and there stop; yet, I suggest, that if man were *perfect* in any one quality of intelligence, he would be necessarily perfect in them all; and that as intellectual perfection implies *infallibility*, so man, if mentally perfect, would be infallible. But to assert this would be sheer blasphemy and absurd presumption; for the pretension would amount to a vain and proud claim to the plenitude of God's attribute.

Am I right in saying that perfection in one mental quality would be perfection in all? Yes; for there is no definite line of demarkation between the several properties of mind—they are woven into each other and depend upon each other—so that if any one has not the assistance of the rest it could not do its full duty. Thus as a faculty in its action needs help, it is clear that if the help is imperfect the work must also be imperfect. Thus the infallibility of any part of consciousness requires the infallibility of the whole, to which it belongs and in which it rests. Taking one from hundreds of analogies which might be adduced from the material world, and pointing to a quadruped having three defective legs, I ask, Would not this imperfection impair the powers of the fourth, however faultless it might be in itself?

If we were forced to the alternative of asserting either the absolute truth or absolute falsehood of *consciousness*—if there be no middle term between the perfection of our sentient powers and their non-entity, then we are placed in a dilemma between two fallacies: 1°. We would have on one side the sophism of the unconditional realists, who rely upon the data furnished by consciousness itself to prove its own veracity, which is *begging the question;* for the very thing denied cannot be taken as the basis of an argument concluding to its own truth. How can a witness be heard to prove his own credibility? 2°. On the other hand, we would have the fallacy of the nihilists, who argue upon the data given by consciousness itself, in order to conclude against its very existence, which is *felo de se;* for if consciousness has no reality it cannot be the basis of any conclusion whatever. Thus we are forced into a middle position, which is simply this:

1°. That which consciousness declares is the beginning and basis of all knowledge—the *centre* from which all we know radiates, so that every attempt to prove or disprove it fails for want of a legitimate major premiss; for if this basis, beginning, or centre of all reasoning, could be proved or disproved, there would be a major premiss or fact still more primary and universal, so that consciousness would not be the beginning or centre. But as we know of no other ground more universal, further removed, or nearer the core, all our arguments must admit the deliverances of consciousness *as fact* though unproved and unprovable. These deliverances are like the testimony of a single eye-witness to the allegations of an indictment or declaration. It would certainly be absurd to ask *him* to prove what he says; for that would be requiring two witnesses when there is really but one in existence.

2°. But while we *must* take consciousness as fact simply because it is the fact of facts, and contains all in all,—because there is no other and it is our very self; this implies that we must take it *as it is;* for we cannot take it otherwise,—yet, for the same reason, we must admit it and all its imperfections, self-impeachments, and self-corrections: admit its declaration of an objective not-self—admit this not-self as known only in the self—admit that self and not-self are frequently confounded—admit that what consciousness positively avers to day as true, it holds to-morrow as false; and still is just as positive as ever.

The way to discover the truth in a case like this, is to cross-examine the *only* witness; so that he may correct himself if he was mistaken, and he will not hesitate to do so; for his *honesty*, at least, is certain, since it is for himself and to himself he gives his testimony.

Indeed, it is necessary that there should be a starting point of knowledge, or *prima ratio;* for if there were not one, we would be constantly driven from position to position in all reasoning. Thought would fall backwards down the abyss of " *infinite series*," or pursue an ever distant *ignis fatuus*.

With all its imperfections consciousness therefore subsists as the *criterium veritas*.

Of these imperfections it behooves us not to complain: God alone is perfect. For what he has given, let us be thankful, since it is life and intelligence; and since it fulfils the requisites of the mortal clay, while it connects us with HIS eternal essence.

The Senses may be considered as one: that is, *touch*. When we perceive an object by touch, we ascertain its form, its size, its number, its arrangement, its density, its weight, its force, its position, its texture, its temperature, its movement, &c., and by a succession of touches we might even measure time. All of the qualities may with more or less adequacy be perceived by sight; and *sight* adds color. *Hearing*, in common with touch and sight, perceives time and motion, and adds sound. *Taste* is so closely allied to touch, that absolute contact is necessary in using this sense. This is also true with regard to *smell*. Indeed, not only taste and smell must be *touched* into action, but so also must sight and hearing; for it is by the immediate percussion of light and sound that the eye and ear are impressed. So that we may consider the four last as higher developments, indistinct modes of the sense of touch.

When we perceive an object the first impression is concrete.

Suppose, for instance, an apple: the first notion its presence affords is unital—it is the concrete notion of an apple. Color, smell, taste, form, &c., are not considered abstractedly, but all inhere so intimately that no idea is conceived, but of one entire object.

In mathematics this is concrete numeration.

In language this is the noun, which certainly came before the adjective, and even before the abstract substantive.

The unity of the senses is implied in the fact, that though we may conceive the abstract notion of color, smell, taste, form, &c., yet the hand, the palate, the eye, the ear, the nose, unerringly refer these qualities to the same object presented, when, in truth, they are united in that object. The senses do not present as many severalties as there are qualities. The idea of severalty of objects does not arise in consequence of the severalty of the senses; but the senses declare *one* object with several qualities. In the case of the apple:

the color which the eye beholds, the taste which the palate obtains, the odor which the nose scents, the sound which the ear admits, the density which the hand feels, are all known as being of *that* apple. The apple which touch ascertains as a solid is known *to touch* as being the *same* apple which sight beholds as red, taste relishes as sweet, smell appreciates as fragrant, and sound hears as husky; and so it is conversely from one sense to the other. Even when objects are distant, the sound suggests form, smell, color, &c. Evidently there is a medium of interchange between the senses, or a common basis of feeling. There is certainly a communion between the senses, whereby, in union, they become aware of the *identity* of the object in which each of them finds a distinct quality. There must be an inherent property common to all the senses, or a central focus to which external impressions converge, and in which they all unite. Outwardly this would be the touch, which is common to the four other senses—inwardly this would be the mental *image*, so often acknowledged by psychologists. No other than one or both of these hypotheses would fit the facts.

Here we should note a class of facts of the greatest importance to the philosophy of sensation and of thought—it is that crude collection which constitutes the science or art of Animal Magnetism, Spiritualism, &c. Left in the hands of charlatanism, credulity, and superstition, the real facts which these pseudo sciences possess have been so intermixed with errors and falsehoods, with so many gratuitous assumptions and imaginings, that the majority of serious and practical minds have found it safe to reject the whole. This absolute rejection will not, however, bear the test of time and experience; for facts are now and then presented, so authentic and yet so entirely dehors the routine of classic metaphysics and psychology, that to ignore them is to be wilfully blind and deaf. The philosophy which omits them must be incomplete, as excluding a class of positively ascertained phenomena. It is therefore time that men of true science, strict observation, and logical intellect should examine these facts, and assign them their real value and place. Their positive meaning is to be found.

Among these facts the following is well attested and may be verified: Persons have been found who, in certain conditions, can read with bandaged eyes, see through the thickest substances. I have witnessed this phenomenon myself. Here then is a case of seeing without eyes—the special organ of vision is dispensed with. The same apparently supernatural fact has been witnessed in regard to the organs of taste, hearing, and smell. Now, how can we explain this physically? I find but one answer. It is that there is a central seat of homogeneous substance or continuous surface of sensation, which, when excited, dispenses with the medium of the special organs, and performs alone their functions. If this be so, here would be another proof of the common basis of the senses.

It is nevertheless plain that the abstract fractions of the sentient unit are gathered severally. Each sense performs at least one distinct function—does what the others are totally incapable of doing. Thus the sound the apple makes as I bite it, is cognized by the ear and not by any other organ; the savor I find as I masticate it is taken by the palate, and not by any other organ; the odor it exhales is caught up by the nose and not by any other organ; the colors it possesses are perceived by the eye and not by any other organ; the hardness of the substance is disclosed by the feel and not by any other sense. Moreover, the non-existence of any one of these organs of sense would exclude the conception of the quality it is most specially destined to distinguish. It would then be to us as if there were no such quality in existence. If any one of the senses (except touch) were extinguished, the others would remain unaffected, and would continue their normal operations.

Thus it appears that the senses have each a separate individuality.

But I have already shown that each sense, *while it lives*, is so closely interwoven with the others, through the common bond of *touch*, that no independent action of any one sense ever practically takes place.

The senses therefore are—MANY IN ONE.

"The senses are many in one:" such is the resultant expression of five simple operations: 1st. The primary *enumeration* of the five senses, as existing and distinct integers; 2d, the *addition* of the five in one *sum* or term—sensation; 3d, the *subtraction* from sensation of four of the integers: smell, taste, oyer, sight, by which we find that touch remains; 4th, the *subtraction* from sensation of only one of the integers, touch, by which we find that nothing (zero) remains; for the elimination of the feel carries away all sensation; 5th, the consequent equation is: touch=sensation.

Thus, insomuch as they are distinguishable from each other, we may treat the senses as severalties. Accordingly, we may endeavor to enumerate the direct functions of the senses, apart from all that appears to be composite, apart from all complexity, and from what is consequent upon other powers of the mind.

TOUCH, we find spreads its net of nerves to every part of the body; yet the same things or forces produce different grades of feeling at different points of the body. This is in the ratio of the delicacy and fineness of the skin. Alcohol or pepper, for instance, will burn with more intensity when applied to the eye, than when touched by the hand, &c. Yet the feel of any given object is always *in esse* the same: the difference is in degree only. At the same time in the touch of different things we find a great variety of sensation, not only in degree but in quality. Hence we are able to give names to various feelings experienced by touch: Density, Rarity, Texture, Contexture, Pulverulence,

Adhesion, Warmth, Coldness, Shocking, Soothing, &c., or hard, soft, firm, fluid, thick, thin, viscid, friable, tough, brittle, rigid, flexible, rough, smooth, slippery, tenacious, &c. These, with their co-ordinates, are the names of the principal sensations of which we become conscious directly through touch. They are the *units* of or numerators of touch, and touch itself is the name given to their common denominator.

TASTE directly and individually cognizes a great variety of sensations. The number is so great that no classification of them has ever yet been undertaken, nor does language as yet afford the terms necessary for their systematic arrangement. Only a few specific units of taste are distinguished by words essentially their own. Sweet, sour, bitter, pungent, are the only abstract names for tastes which occur to me now. The other tastes are named after the objects in which they are found, such as—sugary, honeyed, salty, spicy, &c., &c.

SIGHT proclaims color, light, and shade in all their combinations. The abstract units of sight are not more numerous than those of any other sense; but it is the principal instrument by which we become conscious of *concrete* units; for it enables us to perceive (at a given point of time, or space) an assemblage of parts forming a whole, such as a man, a beast, a vegetable, a mineral, &c. It is the organ to which we owe "the *images*" formed in the mind. Yet, as we have already shown, the other senses (touch more than the rest) are contributors and rectifiers. Hence we err when we attach the ideas of space, motion, number, order, place, form, size and the like, exclusively to sight; and a closer analysis forces us to acknowledge that the *direct* function of sight is the perception of color and shade.

OYER cognizes sound. It furnishes units of great precision; and *Music* with its seven well-marked notes, &c., is its offspring. Some have thought it possible to form a gamut for the use of touch, or sight, or taste, or smell, with names of degrees, as clearly marked as in music. Indeed, Newton and his disciples have already done this for color; and we see no valid reason for declaring it impossible in the domain of taste, smell, or even touch. Oyer, however, for the present is in the advance. Its sensations are measured, numbered, weighed, classed, and named with a perfection truly admirable.

SMELL is the most isolated of the senses, so that its direct functions and feelings cannot be mistaken; yet, whatever may be the cause, nearly all its feelings are, like those of taste, named after the experiences of the other senses. We have but few words for smells which are not the mere transformations of the names of concrete objects. No measured units of smell have, as yet, been discovered; and its ut-re-mi-fa-sol remains to be framed. Fragrance, stink, perfume, fetor, are so general, they cannot be considered as designating units.

In the preceding paragraph we considered the functions-*proper* which impart severalty to the senses. In doing this the functions-*common* forced themselves upon our attention. While we mentioned the distinct properties which make the senses *many*, we could not help recognizing the general characteristics which make them *one*. We could not help this, because, while we were subtracting from all the properties those which were special to a particular sense, we found the common phenomena so united, co-existent, and co-operative with the more limited, that one class could not be observed and noted without the other being present in the view and in the language describing it.

After enumerating:

1. TOUCH, perceiving *substance* and its densities;
2. TASTE, perceiving *savor* and its phases;
3. SIGHT, perceiving *color* and its shades;
4. OYER, perceiving *sound* and its tones;
5. SMELL, perceiving *odor* and its varieties

the fact that touch extended its properties to all the senses, and was their common element, became apparent, and we have noted it.

But this communion shows itself by other evidences.

In all the senses there is a consciousness of intercourse with—

1°. PHENOMENA, or the Concrete and Ostensible;
2°. FORCE, or Impulse and Motion:
3°. LAW, or Necessity and Equilibrium;

4°. SPACE, or Extension and Place;

5°. TIME, or Duration and Moment.

1. Phenomena, as such, could never be the data of thought without being felt in Sensation as the evolution or resultant of some Power or Force.

2. Force and Phenomena would be *as chaos*, if sensation were not conscious of the subjection of the *external* world to absolute and perpetual laws.

3. Law, Force, and Phenomena would be *as dreams*, if Sensation did not realize Space as containing them.

4. Space, Law, Force, and Phenomena would be *one eternal now*, if Sensation did not divulge the succession of Time.

5. Time, Space, Law, Force, and Phenomena would in their turn be "unthinkable"—that is to say, never become any thing more than driving and drawing motors of instinct, were it not for the *elementary* and *egressive* powers of Thought, of which I will treat in the next chapter.

Physiology confirms these views, and enables us to define not only the offices of general and special sense, but also to find the distinction between Sensation and Consciousness in one degree, as well as between Instinct and Thought in the next.

Physiology shows that the nerves of vision, when shocked by a blow, or a current of electricity, emit flashes or appearances of *light;* that diseases of the ear-tubes sometimes give a "*singing in the ear*," or other sensation of sound; that the nerves of vision are insensible to sound, and those of hearing insensible to light; and that for the protection of the eye-ball nature has provided it with nerves of touch distinct from the optic or light-perceiving nerves, &c., &c.

On the other hand, however, Physiology teaches us that in the absence of sight and hearing, touch will enable us to ascertain Direction and Form, Size and Order, Time and Space; or according to common parlance, which is scientifically correct, the "strength of the wanting sense goes into the other," which becomes more intense, and fulfils the office of the two, so that the blind do find their way and the deaf can learn to speak.

Physiology shows, too, that the trouble of the born-blind who acquire vision, is to find the harmony and common properties of Touch and Vision.

When they become conscious of the common centre of the two sensations, their tribulations cease, and confusion is gradually dispelled.

Dr. Wardrop gives a very interesting account of the circumstances which followed the acquisition of sight by a lady, on whose eyes he had performed an operation. The details are lengthy, and I must confine myself to citing one or two passages: "On the sixth day she seemed indeed bewildered from not being able to combine the knowledge acquired by the senses of touch and sight, and felt disappointed in not having the power of distinguishing at once by her eye, objects which she could so readily distinguish from one another by feeling them. On the seventh day the teacups and saucers fell under her observation. 'What are they like?' her brother asked her. 'I don't know,' she replied; 'they look very queer to me, but I can tell you what they are in a minute if I touch them.' She noticed an orange on the chimney-piece, but could form no notion of what it was till she touched it. On the eighth day she seemed to have become more cheerful, and entertain greater expectation of comfort from her admission to the visible world," &c.

Physiology also ascertains the homogeneity of the substance or matter of the nerves. Hence, though Touch, Sight, Smell, Hearing and Taste, Sensibility and Motion, have their special nerves, these nerves are all endowed with the same primary qualities, chemically and organically, and the development of distinct functions is evidently due, not to a diversity or contrariety in essence, but to *modifications* of that essence.

INSTINCT, that machinery which drives and adapts the actions of animals in the most complex works, does not (with the introduction of consciousness) desert the Vertebrata. Hence, sometimes when they act from pure instinct, their apparent freedom, and the consciousness they exhibit, create an inference of rationality which does not really exist.

As man possesses consciousness in a high degree, and can comprehend its operations, while he has hardly any gift of instinct, and can barely conceive what instinct is, he is prone to attribute the instinctive acts of animals to the powers with which he is familiar, and which are at his service. The acts which some beasts and insects perform instinctively, man may often perform by the aid of reason, (and without the help of instinct, which for many purposes is refused him;) so that he naturally imputes the actions of beasts and insects to faculties like those possessed by himself, and by which he is enabled to accomplish what he sees them do. It is not till beholding them proceed without education, experience, or reflection, that he clearly apprehends the existence of instinct, the operations of which he can only understand when he observes his own reflex actions in nutrition, sleep, generation, &c.

It must not be inferred that I underrate the force of instinct *in man*—he is much indebted to this property.

In the study of Vitality I have alluded to many proofs of this. Most every thing he does in the act of feeding is instinctive, so in the acts of fighting, of walking, of keeping his balance, and of sexual connection. But thought constantly intervenes and intermeddles, so that it is difficult to separate the share of intuition from that of deliberation. Philosophy has still great labors to perform, in making a careful analysis of particular acts, so as in each to assign the specific shares of vitality, instinct, consciousness, and thought. Certain it is they are all four present in almost every movement of the human body.

Now, starting from the facts clearly established in our study of Vitality, to wit:

That the ablation of the cerebrum removes consciousness;

That (notwithstanding the removal of consciousness) certain acts, necessary to life, are determined by sensation, and are duly performed;

That the nerves of special sense have a *direct* action upon the nerves of motion;

That the INVERTEBRATA, and many fishes, have no cerebrum, and yet perform acts determined by the nerves of special sense;

I infer—

That sensations and consciousness should be distinguished; should be as positively discriminated one from the other, as any one special sense can be known from another—the distinction is as great.

That consciousness is a modification or special development of sensation—just as taste or smell is a modification of touch; and that the differences between the basis and the mode are as positive in one case as in the other.

It may be difficult for us to conceive how, for instance, Bees can work and act without experiencing what is known to us as CONSCIOUSNESS—that is to say, without the faculty of combining several simultaneous sensations into *one* picture or idea—*one* co-ordinate assemblage or "*ensemble*" as the French express it.

Yet it is so; and must be so; for, insects have no cerebrum.

But some one may say: "*perhaps* the nerves and ganglia of special sense, *in insects,* do the office of Consciousness or of the Cerebrum." To this I reply: your "*perhaps*" is no argument against a plain induction from ascertained facts; your "*perhaps*" contradicts the speciality of the several kinds of nerves, and gives to each kind *two* special functions; your "*perhaps*" is at war with the economy of nature in the plan of "*division of labor,*" which she strictly observes, and in her other plan of "*doing nothing in vain,*" a rule from which she never departs. Surely nature would not have made a new organ (a cerebrum) to evolve consciousness, if the special nerves had been capable of it, and if it already existed by their evolutions; for in that case the accession of a cerebrum would have been wholly unnecessary.

If we cannot implicitly rely upon the economy and constancy of nature, all reasoning must cease.

Relating *in detail* the acts of Bees and other insects, those who suppose the necessity of consciousness for these acts, exclaim: "How can we understand doings so wonderful and complex, unless we admit a consciousness in the actor? How could these acts be done without a combined assemblage of phenomena in perception?"

I answer:

Though the How and the Why be unknown the fact is not the less certain; and if we cannot form a clear conception of the cause and process of action *without* consciousness, neither could we *with* it; for, as I will presently show, consciousness would explain nothing—the mystery, if mystery there is, would be as great as ever.

The insects go directly to their work and do it to perfection, *from the instant of their birth.*

They erect a complicated castle, and its architecture conforms to the most abstruse laws of physics and mathematics, though they have received *no education in the art they practise.*

Each does a share, executes a distinct operation of the process; one carries the material, and another scoops out the cell; they are all working at the same time, order and system prevail in their manœuvres; and a beautiful edifice of harmonious parts and adapted totality is constructed, yet *none of the workmen ever did or saw such work before.*

Hence, the argument drawn from the complication or design of the work amounts to nothing in favor of consciousness; for if the works are performed without previous knowledge, instruction, or experience, and only by virtue of an innate impulse and direction, as they evidently are, of what *use* would consciousness be to the workers? Of no use, since they do not obey consciousness, any more than do the spindles and looms of a cotton factory.

True it is their work exhibits evidences of design, but the design is not theirs: it is that of God—the Universal Mind—the Grand Archeus of the Universe.

Is it reiterated that the insects go and come—that to find their food they must seek it, that to gather it they must *know it,* when found. I answer again; sensation, direct mechanical sensation, under the compulsion of a predestined organism, is the sufficient and only solution consistent with all the facts—consistent, for instance, with the fact that each kind of worker is formed peculiarly for a specific species of labor; and the fact that among many tribes of insects the parents die before their progeny are born; and among others the eggs of a brood are hatched by the elements; and yet the work of every generation is duly done. Thus, it is not a whit more wonderful that they should seek their food without being conscious of it, than that they should build their palaces without *knowing* how.

Certain it is they have not *the organ;* and, therefore, cannot possess a consciousness.

CONSCIOUSNESS is the union of various simultaneous

sensations into one—so as they all together form one tableau or idea.

Consciousness is the combining of many direct sensations in due accordance with present reality.

Consciousness, as well as sensation, is revived in Memory; but the Memory of consciousness is concrete.

Consciousness is therefore the summary of sensation.

The seat of consciousness is the cerebrum, and it determines action *through* the cerebellum; and the Vertebrata are therefore endowed with consciousness.

It does not give liberty; for its operations are positive or imperative; but it imparts greater variety and complexity of *motives ;* and consequently of action.

Hence, when we see the Orang-Outang, the Elephant, the Horse, the Dog, the Fox, the Rat, &c., deceiving, or decoying foes, practising cunning ruse, selecting the fit mode within their reach to attain an object, when we read the thousand and one anecdotes related of their so-called "intelligence," we will not be able to find any thing in them beyond the *spontaneous* suggestions of their *concrete* Memory and Consciousness, aided in many instances by the still more wonderful incentives of their instinct. We will not fail to observe that the motives which appear to their consciousness, are *obeyed without deliberation ;* and that if not checked or deterred by the accidental and intervening occurrence of another *direct* perception, the animal will unhesitatingly fulfil the dictates of feeling on the one side, and seize the means of gratification presented to consciousness on the other. Impelled by hunger, self-preservation, fear, anger, &c.,—aided by the acuteness of their senses,—while the scene around them is lighted up by consciousness, they do all that man could do, if he were deprived of his powers of abstraction, meditation, &c.

When the acts of sub-human animals cannot be traced to direct *propelling* motives they may appear to be free and rational, simply because we do not sufficiently consider the variety of *attracting* forces which consciousness subjects them to, when it reveals the whole scope of the horizon to their view and activity.

But it is not until we come to the study of *human thought*, and have discussed its distinctive traits, that the true nature and purview of consciousness can be made fully apparent. At present we content ourselves with the remark that man seeks, finds, *makes motives*, subjects them to examination and revision, accepts or rejects them, but other animals cannot do it.

Since consciousness unites all the sensations of feel, sight, sound, taste, and odor—blends them together—the faculty of suggestion necessarily arises; for fusion and conjunction of several sensations implies an interchange, and therefore suggestion. Each sense brings its message to the common centre, and an entire picture is formed. Each with its *special* impression of quality, brings its indication of time, place, force, and motion.

Of these four last mentioned, and perhaps in others, they have a common susceptibility, and are therefore able to correspond with, and react upon one another.

Association of impressions takes place; and hence the "scalded cat dreads cold water."

But what is the definite purview of *Consciousness?*

If we could bring our mind, notwithstanding the constant interference of thought, to conceive its state when first perceiving a novelty, and before *turning* over the perception in reflexion, we would have a clear idea of the purview of consciousness. The image of the objects would be distinctly within the sensorium, with form, color, space, time, motion, totality, and such like, before being analyzed, classified, referred either in whole or in part to an essential type, and before being numbered and measured, according to any standard.

The image thus given might occasion pain or pleasure, revive the *memory* of some other previous impression, start some reaction of motor nerve; but no reasoned conception would exist.

Now suppose we were incapable of subjecting the image to any revision, that we were not conscious of any *laws* of nature, or grounds of deduction and induction, and the image would work upon our sensorium uncontrolled by ourselves, and should provoke a determination of action without deliberation on our part: if we could realize to ourselves a condition like this, we would then have a correct conception of the sensational consciousness of fishes, reptiles, birds, and beasts.

There are *degrees* of consciousness.

In FISHES the cerebrum is in a rudimentary state; in REPTILES it begins to assume a somewhat more distinct but still undeveloped form; in BIRDS it presents a notable improvement, but there is yet no separation of the hemispheres; in MAMMALIA it unfolds all its principal parts, and in man its formation is completed.

But it is not only from class to class that this progression takes place, but it is also observable through the orders of each class—till the cerebrum of man is attained.

The first appearance of the cerebrum in fishes, is that of a small bulb of nervous substance without ventricles, convolutions, &c.; but, as the seriation advances, the softer portions are deposited on the exterior and the more solid matter in the centre; the gray matter makes its appearance; the radiating fibres, the commissural fibres; the corpus callosum; the ventricles; the convolutions, &c.; while each particular part after first showing itself as a simple germ in one class, becomes embryonic in the next, takes a distinct shape in the next, and finally developes itself with granules, threads, converging and diverging radii, striata, &c., in man.

But as between man and the higher Mammalia there are *no new parts* yet discovered by comparative anatomy, nothing to indicate a new organ. There is greater elaboration, more distinctness, more details—the threads cross each other with greater complexity; but there is nothing to divulge any new function.

Consciousness alone is perfected.

Hence, in conformity with what we know of the grades of *consciousness* as displayed in the *actions* of animals, we see a seriated development of the organ; and find that the bodily formation and active display proceed in parity.

Hence the powers of *consciousness* in man, are and must be more intense and complex than in any other creature.

Beyond sensational consciousness, the sub-human animals do not go. Mere perception of direct or immediate phenomena, in concrete aggregation, is sufficient to explain all the wonderful stories told of their so-called "intelligence."

Hence it is I am led to believe that phrenologists, in *naming* several organs of the cerebrum, have humanized them too much. The rational element of humanity is so constantly involving itself with all our acts, vital, instinctive, or conscious, so modifies and commands memory or suggestion, that we can hardly separate the ingredients even in nomenclature; and consequently phrenology has in some instances imputed a *rational* essence to some organs of consensual perception. Revising the names of this portion of the organs, I would regard their functions to be,—

*Individuality*, but not Combination;
*Eventuality*, but not Operation;
*Locality*, but not Circumscription;

*Form*, but not Symmetry or Proportion;
Extension, but not *Size* or Dimension;
Force, but not *Weight*, or Resolution of Forces;
*Color*, but not Catoptrics;
Interjacence, but not *Order;*
Severality, but not *Number* or Computation;
*Time*, but not Chronometry;
*Tune*, but not Rhythm;
*Language*, but not Grammar.

In one word:
Quality, but not Quantity.
Imagery, but not Measure.

And I now add to this list of Sensations even those two mighty faculties miscalled intellectual or reasoning faculties.

COMPARISON, which is simply the *perception* of identity and variety.

CAUSALITY, which is simply the *perception* of connection and disconnection.

What! exclaims the reader, are these two grand faculties to be reduced to the category of mere sensations? these *reasoning* faculties which belong to man alone—these *rational* organs which invest us with our superiority over the brutes, are they to be given up to our animality, at the expense of our humanality?

Indeed, it must be so, for observation commands this classification; and when I come to the study of

Thought, I hope to be justified; but, in the mean time, I beg attention to the remark—that if we doubt a dog's faculty of COMPARISON, we must deny his ability of distinguishing his master from another person *at* sight; or if we doubt his CAUSALITY, we may try whether when we pick up a stone and offer to throw it at a dog, he will run or not.

Then, what is there left for man alone? Much—much more than he has, so far, fully appreciated as his exclusive property: an atom of the divinity—a spirit—an Archeus—not only superior, but different from any material or physiological endowments. What is it? I will attempt an answer, but before doing so, I must dispose of the emotions.

# III.

## EMOTION.

What are those vibrations, agitations, calms, thrills, tremors, shocks, quietudes, ardors, apathies, quickenings, reactions, and even indifferences we feel *within* ourselves, and which cannot be identified with either Vitality, Sensation, Thought, or Action?

They are what we call Emotions, of which there is a great multitude, and of this multitude, each unit has a known character and name; the principal ones being, according to Phrenology, Amativeness, Parental Love, Adhesiveness, Inhabitiveness, Constancy, *Vitativeness*, Combativeness, Destructiveness, *Alimentiveness*, Acquisitiveness, Secretiveness, Cautiousness, Approbativeness, Self-Esteem, Firmness, Conscientiousness, Hope, Faith, or Spirituality, Veneration, Charity, or Benevolence, Constructiveness, Ideality, or Beauty, Sublimity, Imitation, Mirthfulness, and Human Nature.

They cannot be confounded with Sensation, Consciousness, or Thought, but may be influenced or aroused by either.

They are not Sensation, for Sensation sometimes *causes* them, and to identify them with Sensation, would be to confound effects with causes.

They are not Consciousness, for Consciousness is a mirror, and to identify them with Consciousness, would be to confound the reflector with the rays it radiates.

They are not Thought, for Thought is their judge and mentor, and to identify them with Thought, would be to confound force with law; the steam with the engine.

Yet we *feel* the Emotions, we are conscious of them, we can think them; but, in doing so, we become more fully aware that they are the vibrations of our organism when played upon by Sensation, Consciousness, and Thought; as distinctly so as are the vibrations of a harp string from the hand that strikes them.

Besides, the Emotions are sometimes awakened by Sensations alone, sometimes by Consciousness alone, sometimes by Thought alone, and sometimes by all three *together*—thus showing that neither of these *three* can be Emotion itself, as it exists sometimes without sensation, sometimes without consciousness, and sometimes without thought, and therefore is not a property of either.

Without Sensation? Yes; for the loves of the plants; the special warmth and excitation evinced by their organs of generation at the time of conjugation; the recoil of the Mimosa when touched; the combat of the Dionæa with every insect that touches it; the tendency of all plants to *seek* for heat, light, electricity, and food; the loves and acts of those insects which have no nerves, no organs of sense, and which are only distinguishable from plants by their mode of nutrition and growth; and even the loves of the turtle-dove, which attaches itself to its mate, not by virtue of any disclosure of sense, but by virtue of a predetermined instinct which nothing can revoke; the gregarious feeling of many animals, such as ants, bees, sheep, and men, which gregariousness being in these species and not in others, no operations of sensation suffices to explain—all these facts, and many others too numerous to mention, clearly show that emotion may exist without sensation.

Without Consciousness? A *fortiori*, if emotion may exist without sensation, it may without consciousness, which is only the summary of sensation; and, moreover, we know that the Bee, the Wasp, &c., who evince anger, combativeness, fear, and other emotions, have no cerebrum, and therefore no consciousness. They have sensation only, and *through* it their emotional properties may be excited; but the fact that emotion existed before sensation, having forced us to conclude that emotion was identical with it, we must conclude that it only opens a new avenue to sensibility; and that consciousness is only another avenue which may, or may not, exist. But it is in man that the non-essentiality of consciousness to emotion is the most apparent; for man is combative, secretive, destructive, cautious, acquisitive, &c., by innate instincts, which, far from originating with consciousness, control it, sway it, and subject it to their tendencies and uses.

Without Thought? None will contest the non-identity of emotion and thought; and many would be ready to assert a repulsion to exist between the two. In fact, the frequent clashings between judgment and inclination, will and desire, is sufficient, at least, to prove that they are distinct. Happy is the man who, in accordance with the designs of the Grand Archeus, succeeds in harmonizing these two elements of self, and sets them to act in unison with each other and with the laws of nature.

Attempts have been made to confine the idea of Emotion to the mere *pain* or *pleasure* we feel on becoming conscious of certain sensations; but this definition, for several reasons, will be found inadequate to convey a correct understanding of what Emotion is.

It is not enough to say that Emotion is pain or pleasure, for it is evident that to feel either of these, the organism or medium must be gifted with *properties* or *energies*, which render it susceptible or prone. A stone cannot feel emotion. Why? Simply because it possesses no property of excitability within itself, it has no innate energies resolvable into emotion.

Pain and pleasure are only two of the most general *effects* of emotion. They are not emotion itself, for to describe the emotions, we are compelled to use other terms than "Pain" and "Pleasure." We must say:

affection, content, regret, cheerfulness, dejection, joy, sorrow, beauty, hope, despair, fear, diffidence, courage, wonder, pride, vanity, humility, modesty, friendship, enmity, sociability, melancholy, love, hate, benevolence, pity, gratitude, respect, veneration, contempt, piety, and a thousand other terms which may or may not imply any suffering or enjoyment; sometimes neither, and often either, according to circumstances.

It would be impossible to include *all* the emotions in a classification comprising only the two heads of pain and pleasure. Many would come under neither; and even those which might be ranged on one side or the other, might, by a rising or sinking of intensity, exhibit the opposite condition. Thus, Benevolence may become Pity or Sorrow; Shame may be softened into Modesty or Bashfulness.

It has, doubtless, already been remarked that in separating Emotion—in distinguishing it from every thing else, I have not excluded vitality; and the inference to be drawn is, that I can find no essential difference between Vitality and Emotion.

Is there any?

If there is, it must be deduced from the following definition, which I believe to be true:

EMOTION *is the manifestation, within the organism of the motive properties of Vitality.*

This manifestation may be determined in different modes:

1. It may spring up in Vitality by virtue of the vital force itself.

2. It may be quickened by Sensation.

3. It may be illuminated by Consciousness.

4. It may harmonize, in sympathy, with Thought; or,

5. It may be developed by two or more of these forces acting in different proportions and under different conditions.

Hence according to this theory, if Emotion be distinguishable at all from Vitality, it is not otherwise than as Form from Matter, Color from Light.

And this is indeed an important and strongly marked difference; for there are few minds that cannot realize it as a valid distinction.

None who feel themselves will deny that emotion is vital—that all we know of it is in the modifications of our vital feelings; but every one admits a positive discrimination between properties and the phenomena they evolve. How many, for instance, are the modes in which gravitation appears, the falling apple, revolving worlds, flowing waters, &c., yet we all concede the necessity of not confounding weight and motion. So it is with fuel, heat, and light; and thus, among many other comparisons, we might give this one: Vitality is a flame radiating its own heat and light, or emotions, stirred by the poker of sensation, reflected in the mirror of consciousness, conducted by the flues of thought, burning its own elements, and dying if the fuel is not renewed.

Whatever excites emotion in one person, may not affect another in the least, or may induce a very different feeling.

Thus, noise may irritate and *anger* the nervous or studious man, but does not disturb the phlegmatic, and would please a child. The corrupt smile at vice, but the pure behold it with indignation. Merriment enlivens the happy, but shocks the miserable man.

Since the causes of Emotion are so multiple; since our mere vital condition, state of health, &c., has so much to do with them; since every shade and kind of Sensation may move them; since every aspect and phase of Consciousness may evoke them; since every evolution of thought may influence them; and since all these determining powers cross and intermingle in so many ways and proportions, the number of complex emotions actually felt must be very large; they must be as numerous as could be the *permutations* of many numerical digits arrayed in twos, threes, fours, &c., and this would be *millions*.

At the same time as it is only through the what-is-felt—only in the concrete feeling just as it presents itself, that we know of emotions; so by this feeling do we *name* them. Hence we have in our dictionaries a multitude of terms to express and designate various *complex* feelings; and but very few (I ought rather to say none) for any unmixed and strictly abstract emotion.

Nor do the complex terms, at our command, suffice, for we are constantly obliged to resort to whole phrases and sentences to express the conditions and movements of the Soul.

But, confining our attention to the words singly, we find that language (having been formed apart from any view to abstract analysis or exhaustive classifications, but under the pressure of direct and compound necessities) gives us terms only for the what-is-felt, as it is felt; and hence the Dictionary, beginning at "Abash" or "Abashment," and ending with "Zealousness," contains, at least, two thousand words expressive of states or disturbances of feeling; while also every one of these words conveys a composite meaning.

There is, for instance, in "Hate," as well as in "Contempt," a sentiment of antipathy or repulsion; but, in one case, it is mingled with an idea of the harmfulness of the object, and in the other of its impotency. In one the basis of feeling may be the hostility of Vice to Virtue, or of Justice to Wrong, while, in the other, it is often the opposition of Gravity to Futility, or the like. Nor are these terms even so simple as to require us to stop the analysis at this point. Hate has, for instance, its degrees: it may be only aversion, grudge, spite, resentment, or it may be disgust, malice, detestation, abhorrence, abomination, implacability, &c. In Hate, too, if it be caused by an act of injustice, and not by mere instinctive repulsion, the intellectual powers may be concerned; for, in this case, hate *depends* upon the judgment of right and wrong, and may cease through any detection of error in premises or conclusion.

Hence, it would be a difficult task, indeed, to form a satisfactory list or catalogue, or classification of primary uncompounded emotions. We have in Physics the primitive colors, in Chemistry we have the "elementary bodies;" but, in Psychology, the radical emotions have not been completely ascertained. Language, in its present state, almost precludes a systematic classification; for the terms at the disposal of the philosopher, are not only complex in themselves, but run into one another, and any one word will imply some condition or meaning belonging to many others having with it apparently no connection.

Phrenology has attempted the desired classification of Emotion; and even were we to discard its Anatomical and Physiological pretensions, Phrenology would still hold a high rank among Psychological systems.

The phrenological theory is, that—

All the functions and faculties of man are the source and seat of emotion. Knowledge supplies motives, and feeling induces thought and action. The motor nerves have direct or indirect intercourse with the whole man. His vital, animal, and rational nature, separately or together, vibrate in emotion, so that it may be said every feeling or thought is emotion; and thus we would have

1°. Love of Being, represented by the vital instincts.

2°. Love of Having, represented by the Propensities.

3°. Love of Doing, represented by the Sentiments.

4°. Love of Knowing, represented by the Perceptive and Intellectual organs.

5°. Love of Speaking, represented by the organ of Language, moved by the rest.

But they are all concerned with each other, and it is difficult to group them.

Taking the emotions, as represented by the Phrenological synopsis, it will be found that they will admit of the following division:

1°. The *love of Life* or Egotism, represented by the Selfish and Domestic Propensities, or as I would prefer to call and class them Subjective and Objective Selfishness. The *subjective* or wholly selfish are Self-esteem, Approbativeness (?) Cautiousness, Combativeness, Secretiveness, Acquisitiveness, Distinctiveness, and Alimentiveness, which descend from the stem of Selfishness. The *Objective* or Selfishness, in objects of affection or propensity, are Amativeness, which is a selfish desire to gratify the genital functions; Philo-progenitiveness, the attachment to one's own progeny; Inhabitiveness, which is selfishness, applied to locality; Adhesiveness, which is selfish pleasure in gregariousness, or in chosen objects of companionship; and Concentrativeness (?)

or rather Constancy, which produces continuity of *affection* towards the objects chosen. CONSTRUCTIVENESS, which is the selfish instinct whereby birds and insects are enabled to build their nests, or beasts and fishes their lair, as the bee its hive, the beaver its lodge, &c. The language of these organs is: *My* Wife, *My* Children, *My* home, *My* friends; may *I* never be parted from them.

2°. The love of KNOWLEDGE or Curiosity by the Perceptive Faculties, of which we have already treated in the study of sensation.

3°. The love of *Truth* or Hope represented by a group composed of Conscientiousness, Firmness (?), and Hope.

4°. The love of BEAUTY or Faith, represented by a group composed of Veneration, Marvellousness, Sublimity (?), and Ideality.

5°. The love of *Morality* or Charity, represented by a group composed of Benevolence, Imitation (?), Mirthfulness, and Language. Some would add Human Sympathy and Suavity.

I have marked some of these names with a point of interrogation, in order to suggest, that—

1°. Approbativeness is a perfectly selfish faculty: it seeks to please only for the sake of self-glory or vanity; it fears the ill-will of others; it delights in their praise, but it does not love *them*, or care for them, otherwise than for the *flattery* they may offer.

2°. Concentrativeness is a misnomer. It ought to have occurred to Combe that nature in her consistent symmetry would not have located an intellectual organ among the propensities; but that the continuity evinced by those whose heads served him to mark this organ was the continuity (and therefore the concentration) of *affection*. Indeed, Spurzheim did not concur in Combe's opinion, declared that his experience was in contradiction with them, and Combe himself only gives the name as *conjectural;* and the mistakes made by practical phrenologists, who have received the conjecture as demonstration, might serve to discredit their art, if in other respects it not redeem itself. Continuity of affection, instead of continuity of thought, is probably much nearer the truth.

3°. Imitation is evidently *sympathy*, a sort of identification of self with others and their feelings. I have therefore placed it among the social emotions. It is by this chord that the Actor, the Orator, and the Poet are able to set an assembly or community to a unison of feeling and of action.

4°. Firmness is the organ to which concentration of mind, or of continuous trains of thought, really belongs. Firmness implies fixedness of *intent*, or of *design*, so that he who has this feeling will, if his intellect is once attracted by any question, pursue it to the end.

5°. Sublimity was I believe discovered by Fowler & Wells. I have placed it among the Artistic Organs, as it seems closely allied to the unawed advance towards unlimited perfection, evinced by the inventors and progressive men of the age. It is of higher rank than the mere constructive instinct, which works upon a predestined model; for it is free to receive its impulse from intellect and ideality, which delight in adaptation and beauty.

But in all these definitions of emotions, there is always some term or phrase implying some element of thought or option, which does not and cannot belong to them. The emotions cannot be considered as intelligent, nor should their definition convey a compound notion, for if they were either capable of rational judgments, or of multiple components, they would not be emotions, but modes of reflection and judgment.

The stamp of reason they acquire in man, is due not to any quality of their own, but to man's intellectual nature, which not only modifies and enlightens them, but soars above them, above their animality, and descends from the Spirit of God to inspire them.

The ideas man forms of his emotions, and the names he gives them in consequence of these ideas, involve sensational impressions and intellectual operations, which constantly accompany the passional involutions. Man's FIRMNESS, for instance, is interwoven with the judgment, whether correctly or incorrectly formed, of what is to be done; his CONSCIENTIOUSNESS contains the idea of what *ought* to be done; his HOPE exists with an appreciation of probability or possibility, as well as with some desire; his SUBLIMITY is moved in common with the presence or recollection of great force, and the simultaneous recollection that this great force is adapted to some mighty *design* of God or man; his CONSTRUCTIVENESS is associated with a capacity for the processes of thought the architect requires, viz., the computation of measure, proportion, fitness, &c. Thus were it not for the PECULIAR *impulse* or *thrill* of each of these emotions, and for the fact that we know several of them to exist independently of consciousness, we would be apt to regard them as purely phenomena of the intellectual or rational power in the agent.

It is in man that this admixture of the rational element with emotion is peculiarly felt; and therefore if we were to confine our attention to man alone, we could not hope to unravel the apparent confusion thus created; but the instincts of the lower animals, those instincts which are clearly and positively automatic, owing nothing to education or thought, have furnished us with appreciable distinctions. Hence in vain have philosophers shown the sensational and intellectual characteristics of the *human* emotions, and have argued, with Condillac, that sense necessarily produces consciousness, and that consciousness necessarily produces thought and emotion; the Phrenologist turns and points to senseless vitality, or to preordained instinct as his witness.

Still the difficulties of elementary nomenclature, and abstract definition remain, preventing any clear demarcation; and it would seem that man might with this or that faculty perform the acts for which another organ has been given, or appears to be destined. Hence, for instance, what need of Constructiveness if we have Order, Comparison, Causality, Ideality, &c. But the confusion is merely verbal, turning more upon the meaning of the name than upon the essence of the emotion itself.

But, notwithstanding this nominal indistinctness and verbal admixture as between one emotion and the other psychological elements, there is one clear and well-marked distinction to be drawn. It is between the selfish and the social feeling. One set of emotions tend evidently to self or egotism; they are concentric; but another set tend to society and man in general; they are expansive and disinterested. On the one side we may place all those sentiments having communion with Humanity and God, while on the other, we may range the propensities peculiarly animal and vital.

This gives us at once the grand distinction which pervades the philosophy of Jesus, and which constitutes the ethics of the New Testament.

Thus is our attention called to the

## JESUIC PHILOSOPHY OF EMOTION,

in relation to which I will now proceed to give my views.

Many, before reading this Study, would like to know what sect the author belongs to; but neither this preface nor the book itself will gratify their curiosity in this respect. The disclosure is refrained from simply because it would be an idle thing in a work which does not propose to consider the character and teachings of Jesus in a religious or theological point of view. It is only of the man and his philosophy that the following pages are written.

Of Jesus, the Christ, there are apostles who have promulgated the revelation, martyrs who have perished in the name, priests who have preached the dogmas, worshippers who have professed the faith, and theologians who, in thousands of volumes, have expounded the word; but of Jesus, the man as distinguishable from God, few have separately treated.

And may we not without irreverence consider him in this view? Is it not taught that he was both man and God—that he had a true human body—that he ate, drank, walked, worked, and grew weary—that he groaned, bled, and died on the cross—that he assumed our whole nature, soul as well as body—that he was capable of human feelings, such as amazement, grief, joy, &c.—that his human nature must not be confounded with his divine—that though there is a union of natures in Christ, there is not a mixture or confusion of them or of their properties—that his humanity is not changed into his deity, nor his deity into his humanity; but that the two natures are distinct in one person?

If, on the one hand, the Unitarians have been condemned for doubting the divinity of Jesus, on the other Marcion, Apelles, Valentinius and many others were declared heretics for denying his humanity.

It is therefore without the fear of incurring the blame of any Christian that, eliminating every theological view, and considering the *ethics* promulgated by Jesus and his apostles in a purely rational aspect, I shall endeavor to expound and commend his *law* as a systematic philosophy. I hope to show that, even without the sanction of divine authority, and when measured by right reason alone, this system is *logically* and practically the true one, and the only one suited to the nature of man as a social creature.

In doing so, I shall not, I believe, find it necessary (as do the most approved authors, who nevertheless are considered as good Christians) to tamper with, palliate, or evade any of the moral precepts of Jesus, so as to pander to the exigencies of selfishness or vanity, or to any of those punitive feelings which influence the prevailing ideas of Justice and Right. Unfortunately this is the fashionable course ; and in the most popular works on ethics we still find Brotherly-Love hewn square with the "four cardinal virtues" of the Greek and Roman moralists. These I think should be discarded as insufficient and as leading man astray. I accept the *new law* in its broad and absolute meaning; and it is in this uncompromising sense that I shall maintain it to be the true and perfect standard of human action.

From a perusal of the works of scientific thinkers of modern times, it would appear as if the majority of them had taken it for granted that Jesus has not disclosed the innate moral criterion, but has left it to them to find and proclaim the natural stand-point of morals, law, and politics.

In this, I think, they have been mistaken. By the rules of action prescribed and exemplified in the New Testament, by the enunciation of the *principle* or basis of these rules, and by the *reasons* given to fortify them, we are furnished with a complete system far better than any ever formed by the philosophers of ancient times, —a system containing within itself *psychologically*, the essence, and *logically*, the rationale of the moral law; while the whole is practically illustrated by the sublime and beautiful *acts* of the author and his apostles.

But the scientific moralists were far from perceiving this. They have continued to explore the world of mind and action to find some *new* theory, some hitherto unknown resting-place for the olive-bearing bird of true virtue. They all, no doubt, desired the moral perfection of man, but the wish for the glory of discovering the test principle and focal point of ethics, and social economy, had certainly much force in determining the course of many of them, and prevented them from seeing—1°, that the precious jewel had been found—2°, that they were not the finders.

I regard many of the works of these philosophers as serving to exhibit the miserable aberrations and ingenious shifts of which the human mind is capable when seeking to reconcile the animal and selfish development of the passions with the dictates of reason and the true instincts of nature. On the other hand, the efforts of many writers to disclose a pure criterion is of itself sufficient to show the existence of an inherent impulse in man which prepares him for love and aspires to truth; but they have failed, in a greater or a less degree, to attain the goal of these impulses and aspirations.

The ancients in their failure, being ignorant of the Jesuic doctrine are entitled to our indulgence; but the moderns, though often displaying laudable motives and aims, are less excusable; for they had the benefit of the Jesuic record, and yet disregarded it to follow the Greek and Roman models. Thus, in lands professedly Christian, where the Jesuic record is held as divine and as containing the revelations of God in theology and morals, we see men profoundly learned, who (though seeking for the pivotal truth) have hardly noticed *the book* which was before them, and which contained the truth they desired, written in blazing characters. They ransacked the mazes of metaphysics, and racked their brains with cunning and abstruse speculations to solve the problem which had been worked out, centuries before, by him whom they were wont to call their God. Strange to say, this book and revelation, which they all had in their hands, remained, with respect to the *fundamental principle* it contains, sealed to their intellectual eye; and though they read it over and over again, they found but little in it besides texts for theological controversy. Having eyes they did not see, having ears they did not hear. True, they have professed a profound respect for the book, and ostensibly bowed to its authority; but it was only to betray or forget it with impunity; and they passed it over with scarcely a thought (not dreaming it contained the treasure they were seeking) to follow after their own theories or those of Socrates, Plato, Aristotle, Zeno, Epictetus, &c.

It must, however, be admitted, that approaches have been made towards the true criterion; and that of late years the philosophers are beginning to see that the New Testament is the way to true ethical knowledge, "*subjectively*" as well as "*objectively.*" At present, they are not far from converting their favorite terms of "Suggestion," "Sympathy," "Conscience," and "Moral Sense," into the more primary and definable ones of—1°, "Love to God," and 2°, *Social Feeling*, or "Love of Man." All that is now necessary is, to show them that these two are the plain and positive innate attributes of man. The time is fast approaching when no ethical works will be esteemed except periphrases, commentaries, amplifications, illustrations, and demonstrations of the Law of Love, as stated by Jesus, and as exemplified by him eighteen centuries ago.

Indeed, we are already arrived at the point when we are able to perceive with clearness, not only how the nominalists and realists, the sensationalists and idealists, divisionists and communists, the protectionists and freetraders, have demolished one another; but also how it is that nothing of their several systems remains standing, except the few pillars they had borrowed from the intellectual and moral temple of true Christianity. It is curious, in looking through the works of the great thinkers of these schools, to see, apart from their verbal peculiarities, varied nomenclatures, and singularities of logical process, how they in substance agree together, how they all tend in their material points of agreement to establish the Jesuic doctrine, and how the omission or denial of some one of the ingredients of the Jesuic philosophy, or an isolated development of only one of its principles, has been the cause of all the errors of which they have convicted one another.

This has been perceived by most of the master minds of the present century, and many of them have already pointed out and contributed to the growing tendency towards Jesuism. This book is a humble tribute to that tendency.

Let it not be imagined that I confound religion with ethics. Yet, though not confounded, they should never be separated. Ethics without religion is a body without life. But, I insist upon it, a complete and perfect system of ethics, properly so called, is published and expounded in the New Testament.

Nor let it be thought that what I call a system of ethics, is merely a series of precepts inculcating certain duties, without reference to any primary and general principle. No. My aim is to show that the New Testament contains not only the precepts of true virtue, law, and social organization; but also the repeated enunciations of the original cause, intellectual essence, prime motive or logical beginning from which all the rules it contains are derived, upon which they depend, and by which they are proved, in such a manner that the existence of the first great truth being once made evident, all the commandments follow as strictly rational deductions. Even an atheist who might obstinately choose to separate the ethical principles and ordinances contained in the New Testament, from the religious dogmas with which they are interwoven, would find more to satisfy his best feelings and his reason than in all the essays of the sages of antiquity. Indeed, the peculiar beauties and advantages (as well as the progress) of modern philosophy are due to the direct or indirect influence of the lessons of Jesus. This is the light which enabled Butler and his successors to see more clearly through the difficulties of their subject, and to discover moral analogies which had been hidden for ages. As we progress, the surpassing excellences of the Jesuic system will, at every step, become more and more evident, until their final triumph in theory and practice be achieved.

If I can forward this object in the slightest degree I shall rejoice.

The ethical system of Jesus may be set forth in consecutive order, as follows:

That God is our common father.

That, as children of one father in heaven, we are brethren.

That God loves us all as his children.

That God, by his impartial bounties, gives us the example of universal love.

That, as the children of God, we should love him.

That, as brethren, we should love one another.

That, by this parentage and brotherhood, we are equal before God and each other.

That God has implanted the social feeling within our nature.

That, by his will, we are not only children of our father, but also members of society.

That, as members of society, we are members of one another.

That, as members of the social body, we are identified in interest and feeling.

That, by this identity, whatever affects one affects all, and whatever affects all affects each.

That, as we cannot sever this union of one and all, the love of others should be equal to the love of self.

That, as each of us is but a fraction of society, mere members of the social body, there exists a general human solidarity.

That, as our weal depends upon the common weal, so therefore the welfare of society is the paramount law.

That we each possess an immortal soul.

That, by our immortal souls an eternal connection exists between us and God.

That, by this connection, death is powerless to sever us from the heavenly family.

That, by the assurance of an eternal life and brotherhood, all fear is banished.

That, by banishing fear, all self-denial, self-sacrifice, and even martyrdom, may be cheerfully incurred, to serve the people.

That, by the equality of self-love and social feeling, we are free agents.

That, by free agency and immortality, we are responsible beings.

And that, finally, by the power of these great truths of Faith, Hope, and Love, the kingdom of God will be established on earth as it is in heaven.

This hope is the sanction, the cement, the vital force of the whole Jesuic system; for, without it, who would die for the people, who would not consider his own interest as distinct and supreme? Without hope in heaven, the individualizing and dissolving influence of egotism might, in spite of the social feeling, prevail, and ever torture the bowels of society with every disorder. Mankind would forever live like wild beasts chained to each other, antagonistic, yet linked together by the social bond, and each would try by every mode of force and stratagem, to save himself from the general fate.

This is a faint outline of a few of the main features of the Divine philosophy of Jesus, which is summed up in three words: Faith, Hope, and Charity, these three, but the greatest of these is Charity; for all the law is fulfilled in one word: thou shalt love thy neighbor as thyself. The beginning and the end of this system are expressed in one line: He who loveth God loveth his neighbor also.

Jesus was the author, the first promulgator, the founder of this synthesis of ideas, this arch of principles, this harmony of ethical truths, and he gave it to the world as a *religion*, so that when I claim it for religion, I merely assert a fact and an undeniable copyright, an unquestionable title.

But many have not been in the habit of associating these ideas of Equality, Socialization, Solidarity, and Liberty with the religion of Jesus.

I know that the moral and social ideas of Jesus have been most commonly forgotten in sectarian creeds and theological contests—that substance has been made to yield to form; but take the book and read it for the lessons of divine and social love it contains, and you will find that the New Testament confirms on every page every word I say, and nowhere contradicts me.

If in the voluminous writings of Confucius, of Plato, or of any other sage, one or two passages may be found, which resemble some of the words of Jesus, be assured that they are disconnected and loose, forming no part of the structure which they accidentally adorn. In the New Testament, on the contrary, these principles are there as the foundation of the entire edifice, as an integral part of the whole, as the key of many exemplifications, as the spirit of the general context. Jesus was the first to point out the supreme value, the all-pervading truth, the infinite power, and the intellectual connection of these principles. It may well be said of the main precept of the Jesuic system, that the stone which the builders rejected has become the head of the corner.

Jesus did not profess to give *existence* to the truths he disclosed, no more than Newton professed to create gravitation. Yet no man who might have previously written or said that an apple had fallen from a tree to the ground, could claim to be the discoverer of attraction. With no more reason could any one who may have said—" do unto others as you would that others should do unto you," be set up as a rival of him who developed the source, reason, consequences, and connection of this precept, and who gave it a place in a plan where it shines harmonious with the rest—a jewel bright—but not by far the brightest among many others, forming with it a symmetrical diadem of glorious truth. Jesus came not to disturb the eternal laws of heaven; but he appeared in the moral world, as Newton did afterwards in the physical, to make known the mystery which had been hidden from the foundation of the world.

The ancient sages spoke here and there a detached phrase of the divine law; but they uttered it, as it were, casually and unconsciously, for we see nowhere a persistence in the train of thought. On the contrary, they depart from it instantly, to expound ideas of punitive Justice, interested Prudence, selfish Temperance, and angry Fortitude. In some places they merely crossed the path of truth—they did not follow it. They said just enough to prove that the Jesuic system is not an artificial one, but grows out of the true nature of man, as endowed from the beginning by the Creator. If all the scattered Christian sayings of the ancient philosophers were gathered together, and attributed to a single sage, he would remain but a pigmy alongside of the giant Jesus.

1. THE CRITERION PROPOSED.—The majority of moralists whose wisdom has enlightened the world, in ancient and modern times, have made researches, to ascertain the prime mover or single fundamental rule of human conduct; and each has fondly cherished a belief in his own success. Most of them have respectively designated some feeling of the soul, some instinct

of nature, or some universal maxim, as the main instigator or true guide of action. The primary sentiment, or synthetic precept thus found, is given in their various theories, as the touchstone or criterion by which the acts of men are to be tested. Thus Egotism, Sympathy, Conscience, Interest, Utility, Experience, Honor, Vanity, Ambition, Reason, Justice, Pleasure and Pain, Use and Abuse of faculties, have in turn been made the supreme law of man.

The unanimity with which philosophers of note have sought for a great pivotal truth, or some general principle of right and wrong, shows of what importance the discovery of such a truth or principle would be.

Such a criterion once established, all the difficulties of the science of ethics would at once disappear; for then we would have a common standard, by which every action might be immediately weighed and measured, an axiom from which all minor precepts would clearly and logically flow.

Indeed, a just conception of the infinite wisdom and mercy of God, should, of itself, give the assurance that he has not left us without an inward capacity in harmony with his eternal justice.

If such a master-law or capacity really exists, it is to be presumed that Jesus, the Christ God, must have revealed it, or that Jesus, the man and philosopher, must have sought to discover it.

Viewing him in his human aspect, that of a virtuous and profound philosopher, whose love of mankind knew no bounds, we must remain satisfied, from the fact of that boundless love itself.

That he must have endeavored to do what others have striven to accomplish : to unveil the mysteries of the human heart, and to find within the mind a genial soil in which the tree of life might grow.

That he sought to base his ethics upon the nature of man, as organized by the Creator.

That he did not, wilfully, when God had given us irradicable impulses to go in one direction, instruct us to proceed in another.

That he did not, wilfully, subject us to a rule which, from its being contrary to the laws of our mental and physical organism, is impossible.

This prompts us at once to inquire whether the philosophy of Jesus, as found in the New Testament, does not disclose some all-pervading element, inherent in man, and designed by the Deity to govern the moral and social world ?

2. THE FLESH AND THE SPIRIT.—We find, in reviewing the sayings of Jesus and his apostles, a clear line of demarcation drawn between—the Flesh and the Spirit—the lusts of the flesh, and the triumph of the Spirit—things carnal, and things spiritual—the old man, and the new man—the works and fruits of the flesh, and the works and fruits of the Spirit—fleshly wisdom, and the grace of God—uncleanliness and purity

—things of God, and things of Men—the natural man, and the spiritual man—the works of the Devil, of Satan, of the world, of the body, on the one hand, and the works of the Holy Spirit, of Grace, and of the kingdom of God on the other.

This distinction is so often repeated, and so earnestly insisted on in hundreds of texts, that it is impossible to regard it otherwise than as a main and leading idea of the Jesuic philosophy.

In the very outset of the gospels John the Baptist, the precursor of Jesus, announces him as one who will baptize with the Holy Ghost; and immediately afterwards, Jesus, led by the Spirit (Mat. iv. 1) and ministered to by the angels, (Mark i. 14,) and being full of the Holy Ghost, (Luke iv. 1) is tempted of Satan, and triumphs over him.

In many parts of the four gospels we find the idea clearly conveyed, that Jesus, throughout his whole career, from the event of his baptism through John, down to his crucifixion and death, continued to be filled with this Holy Spirit, and to resist the Devil and his lusts.

On one side he places *the soul* and on the other *the body*, and counsels his disciples to mutilate the members rather than to permit their lusts to overcome the spirit. (Mat. v. 30, xviii. 9; Mark ix. 23.)

In the same discourse he places God and Mammon in juxtaposition, and warns us that they are irreconcilable, and that we cannot serve them both. (Mat. vi. 24.)

And then when on his way to meet his death he again, in his rebuke to Peter, gives an emphatic sanction to this distinction: He turned, and said unto Peter, Get thee behind me, Satan; thou art an offence unto me; for thou savorest not of the *things that be of God*, but of those that be of *Men*." (Mat. xvi. 23; Mark viii. 33.) Jesus here clearly designed to distinguish between the spiritual and sensual feeling; for we shortly afterwards find him enjoining Peter thus: Watch and pray, that ye enter not into temptation, for the *spirit* indeed is willing, but the *flesh* is weak. (Mat. xxiv. 41; Mark xiv. 38.)

The exordium of the Gospel of St. John contains a plain enunciation of this division. He describes the sons of God as those who believe in the name of Jesus, as those who " were born not of blood, nor of the will of *the flesh*, nor of the will *of man*, but of God." (John i. 13.) A little further he says, (John iii. 6:) That which is born of the *flesh is flesh*, and that which is born of the *Spirit is spirit*. These are recorded as the words of Jesus himself, in his dialogue with Nicodemus, about the necessity of being born again; and he repeats on another occasion: It is the *spirit* that quickeneth—the *flesh* profiteth nothing. (John vi. 63.)

The importance of this distinction, as taught by Jesus, was strongly felt by his apostles; for we find them constantly urging it in all their epistles, and in a variety of forms. If it were necessary, a multitude of texts could be quoted in confirmation of this statement; but there is no reader of the Bible who has not learned to distinguish the *flesh*, its lusts and its works, as the source of sin, from the *spirit*, its holiness and fruits, as the light of the kingdom of God. Yet, I cannot refrain from referring to a few passages forcibly conveying the idea I seek to inculcate, so material do I consider it to be for arriving at a clear understanding of the philosophy we are studying; and so necessary for obtaining a knowledge of the *criterion* that philosophy adopts as its pivot.

Rom vii. 18: I know that in me (that is in my *flesh*) dwelleth no good thing—22, for I delight in the law of God, *after the inward man*. 25, So then with the *mind* (spirit) I myself serve the law of God, but with the *flesh* the law of sin.

Rom. viii. 1: There is therefore no condemnation to them which are in Jesus Christ, who walk not after the *flesh*, but after the *Spirit*. 6, For to be *carnally* minded is death, but to be *spiritually* minded is life and peace. 13, For if ye live after the *flesh* ye shall die; but if ye through the *Spirit* do mortify the deeds of the body ye shall live.

Rom. viii. 6: To be *carnally* minded is death; but to be *spiritually* minded is life and peace.

Rom. viii. 9: But ye are not in the *flesh* but in the *Spirit*.

Gal. vi. 7, 8: Be not deceived; God is not mocked; for whatsoever a man soweth, that shall he also reap. For he that soweth to his *flesh*, shall of the flesh reap corruption; but he that soweth to the *Spirit*, shall of the Spirit reap life everlasting.

Gal. v. 16: This I say then, Walk in the *Spirit* and ye shall not fulfil the lusts of the flesh. 17, For the flesh lusteth against the Spirit, and the Spirit against the flesh; and these *are contrary one to the other*.

Eph. iv. 22, 23: That ye put off the *old man* which is corrupt according to the deceitful *lusts;* and be renewed in the *spirit* of your mind.

Philippians iii. 3: For we are the circumcision which worship God in the *Spirit*, and rejoice in Christ Jesus, *and have no confidence in the flesh.*

Col. iii. 9, 10: Seeing you have put off the *old man*, and his deeds; and have put on the *new man.*

1 Pet. ii. 1: Dearly beloved, I beseech you, as strangers and pilgrims, abstain from *fleshly* lusts which war against the *soul.*

1 Pet. iv. 6: For this cause was the gospel preached also unto them that are dead that they might be judged according to men in the *flesh*, but live according to God, in the *Spirit.*

2 Pet. i. 4: Whereby are given unto us exceeding great promises; that by these you might be partakers of the *divine nature*, having escaped the corruption that is in the world through *lust.*

1 John ii. 16: For whatsoever is *born* of God overcometh the *world.*

Jude 19: These be they who separate themselves, *sensual*, having not the *Spirit*.

In selecting these texts, I have taken only a few of those in which the flesh and the spirit are put in opposition to each other, in the same passage, as they answer my present purpose with more directness; but, throughout the New Testament, THE FLESH, its works, its fruits, now under its name of the flesh, but then as frequently under the name of the old man, the natural man, the body, the world, things sensual, things carnal, Satan, the devil, lust, filth, or impurity—is represented as the great enemy against which Jesus and his apostles contended; and of which they sought to free mankind; and in place of which they offered the Spirit—the Holy Spirit—the Holy Ghost, and through it Grace and Faith with all their fruits. (Titus iii. 5; 1 Cor. xii. 3.)

What I have thus set forth is no doubt familiar to all theologians, and is, I believe, admitted by every one of them; yet I find in these premises the neglected corner-stone of the only true system of temporal ethics, and an infallible and all-embracing rule of human action.

Flesh and Spirit! What definite idea, in a natural sense, should we attach to these words?

Jesus gives us a plain, certain, and beautiful rule by which the meaning of these two terms can be practically ascertained:

Ye shall know them by their fruits. Do men

gather grapes of thorns, or figs of thistles? Even so every good tree bringeth forth good fruit; but a corrupt tree bringeth forth evil fruit. A good tree cannot bring forth evil fruit, neither can a corrupt tree bring forth good fruit. (Mat. vii. 16, 17, 18; Luke vi. 43, 44; et als.)

Applying this rule to the subject before us we find, on the one side, that—

The fruit of the Spirit is Love, Joy, Peace, Long-Suffering, Gentleness, Faith, Meekness, Temperance. (Gal. v. 22.)

And on the other side, that—

The works of the flesh are manifest: which are these: adultery, fornication, uncleanliness, lasciviousness, idolatry, witchcraft, hatred, variance, emulations, wrath, strife, sedition, heresies, envyings, murder, drunkenness, revellings, *and such like*. (Gal. v. 19.)

Is it not evident, then, that these two are the source of moral good and evil, the opposite generators of virtue and of vice?

Nor is this distinction arbitrary. Jesus did not tell us to control the flesh and follow the spirit without any reference to the instincts of our nature. He had, as I will endeavor to demonstrate, a deeper and wider perception of the constitution of man than any other teacher of morals, ancient or modern; and he has given us the *only* law truly adapted to that constitution.

An investigation of the subject will satisfy every impartial mind, that Jesus regarded man as capable of two feelings: one the *selfish feeling*, which corresponds with the flesh; the other the *social feeling*, which is congenial to the spirit, and includes the love of God. (2 John v. 2.)

The selfish feeling is that which confines "love" to the individual; and concedes nought to fellow-creatures but what is necessary to obtain a requital, serviceable to interest or pleasure.

The social feeling is that which extends "love" to all mankind; and concedes nought to the individual but what men enjoy as "members one of another." (Rom. xii. 5; Eph. iv. 25.)

These are the extremes: there are many grades of approach between the two; many mixtures, in different proportions of both.

Hereafter we will see to what extent Jesus admits any of these grades or admixtures.

Certain it is, however, that his moral criterion is all in this distinction between flesh and spirit; and that his rule of moral perfection, *in a temporal sense,* prescribes the full development of the social feeling with all its consequences.

He has taught us the proper method of developing and cultivating it: 1st, by clearly defining the two opposites, so that the line of demarcation cannot be mistaken; 2d, by teaching wherein the works of the flesh or selfish feeling are to be avoided; and 3d, by showing us how to act according to the spirit, and how to reap the sweet fruits the social feeling doth produce.

3. The Selfish Feeling.—In the Jesuic philosophy the Selfish Feeling or the Flesh is personified by Satan or the Devil. All the terms which might be applied to one glorying in all the sins that flesh is heir to are applied to him by Jesus and the sacred writers. Every crime or vice which the most unbridled egotism might suggest is imputed to him. All the offences committed by mankind are attributed to his influence. He is called a murderer and liar, John viii. 44; the God of the *world*, 2 Cor. iv. 4; the ruler of *darkness*, Eph. vi. 12; the adversary, 1 Pet. v. 8; the accuser of the brethren, 1 Pet. ix. 10; a sower of tares, Mat. xiii. 25, 28; a wolf, John x. 12; a roaring lion, 1 Pet. v. 8; the tempter, 1 Thes. iii. 5, &c., &c. He is described as being presumptuous, Mat. iv. 5, 6; proud, 1 Tim. iii. 6; wicked, 1 John ii. 13; subtile, 2 Cor. xi. 3; deceitful, 2 Cor. xi. 14, Eph. vi. 11; fierce and cruel, Luke viii. 29, Luke ix. 39, 42, 1 Pet. v. 8; and cowardly, Jas. iv. 7. We are told that he was the author of the fall, 2 Cor. xi. 3; that he tempted Jesus, Mat. iv. 3–10; that he opposes God's works, 1 Thes. ii. 18; that he hinders the gospel, 2 Cor. iv. 4; that the wicked are his children, Mat. xiii. 38, Acts xiii. 10, 1 John iii. 10; that they turn aside after him, 1 Tim. v. 15; that they do his lusts, John viii. 44; and that he blinds, deceives, and ensnares

them, 2 Cor. iv. 4, Rev. xx. 7, 8, 1 Tim. iii. 7, 2 Tim. ii. 26. The warnings against his power and cunning are so numerous, and the necessity of resisting him, of being armed against him, and of being watchful to avoid his temptations and snares, is so often enjoined, that we can hardly open the book without finding a text on the subject.

All these epithets are applied, all these accusations are brought, all these warnings are uttered, all these sins are denounced against the flesh in texts so similar, and forms so concordant with those relating to the devil, that no doubt can remain that the unsubdued flesh may be regarded as the embodiment of Satan. Rom. vii. 28; Jas. iii. 15; Eph. ii. 2, 3; Rom. i. 21–32; Gal. v. 19–21; Eph. iv. 27; 2 Pet. ii. 4, 10; 2 Tim. iii. 2; 1 John iii. 8, 9; John viii. 44; Heb. ii. 14; 1 John iv. 1, 3.

Indeed, the Jesuic philosophy under this head not only comprises Satan, but, secondly, the *animal body* with its lusts; and thirdly, the *mental spirit* of rebellion and depravity which is opposed to love.

That the animal body is viewed in the New Testament as opposed to the Spirit of God, is evident from the texts which declare: that the law of sin is in our *members*, Rom. vii. 23; that it is necessary to subdue and mortify *the body*, 1 Cor. ix. 27, Col. iii. 5; that the God of the wicked is their own *belly*, Rom. xvi. 17; that the good have *crucified the flesh* and its lusts, Gal. v. 24; that the works of the flesh are fornication, lasciviousness, and other such exclusively *physical* deeds, Gal. v. 19; that the sinful are as natural *brute beasts*, 2 Pet. ii. 12; and that the *natural man* receiveth not the things of the Spirit of God, 2 Cor. ii. 14.

That the selfish feeling (considered as mind) also belongs to this category, appears from the denunciation of the *carnal* MIND, Rom. viii. 7; from the *internal* works of the flesh, such as envy, malice, anger, pride, hatred of God, &c., Rom. i. 21; from the necessity of *cleansing the mind* of filthiness, 2 Cor. vii. 1; from the existence of a *spirit* of disobedience, Eph. ii. 2, 3; and from the declaration that there *are spirits* which are not of God, 1 John iv. 3; minds subject to the flesh.

Thus, a sort of infernal trinity is disclosed: 1, Satan, the God of the world; 2, the sensual spirit; and 3, the earthly body; and it is of this trinity St. James seems to speak, when condemning the wisdom of the vicious, he says, iii. 15: This wisdom descendeth not from above, but is (1) earthly, (2) sensual, (3) devilish.

Hence, as if no part of the comparison should be omitted, we are taught that there is a natural body and a spiritual body, 1 Cor. xv. 44, one which is earthly and corrupt, and cannot inherit the kingdom of heaven, but the other which is changed, redeemed, and is heavenly, (ibid. 35 to 53; Rom. viii. 23.) Of those who hold the one, and live after the flesh, Satan is the father; and of those who inherit the other, God is the father.

In this the children of God are manifest, and the

children of the Devil. 1 John iii. 10. That is, They which are the children of the *flesh*, these are not the children of God. Rom. ix. 8.

4. THE SOCIAL FEELING.—No man—and in calling Jesus a man, I follow the example of St. John, xi. 50, and of St. Paul, 1 Cor. xv. 21; Rom. vi. 15; Heb. x. 12—no man ever displayed a love for his fellow-creatures equal to that which Jesus has shown. During his life all his thoughts, and words, and acts, were for their happiness. Though " he was rich," he stripped himself of every thing for their sakes, (2 Cor. viii. 9;) though he could have enjoyed luxury and power, he rejected them, and became a houseless wanderer, in order to scatter the seed of his word throughout the land; though he was learned, he humbled himself with the ignorant, that he might impart his wisdom; though he was pure, he mingled with the corrupt, for the purpose of reforming them; though his fellow-men rejected and wronged him, he clung to them with unabated affection, and with untiring zeal he continued to travel from place to place, relieving physical infirmities, and curing moral ills—having incessantly before him the single great object of his mission, which embraced the good of all men: no self-denial, no danger, no labor was too great to check his courage and devotedness; and finally, persecution and malice having brought him to the cross, " he died for the people," was a voluntary martyr; and, with his last breath,

(still tenacious in his love even of his murderers,) he uttered the sublime summary of all he felt for us: "Father, forgive them, for they know not what they do."

To prove that in these acts of love and devotedness, Jesus offered himself as an example to be imitated, and that he expects of every man the same intense love of humanity, and the same unmeasured acts of charity, would be to quote the New Testament from beginning to end. But perhaps the best evidence on this point is the declaration that Jesus took upon himself the nature of flesh and blood, "with the feeling of our infirmities, and was tempted like as we are," (Heb. iv. 15;) thus it is shown that he evidently intended practically to demonstrate it to be possible for men in general to feel and act as he did.

Indeed, the ethics of Jesus are not only practically possible, but they are *conformable to our nature*, and are written thereon by the Creator. So thought St. Paul, for he tells us the Lord saith: "I will put my laws into their hearts, and in their minds will I write them," Heb. x. 16. But this is more pointedly shown in the parable of the Sower, and the example of the Gentiles, who do *by nature* the things contained in the law.

The parable of the Sower, Mat. xiii. 3–18, Luke viii. 5–11, represents Jesus as casting the seeds of the word. Some fall by the wayside, some in stony places and among thorns, and some into good ground. The religious feeling and the social feeling inherent in man, are the good ground, which, receiving the seed, enables it to take root, and bear forth fruit. It is the Spirit which quickeneth these congenial constituents, with a holy heat and fervency. He who hath not " root in himself," and in whose heart the seed cannot grow to maturity, is the man who has become hardened in prejudice and egotism. The expressions " good ground," and " root in himself," clearly indicate a natural state of the soul, antecedent to the hearing of the word, and to the infusion of the Spirit. Of this state we have an example in those Gentiles, who having not the law, "*do* by *nature* the things contained in the law," and " show the work of the law *written in their hearts*." Rom. ii. 14, 15.

Now, what is this natural feeling which produces the works of the law?

The example of Jesus answers; every line of the New Testament answers; but there is one line which sums up the response, with a brevity and pointedness which no Spartan could equal. That line contains not a stroke of wit, not a short ejaculation of contempt, defiance, pride, or stoicism: no, it compasses more than all the volumes philosophers have written on ethics; and, in one word, it teaches the wisdom of ages.

St. Paul says, Gal. v. 14:

"*All* the law is fulfilled in one word: thou shalt love thy neighbor as thyself."

Here, then, we have the *love of man*, or in other

words, the SOCIAL FEELING proclaimed as being the pivotal sentiment from which all human virtue doth radiate.

Upon the existence of this sentiment depends all the arts, all sciences, all laws, and all governments, for, without the social attraction, all these things would be useless and vain.

Without this sentiment as a ground-hold, what a mockery would it be to pronounce, as an all-embracing commandment: love thy neighbor (that is to say every man) as thyself.

If philosophers had considered the full force and purview of the social feeling, they would have acknowledged not only its paramount importance, but also that it lies much deeper in the soul of man, than the other motives they have taken as their stand-point.

Egotism, though the very opposite of the social feeling, is in fact necessarily subservient to it; for it can only be gratified in and through society. This secondary rank, for the same reason, must be assigned to Vanity, Ambition, and Pleasure. The so-called moralists, who have taken these words as their pointers, are forced to reconcile them with the social feeling, by showing that Interest and Egotism are well served, Ambition and Vanity are properly gratified, Pleasure and Pain are wisely apportioned, only when they are controlled by a due regard for Society, and only so far as they can be reconciled to the love of Man.

As to Conscience, the Moral Sense, and Honor, they

imply the existence of an index or prompter, which guides or quickens them, and as the inward voice is never else than the echo of a just regard for our fellow beings and society, I conclude that the social feeling is the real monitor.

Sympathy is but a *form* or mode of the social feeling, viewed in a restricted sense, and as attracting individual to individual. The same remark applies to Benevolence.

Experience, Utility, Reason, Use, and Abuse of faculties, are nothing but the watchwords of empirical systems devoid of any cementing or governing principle.

Justice, Equity, and Equality require the discovery of a standard of moral weights and measures; and as Justice, &c., are but the proper *application* of that standard, it is the standard itself we ought to recognize as our principle; but it is in our associated intercourse alone, that any such principle can have any force. Is it not, therefore, the principle of association itself, which governs all social morality?

Thus we find that the Social feeling is after all the source and summary of every virtue and law; for without society virtue and law had never been born, nor could they ever have had even a name. The social feeling is therefore of the *Spirit*, and not of the Flesh.

In accounting for the existence of society, some philosophers have resorted to imaginary accidents and events, by which mankind are supposed, through the necessity of self-protection, and mutual safety, to have been brought together in families, clans, tribes, and nations. Man is supposed to have been at first not only wild but isolated: individual—having no permanent connection with his fellows, male or female. The attacks of wild beasts and of enemies, as well as other circumstances, dependent not upon the internal nature of humanity, but upon a gradual discovery of the interests of the individual, are given by philosophers and jurists in beautiful narratives, as the causes by which man has been, as it were, driven from the solitary to the social state. This theory assumes that man is by temperament or instinct inclined to the solitary state, and that he was, despite natural feeling, compelled, by the force of external causes, to associate with other men.

The evidence of history, geography, and zoology, contradict this opinion: historians have always found men formed, at the origin, into societies; geographers have always seen them living together, even in the wildest lands; and naturalists, who take the liberty of establishing analogies between man and other living creatures, divide the animal kingdom into two portions, the gregarious and non-gregarious, and class man as belonging, by instinct, to the first.

If man were destined by nature for the solitary state, how happens it that he is naturally so weak, so defenceless, and so naked? We find everywhere the natural order of things so arranged, that every animal is formed to harmonize, in all respects, with the condition in which he is to exist. Volumes have been written to show the beautiful adaptation of all things, and creatures in the universe, as illustrative of the wisdom, foresight, and benevolence of the Creator, and, in fact, as proving the existence of God himself. Is man an exception to this rule of general accord, so admirable and perfect in its aggregate and details?

Could the solitary man provide against his physical deficiencies? No: he is left weak, defenceless, and naked, because socialization, for which he feels an innate propensity, meets all the exigencies of this natural helplessness; and moreover, because he is endowed with faculties for which motives of action must be furnished.

These faculties are vast, varied, and mighty. They invest man with the dominion of the globe. Can they have been so lavishly cast upon a creature inclined to a solitary life? To answer affirmatively, is to impugn, without a reason, the supreme wisdom and love, so infallible and constant in all other respects.

If man were solitary, the greatest number of the manifold and extensive powers of the mind (though capable of bringing all things into subjection, and though having the appetite to do it) would be imprisoned in the narrowest circle, would find but few and limited objects and occasions for their action, would be deprived of sufficient aliment and exercise, and would be debarred the full and healthy display or expansion of their natural forces.

All our faculties are social in this: that they have capabilities of development and refinement which naught but society can gratify.

The analytical, synthetical, logical, imitative, idealizing, ordinating, mathematical, and constructive powers of the mind, all require the great field of *social* intercourse, to satisfy their impulses, and unfold their energies.

Deprived of the natural locomotive, aggressive, and defensive members and instruments given to other animals, stripped of all natural physical protection against the elements, and his enemies, man, on the other hand, is endowed with senses, susceptible of and eager for the most luxurious enjoyments. His sense of feeling is so tender that he must have a bed to sleep on, the softest fabrics to clothe himself with, the smoothest implements and furniture to handle. His sense of taste is so critical, and his stomach is so weak, that cookery with its heat and its condiments, must pre-digest and ensavor his food. His sense of smell is so accomplished, that the sweetest and gentlest odors are those which impart him pleasure. His hearing is so nice that it evokes music, with her infinite harmonies and melodies. His sight is so fastidious, that it delights only in lines of beauty and scenes of sublimity.

True it is, some animals have senses more acute than those of man, for some uses; but those uses are of the simplest kind and are single and specific in their ends, while the senses of man are of a complex character, are capable of graduated impressions, of perceiving seriated degrees, of appreciating combined accords and discordances, and demand a supply of subtle enjoyments, which naught but the arts and commerce of society can afford.

To nourish this weak and unagile body, and to gratify those senses, (so delicate and so unfit, by their nature, to dwell among the wild beasts of the forest, or under the inclemencies of the desert,) the man, fulfilling the true inclination of his mind, lives among and with his like, and finds the full aliment and use of his active intellectual powers. His imitative ingenuity creates agriculture; his mechanical faculty invents all the wonders of manufactures and machinery; his constructive propensity produces the comforts and splendors of architecture and viatecture; his analytical powers discover chemistry and botany; his varied appetites generate commerce with its multifarious exchanges and relations; his mathematical genius measures the size, distance, and pathway of the stars, and expounds the laws which control revolving worlds; his musical tastes induce him to frame the gamut and contrive cunning instruments of sound; his logical capacities enable him to trace the intricacies and explore the depths of his own mind; and, finally, his idealizing aspirations procure him elegant and splendid adornments for all his works, and start painting, poetry, and sculpture into life. No pure necessity of self-preservation can account for the formation of the society which evolves these things; but, it is indubitable that all the senses, instincts, feelings, sentiments, and intellectual faculties of man (of themselves and by their own attraction) draw him into association with his fellows. In one word, man is endowed by nature and by nature's God, with a gregarious instinct, the innate desire of society, the *social feeling*.

But what irrefragably proves that man is, by the natural law, a social animal, is the fact that he is created with the gift of language. This gift could be of no possible use to a solitary being; but it is the last and most perfect endowment which God has blessed us with to fit us for our destiny. Vain would it be for me to attempt to enumerate all the consequences which flow from this divine boon. The interchange, the transmission of ideas, the preservation of acquired knowledge, the progress of the sciences and arts, the establishment of commerce, the forum, the pulpit, and the press—all these, which are social phenomena, nay, society itself, could not have existed for a moment without *language*, nor could language itself exist without society; and thus, by the mutual dependence of the two, does it become evident that man is by nature made for speech and for society.

If, then, man is instinctively and organically gregarious and social, if the divinity has formed and endowed him for social life, if he finds the only true pleasurable outlet of all his feelings and faculties in a life of communion with his fellows, if it is only in society and through society that he can be happy, does it not follow that the *social feeling* is the main, the aggregate passion of human nature, the point at which centres every precept of virtue, and the pivot or criterion on which all good morals and all good laws must turn?

In analyzing the moral sentiments of man, we do not hesitate to class as natural and instinctive feelings, Pity, Cupidity, Anger, Love, &c.,—all the passions are assigned a seat in the soul, or (to speak the language of positive philosophy) a location in the cerebral organization of the natural man. In forming the list of our passions, we should not overlook the gregarious or social feeling. In my opinion, for the reasons I have given, it should be assigned the first and most conspicuous place. Sympathy and pity are not sufficient to explain the phenomenon of society. We may, through egotism, or from some other cause, feel sympathy or pity for a dog, a horse, a bird, &c., but there is a gap between such a feeling and that which commands, as an imperious want, the social condition. A man, shipwrecked upon the most beauteous, fruitful, and genial of the uninhabited isles of the ocean, would pine in anguish for the companionship of his like; and if, after a time, his deadliest enemy were cast upon the lonely Eden, the solitary would greet the new-comer with tenderness and joy. Both would fly with exhilaration from their rich and shady groves, to the bosom of society, be its hardships ever so great, or their fate ever so uncertain. The history of hundreds of shipwrecks might serve to illustrate this; and the romance of Robinson Crusoe is only a truthful summary of the observations of travellers upon this trait of human nature.

It is now established, by authentic investigations, that the greatest *moral* torture which can be inflicted, is solitary imprisonment; and the current of opinion has turned against it as a nugatory means of reformation and as a cruel punishment. Why is this so? Simply because in the same manner as we recoil with horror from the cutting and scarring of the physical man, we also revolt against the mutilation of the spiritual man, and must therefore condemn the act which prevents the gratification of the most imperious of our natural passions—*the desire for society.*

Solitary imprisonment excludes all the intellectual and moral effects society is wont to work upon the individual; and consigns him to the complete ossification of all the best impulses of his nature. Like a corpse thrown into the deep grottos of Antiparos, the soul of the solitary prisoner becomes petrified and void of all human sensibility.

An irresistible attraction, far more powerful than self-interest, draws us into social intercourse. Next to life, and the food which sustains life, we require society. Sever us from society, and we feel as if divided from ourselves, a branch cut from the tree of humanity, thrown aside to wither and to die.

5. THE HOLY SPIRIT.—But the Jesuic Philosophy

does not stop here. With the natural social feeling it connects two other facts of equal importance. I mean the existence of God, and the immortality of the Soul. A knowledge of these two facts, whether arising from natural instinct, or reason, or from revelation alone, at once elevates and spiritualizes the social feeling. This knowledge furnishes the social feeling with its highest sanction, and final justification. That sanction is God's economy, and that justification is the eternal brotherhood in the heavens.

"And now abideth Faith, Hope, and Charity: these three; but the greatest of these is Charity." (1 Cor xiii. 13.)

The union of these three in the breast of man, through the grace of God, constitutes in the Jesuic philosophy the gift of the Holy Spirit; and consecrates our body as the temple of that Spirit.

That the gift of the Holy Spirit includes the love of God, the love of man, and the hope of immortality, is clearly taught by the New Testament. "The love of God," saith St. Paul, "is shed abroad in our hearts by the Holy Ghost, which is given to us." (Rom. v. 5.) "Beloved, let us *love one another*, for love is of God, for every one that loveth is *born of God*, and knoweth God." 1 John iv. 7. "For the fruit of the Spirit is all goodness," &c. (Eph. v. 9; Gal. v. 22; 1 John ii. 9, 10; 1 John iii. 14, 15.) "Now the God of hope fill you with all joy and peace in believing, that ye may abound in hope, through the power of the

Holy Ghost." (Rom. xv. 13.) "He that soweth to the Spirit, shall of the Spirit reap life everlasting." (Gal vi. 8.)

These texts, without seeking for numerous others, corresponding to them, are sufficient, in a religious point of view, to show what are the main characteristics of the operation of the Holy Spirit upon us; but it is the connection of the three, which forms one of the most beautiful features of the Jesuic system.

To our ideas of God, which produce feelings of reverence and awe, the Jesuic philosophy adds views, awakening tender and grateful sentiments. Not only is God eternal, infinite, single, all-wise, all-powerful, all-present, incorruptible, immutable, just, true, holy, and glorious, but he is *good* and *merciful*. Nor is this goodness and mercy confined, by the Jesuic doctrine, within a limited sphere; it is rich, manifold, and abundant; it is as infinite and everlasting as the Divinity himself.

God loves man with infinite and eternal love.

He is the common father of all mankind.

Man partakes of God's divine nature, being made in his image, and being vivified by his breath.

Through God, man has the promise of spiritual immortality and celestial happiness.

These are the doctrines with respect to God, which Jesus insisted upon the most, and with which all commandments are connected; and which quicken the physical instinct for society, by the spiritual flame of divine love.

If God's love for man be so great, once conscious of it, we naturally, and as far as within us lies, requite, obey, and serve.

If God is the common father of all mankind, it follows that all men are brothers, and should love one another.

If we are partakers of God's nature, it follows that all his *moral* attributes are ours: love, truth, patience, purity, &c.

If through God we are assured of eternal life, we are immediately prompted to prepare our souls for heaven; and this preparation imports the performance of every sanctifying duty, and the practice of every regenerating virtue.

Nor is this process of argument, which connects all rules of right conduct between man and man with a belief in God, a mere commentary upon the teachings of Jesus. He makes the argument himself, and teaches these opinions in express and direct terms.

St. John gives as a reason for loving God, the fact that "he first loved us." (1 John iv. 19.) In many places of the New Testament Jesus tenders God's love to us, and asks for a return by obedience to his laws, while he makes tempting promises of reward for this return and obedience. (Jno. xiv. 15, 21, 23; 1 Cor. ii. 9; Eph. ii. 4; Rom. viii. 37; John iii. 16; 1 John iv. 9-11; 1 John iii. 1, 16, &c.)

After prescribing love to God as the first and great commandment, he says, the second, inculcating the love of man, "*is like* unto the first," (Matt. xxii. 39,) thus clearly showing the intimate connection he conceived to exist between the feelings of humanity and love to God, and the immediate bearing of these two commandments one upon the other.. Indeed he regards them as being almost identical. (Mark xii. 31.)

He points to the love of God for man in general—of God who sendeth rain to the just and unjust without distinction, as a model of human love for humanity. (Mat. v. 44, 45; Luke vi. 36.)

Love your enemies, says he, "that ye may be the children of *your Father* which is in heaven:" establishing the use of the endearing name of Father, as applicable to the divinity, and establishing also the tender relation of father and child between God and Man, as foundations for an appeal to us as children to imitate heaven by loving even the wicked.

To enforce this relationship, he says: "All ye are *brethren;* and call no *man* your father upon the earth; for one is your Father which is in heaven." Mat. xxiii. 8, 9. Those who love God and obey him, he declares to be "sons of God," John i. 12; Rom. viii. 14; and to those who are obdurate in sin, he assigns another father, the devil. (John viii. 44.)

From such premises, viz., that God is our father, and we (as long as we do not obtain Satan) are his children, it naturally follows that we are "*partakers of the divine nature.*" So indeed is it expressly declared, 2 Pet. i. 4; Heb. xii. 10.

By love to God, by the Spirit of Truth, and by deeds of willing mercy, self-denial, and civic heroism, we are taught that Man, Jesus and God may be as one, in each other. (John xiv. 20; xvii. 21, 26; Acts xvii. 28; Eph. iv. 6; 1 John iv. 6, &c.)

Our body itself is the temple of God, and the Spirit of God dwelleth in us, 1 Cor. iii. 16; vi. 19; our members are his, vi. 15; our spirit is his own, vi. 20.

Such being the case, does it not logically follow, as argued by the gospel itself, that we should love and glorify God in the body and in the spirit, by preserving their purity, and by avoiding sin; for if we defile the body, saith St. Paul, we destroy the temple of God. (1 Cor. iii. 17.)

In one word: "He who loveth God, loveth his brother also;" and "if a man say, I love God, and hateth his brother, he is a liar." (1 John iv. 20, 21.) Can language convey, in more forcible terms, the affinity between the love of God and man?

And as if this were not sufficient to persuade us, the Jesuic philosophy shows, that to God's love we are indebted for the assurance of immortality; and never abandoning the connection between our duty to God, to ourselves, and to our fellow-men, this immortality is made to depend upon the sincere accomplishment of these duties, in spirit and in deeds. (Mat. xxv. 34; Jam. i. 12; &c.) It would be a superfluous work to collect texts showing the necessity of preparing ourselves, so as at all times to be worthy of participating in the joys of the supernal kingdom. Every reader is familiar with this point of the doctrines of Jesus; and every one must at once of himself perceive the reasons which enforce it.

No system of ethics is perfect, or even tolerable, unless it teaches the existence and love of God, the immortality of the soul, and, as a consequence, the universal brotherhood, arising from a common spiritual origin and destiny. All systems devoid of this ingredient, St. Paul properly describes as "oppositions of science, falsely so called;" and of them warns us lest they spoil us "through philosophy and vain deceit, after the rudiments of the world, after the tradition of men, and not after Christ."

The first great commandment elevates man above the beast, links him with the Divinity, and gives a sanction to virtue. Its absence in philosophical treatises on morals is the cause of the multiplicity and contradictions of systems, of the difficulty of fixing upon a criterion or primary motive, of all the uncertainty in fixing upon the fundamental rule of the natural law. The love of God is just as *natural* a feeling, and is as wide in its compassing, as any of the sentiments which have been the basis of learned schemes of morality. Phrenology sustains this opinion, by placing reverence and hope high in the order of moral sentiments. The love of God might therefore be easily made the basis of a professedly "natural" theory of ethics, which would be at least as respectable as those having Egotism, Conscience, Utility, &c., for their foundation.

But the Jesuic philosophy teaches that love to God is inseparably bound up with the love of man, and that they cannot be parted without injury to both. "Keep yourselves therefore in the love of God." (Jude 21.)

Thus it is evident that we might, according to Jesus, define ethics or morals as—

1°. The science of the Will of God; or as

2°. The science of the Salvation of the Soul; or as

3°. The science of the love of man.

But as the three are so closely connected, we should at once say:

Ethics or Moral Philosophy is the science of the moral *will of God*, and teaches us our duties and the reasons of our duties to God, to ourselves, and to others, by Faith in him, through Hope of immortality, and in Charity or Love for all men.

Theology teaches us what to believe: Ethics, what we should do; and, the two together, constitute Religion.

A definition of morals which does not include the DIVINE WILL (whether revealed by prophets, or discovered by induction) as a main component, would not accord with the Jesuic Philosophy. In fact, this philosophy claims the Divinity as its source—it never ceases to speak in the name of God, and it proclaims the perfect performance of all our moral duties as the fulfilment of his will. (Mat. vi. 10; vii. 21; Luke xi. 2; 1 Cor. ii. 6–16; Philip. ii. 17; iii. 14, 15; Heb. x. 36; 1 Pet. iv. 2; 1 John ii. 17.)

Indeed, all definitions of Moral Philosophy should comprise this element. Is it not by the Divine will that "we live and move and have our being"? and has not the Divinity given us this existence for a great and eternal purpose? In this great design and purpose he manifested his will; and if we seek to act in harmony with it, should we not, at once, define the science which teaches us to do so, as the science of the moral will of God?

Certain it is, at all events, that this is the true definition according to Jesus—of Jesus, whose mission as summed up by himself, was the doing and the teaching of the Will of God. (Luke viii. 21; xi. 28; John iv. 34; v. 30; vi. 38–40; viii. 28, 29.)

But if the definition stopped here it would be incomplete, for the mind remains unsettled if left at so great a height to contemplate the boundless space of the heavenly ordinances. A well-marked purview, and brief precision, are necessary in every definition. This brief precision is attained at once by including in the definition itself an index to the triple basis of the whole moral law. Its source: Faith in the eternal reign. Its medium: Hope in the infinite goodness. Its groundwork: Charity to the whole brotherhood of the Almighty Father.

And thus is the social feeling lifted above mere instinct, purified, intellectualized by an identification with Love to God, a reliance in his love of us, and a consciousness of the common origin of the human family.

And thus will the Holy Spirit be made manifest; and "at that day," saith Jesus, "ye shall know that I am in my Father, and you in me, and I in you"—"that all may be one."

Whenever any one of the three characteristics of the Holy Spirit is expressly or tacitly omitted in any definition of morals, or is misunderstood, or is made to predominate, many errors are the consequence; and from the wrong beginning systems are deduced, of which Superstition, or Atheism, or Asceticism, or Sensualism, or Egotism, or Communism, is the ruling feature.

Thus we have :—

Superstition : the affrighted visionary, who beholds hideous phantoms in every rising truth—who fears, but loves not God, resolves all merit into the formulas of belief and rituals of worship; and sends forth her attendants, Ignorance, the eyeless ; Fanaticism, the foaming epileptic; Intolerance, the inquisitor; and Persecution, the iron-hearted, to anathematize science, torture dissenters, drown witches, burn heretics, and massacre whole populations of reformers.

Or we have—

Atheism : the Satanic scoffer, mocking heaven and inspiration, and coupling man with the brute ; he stands before the world with his companions, Pantheism the idolater, and Skepticism the blind astronomer, all reeking with the blood of their fellow-creatures, slain in the name of Liberty and Truth.

Or we have—

Asceticism: the moving corpse without a grave, who severs himself from the human family, avoids brotherly intercourse and love, walks through life wrapped in the winding-sheet of the dead, and hails the Sepulchre as a portal of escape from a land of uncongenial strangers.

Or we have—

Sensualism: the abject satyr, reeling with wine, gorging at feasts, and grovelling in lust—Sensualism, whose God is the belly, and whose law is pleasure.

Or we have—

Egotism: the machiavelic Proteus, the masked bravo, tendering the cup of deception brimful of blood and poison, or kneeling in adoration before his mirrored self, beyond whom he knows nothing and loves nothing; reducing all morals to the casuistry of experience or utility, appealing to vanity under the name of honor, knowing conscience only as the fear of pains and penalties, admitting honesty only as the best policy, teaching hypocrisy and flattery as social virtues, advocating justice but discarding mercy, praising charity but practising it only through penurious alms, and knowing no law but interest, no agent of good but the fetters of despotism or the lash of tyrants.

Or we have—

Communism: the philanthropic Procrustes, who fain like egotism (for extremes meet) would, under pretence of equality and universal justice, compel all men, by fire and sword, to be disinterested and humble, and, in the name of humanity, destroy all liberty and moral responsibility.

It would carry me far beyond the plan of this work to take up each particular Selfish affection, and show in detail the views of Jesus upon it separately. Hundreds of texts might be quoted to show that Jesus, though he did not condemn the innate feelings necessary to self-preservation and generation, made them all *subordinate* to the love of Humanity and the happiness of Society. He raised the marriage institution to that inviolability which gave it a social instead of a private character; for he made the promise of mutual fidelity to depend upon the welfare of the community, and yielded little or nothing to the interests, passions, health, or incompatibility of the husband and wife. He treated the relations of child and parent, of friends and companions, of home and property, as entirely secondary; and required his disciples to leave all, when it was necessary to do so, to follow him—that is to say, to save the people. Self-sacrifice and Civic Heroism are taught in every discourse, and illustrated by every act of Jesus, as being paramount law, by virtue of which the animal instincts and affections find a *common centre* around which they may all cluster in peace, and a *common measure* to which they may all conform without interference and collision.

It is therefore unnecessary to enter into further details. It is only necessary to read the New Testament by this single light and according to this spirit, and the whole philosophy thereof, in its unity and in every application and precept, will become apparent to every intelligent and unprejudiced inquirer.

If Justice can exist at all, it is in the fulfilment *by Society* of its obligation towards each of its members viewed as a limb of its body, so as to secure the good of each through the happiness of all, and thus establish the *equilibrium* of Individual and Municipal Rights.

# IV.

## THOUGHT.

Johnson says: "Thought is the operation of the mind; the act of thinking." "It is," says he in another place, "the action of man's intelligent substance—the first fundamental faculty of man."

Webster says: "It is the act or operation of the mind, when attending to a particular subject or thing; or it is the idea consequent upon that operation."

Locke says: "Thinking is the action of the soul, not its essence;" and in another place he says: "When the mind turns its view inwards, and contemplates its own actions, thinking is the first that occurs."

Descartes held that "To feel and will, is to think."

Condillac, conversely, held that "To think and will, is to feel." In another place he says. "The word thought in its acception comprises all the *faculties* of the understanding, and all those of the will." Also: "Every thought has its proportions and its ornaments."

Laromiguere defines Thought to be "the aggregate of our sensitive, moral, and intellectual faculties."

Bacon concurs with Aristotle, in the apt and elegant remark: "That the hand is the instrument of instruments, and the mind the form of forms."

"The Dictionary of Philosophical Science," published by Hachette, Paris, 1844, says: "Thought (*cogitates*) is the internal movement of the intellect: the evolution which the mind performs upon itself, apart from, but influenced by its properties."

With these definitions before us, we may say, thought involves three things: 1°. An object, 2°. A Motor, 3°. A movement; or, in other words, 1°. *Contents* of mind, whether they be considered as real or ideal, me or not me; for, in either view, they are the *objects* of thought; 2°. *Properties* of mind; and 3°. *Process* of Mind.

1°. Instead of CONTENTS we may say:—Facts, Subject, Object, Reality, Matter, Phenomena, Substance, Time, Place, Duration, Space, Number, Order, Recollections, Images, Suppositions, Opinions, Resolutions, &c., *i. e.*, every thing of which we are *conscious* as a DATA or MATTER of thought, whether we conceive it to be self or not self, subjective or objective, mediate or immediate, presentative or representative.

2°. Instead of PROPERTIES we might say:—Sensation, Faculties, Powers, Affections, Propensities, Passions, Feelings, Sentiments, Laws, Instincts, Appetites, Memory, Imagination, Intellect, Motive, the power of Judgment, of Reason, of Comparison, of Association, of Abstraction, of Generalization, &c., *i. e.*, every thing of which we are conscious, as *internal* FORCES or POWERS *inducing* any mental action whatever.

3°. Instead of PROCESS we might say:—Logic, Computing, Measuring, Analyzing, Synthetizing, Generalizing, Inducting, Deducting, Comparing, Classifying, &c., *i. e.*, *the acts themselves and their laws*, as exhibited *in* the movement of the thinking mind, while performing its rational function.

Let it be noted that in making this summary, I take the definitions of thought given by philosophers, *as I find them*, and do not here assume a theory of my own; and even in those definitions, I take as true only such facts or points as are agreed upon by all the professors of every school.

Thus our beginning is upon conceded ground; and, secure in undisputed premises, I start to find new footholds of progress.

Wherever the professors of *philosophy* have differed, I will investigate for myself; and invite the reader to join me.

At this stage we may, at least, say:

THOUGHT is the *movement* (Process) of the mind upon *itself* (Contents) as influenced by its own *capabilities* (Properties).

Thought must have a beginning, or what in figurative language is called a basis, a foundation, a pivot, a fulcrum, a stand-point, a centre, &c. If it had not this it never could be positive, never be fixed, never act with certainty; for the very idea of certitude implies an initial fact behind which thought cannot go, a primary truth which the mind cannot contest, and out of which all argument must proceed—and which like the star-needle to the mariner must command our faith.

This initiatory act is (we deferentially suggest) Numeration, or Enumeration. It is the beginning of thought; for it furnishes all the materials of reasoning in all science and art, and it contains within itself the primal law of intelligence.

This act of enumeration is performed by sensation and emotion, in conjunction with an inherent power of the mind, which enables it to take, to form, to assume, to evolve A UNIT.

In mathematics this fact is indisputable. In every other science it will be found, upon scrutiny, to be equally undeniable.

A little attention to facts will enable us to know that the mind in receiving or gathering its sensations, does nothing but enumerate.

Indeed, if sensation were to stop short of embodying integers, or concrete units, where would our knowledge of any thing be? What would that knowledge consist of without units of matter, motion, time, space, substance, force, quality, quantity, body, spirit, or definition, whether expressed by a name or a number? Without a numeral unit, no fraction, no addition, no sum, no mathematics could be conceived. So without an abstract or concrete integer described or defined with certainty, no analysis could be made, no synthesis could be known or found, no induction or deduction could be carried out, and logic could not exist. True it is, units which might be treated in arithmetical numbers do not abound in philosophy, morals, law, religion, and the like; but at the same time, it is equally true that these sciences are strictly to be considered as sciences only so far as their contents can be *named* and defined, which is equivalent to enumerating them. As we progress in finding clear limits to the entities named, or as the name given approaches to a distinct unit, so does the science improve. As the parts of which its synthetical unit is composed, also acquire this clearness of limit, so does a science approach perfection. Outside of exact integers there is no science worthy of the name, and hence we are induced to assume the laws of number and measure as the laws of all reasoning in legislation, ethics, politics, &c.

I do not mean by this that these sciences can be treated in arithmetical numbers or geometrical figures; but that as numbers and figures are the data of abstract mathematics, so names, definitions, and stated facts, are the algebraical signs of every concrete science, whether it can be reduced to numbers or not; and that the *same laws of thought* govern in reasoning with these names, &c., as in reasoning with arithmetical numerals or geometrical figures.

Hence, my general proposition is:

1°. That—*the initial act, germ point, or focal centre of all thought* is THE IDEATION OF THE UNIT; and, therefore,

2°. That—from the ideation of the unit all evolutions of thought proceed, and to it all compositions and decompositions of thought recur.

In showing this I begin with—

## LOGICAL ENUMERATION.

We have already seen that the subject matter and end of all thought is *fact*. Reasoning is a procedure from fact to fact.

We have also seen that there are certain data given by consciousness which are by necessity the *initial premises* or *prima ratio* in all reasoning, and behind which we cannot find a stand or starting point. The facts thus exhibited to thought by consciousness are its materials.

But what is a fact?

A fact is any *single* state or act which can be declared by a simple sentence. Examples: 1. "I am;" 2. "The Jews cruelly crucified the divine Jesus."

In these two examples we have simple sentences—there being only one verb in each example.

But the first example cannot be multiplied into a greater number, while the second example might serve to form several simpler sentences; thus:

The Jews crucified Jesus;
The Jews were cruel;
Jesus was divine, &c.

So it appears that a single fact may be either simple or complex.

1. A *simple* fact, is that which may be declared by a simple sentence, that is to say, a sentence which cannot be multiplied or divided into several without adding to the sense.

2. A *complex* fact, is that which is declared by a complex sentence. A compound sentence (which is defined as one which can be resolved into clauses) always declares two or more simple or complex facts; as: "Plato and Aristotle were men of great wisdom; but their philosophy was inferior to that of Jesus."

Besides being simple or complex, facts are either direct or indirect.

1. A *direct* fact, is that which is perceived by consciousness without the aid of any process of addition, subtraction, multiplication, division, reduction or ratio. It is the pure enumeration or remembrance of what is felt, as it is felt. It may be either the present sensation and feeling, or an image supplied by memory, or a definition and conviction heretofore sanctioned and now relied on as an axiom. Its essential characteristics are: 1°, immediate recognition by the mind as truth, *without discussion or doubt;* and 2°, completeness or totality—that is to say, not requiring before recognition the conjunction or elimination of any other fact or idea.

2. An *indirect* fact, is one which (whether simple or complex) is joined to, taken from, or measured with others to form, leave, or find a previously unknown or unperceived entire truth.

Now for the Unit.

In mathematics the idea of the unit involves the possibility of *repetition*, one, two, three, &c., numbers of times; but this is not the positive and true idea of the unit. A thing may be a unit though there be only one of its nature in the universe. The fact that it is one is enough to constitute it a unit, though it cannot in fact be repeated. It is one, whether there be another one or not. When it can be repeated, what do we say? We say, that there are many units of the same denomination. Each is of itself a unit; and as such it does not depend upon the existence of any other thing like or unlike it. God is *one;* yet the true idea of God precludes the possibility of repetition. The sun is one, the moon is one; and they are units in themselves whether there be other suns and moons or not. In the science of numbers, what is meant by two, three, &c.? Two simply means one and one; three means one, one and one: the same can be repeated as to four, &c. The figures 2, 3, 4, 5, 6, 7, 8, 9, merely serve as a shorthand to express the repetition of units of the same kind; but if units of different kinds are taken together this form of short-hand is no longer applicable, and we are obliged in lieu of numbers to call each thing by its substantive name. Thus several objects are before me—they are: Apple, Horse, Diamond; I do not count them; but by the giving of these names an act of enumeration is performed. Indeed, even in the science of numbers, things of different kinds are reduced to a common denominator, to render their computation in arithmetical characters possible. Thus we say: two, three, four, &c., " things," though these things thus numerically designated may be totally dissimilar in themselves.

A UNIT is any single entirety. It is any single and entire thing, person or fact, being, act or quality.

Upon considering the facts embodied in this definition, we find:

1°. The PURE or ABSTRACT unit, which is the idea of one independent of any auxiliary object; or the mere elementary number or measure of its like without regard to any interposed standard of substance or force. The pure unit regards only itself. The semibreve is the pure unit of musical sounds. Thus the mere sign of unity—the figure 1—may be regarded as constituting a unit in itself, and from thence all the operations of pure arithmetic may be demonstrated, without ever thinking of any application or relation beyond that of the signs among themselves, as mere conventional assumptions.

If a mathematician deals *habitually* with PURE arithmetical numbers, algebraical tokens, and geometrical figures, apart from any direct applications, his aggregate intellectual force will diminish, while if he *constantly* applies his rules and processes, as a form of reasoning, to all practical questions, the acuteness, strength, and clearness of his mind will increase.

2°. The STANDARD or COMMON unit, which is the applied standard of weight, force, value, time, distance, capacity, &c. It involves the idea of a positive relation between two (or more) *real* things—one of which serves as the measure. It differs from the pure unit in this, that it is juxtaposited with another something. Ex.: a Cent; a Man; an Animal, &c.

3°. The CONCRETE or PROPER unit, which is any definitely limited and single thing, or person, including several qualities or circumstances as parts or attributes of its unity. Ex.: *the* Man; *that* Horse; Adam, &c.

4°. The COLLECTIVE or MULTIPLE unit, which is any single term, or name, including many individuals. Ex.: Men; Synod; Committee, &c. All plural nouns and plural integers are collective units.

5°. The COMPLEX or VERBAL unit, which is any *single* fact or declaration including a subject or a predicate considered together. Ex.: What I feel; my Love; &c.; Thinking; Dreaming, &c.

Euclid says:

"UNITY is that according to which each of existing things is called *one*."

"Any thing may be unity for other things of its own kind."

Two other distinctions of great importance remain to be noted.

Units are either
>I. Constant or Variable.
>II. Numeral or Ab-numeral.

### I.

1. CONSTANT units are those that retain the same value in the same expression.

2. VARIABLE units are those which admit of an indefinite number of values, in the same expression.

### II.

1. *Numeral* units are those which are computed by means of numbers.

2. *Ab-numeral* units are those which are computed without the use of numbers.

Davies, in his Logic of Mathematics, says:

"Algebraic symbols may stand for *all numbers*, or for all quantities which numbers represent, or *even for quantities which cannot be exactly expressed numerically.*"

"In Geometry, each geometrical figure stands for a class; and when we have demonstrated a property of a figure, that property is considered proved for every figure of the class."

The whole process of reasoning by *numeral* units,

is explained in Arithmetic; and it is not our object to treat this branch of our subject further than to show the identity of its principles with the process of reasoning upon instances of ab-numeral units.

The numeration of Arithmetic, and the enumeration of general logic, differ only in appearance—not in essence.

The arithmetician does not find it necessary to give a distinct name to every quantity which enters into his process.

The standards of the quantities with which he deals, their commeasurability, enables him to use the shorthand of *digits*.

The general logician, on the contrary, encounters the necessity of distinct names for the several quantities he operates upon; and he finds it almost always impossible to apply numbers to these quantities.

Yet he always regards them *as quantities*, and though he does not enumerate them by digits, he names every item of his computations, and is able to measure them, at least so far as to declare that this or that term is—" more or less *than*," " increased or diminished *by*," " added to," " taken from," " the equal of," &c.

The algebraist keeps his quantities distinctly apparent throughout his process, by means of signs: $a$, $b$, $c$, $x$, $y$, $z$, &c.; the general logician uses names, definitions, phrases, in fact every form and artifice of language; generally keeping the terms of his computation distinct under their respective marks, as in algebra.

The logician is, however, frequently enabled to merge the manifold terms of a ratiocination into new and comprehensive titles, and like the arithmetician, he often sums up or solves with a precision not to be surpassed in numeral logic.

But we are anticipating.

It is sufficient at the present stage to note this: that when the materials of an argument cannot be *counted*, when numerals cannot be used to compute them, they are only INVENTORIED. A list is made of all the items, by titles, phrases, and names; and this is logical Numeration or Enumeration.

The principles which ought to govern such an enumeration, will be better understood after an exposition of the operations of addition and multiplication, subtraction and division, reduction and ratio, which may take place apart from any digital numeration; and only by names and grammatical signs.

In the mean time I remind the reader:

1°. As to identity of names with number: that when Pythagoras was asked which being he thought was wisest? he answered: "*Number.*" Which the next wisest? he answered: "*That which has given* NAMES *to things.*"

2°. As to the initial act of thought: that in Genesis ii. 19, it is written: "Out of the ground the Lord God formed every beast of the field, and every fowl of the air, and brought them unto Adam, to see *what he would* CALL *them.*"

## ADDITION.

How are we to add together terms not commeasurable, terms of different, of mixed, of irregular values, denominations, qualities, orders, and natures?

Algebra, which deals only in such quantities as can finally be *reduced* to exact numbers, nevertheless suggests an answer to our question; for it marks the quantities by artificial names: a, b, c, x, y, z, &c., and treats these artificial names as positive entities, till a convenient period in the operation presents itself for making the reduction.

Logical addition proceeds in a similar manner; and differs only in the form of the reduction.

Instead of merging the items into a sum total of exact numbers, it finds a total name, or phrase, which *sums up* all the terms of the problem.

For example:

Add together the following terms:

> A thing,
> A price,
> A receiver,
> A deliverer,
> A consent to receive,
> A consent to deliver.

The sum total is: A contract of "Sale."

The sum total of this addition, instead of being expressed in figures, is set down in the word "Sale," which is just as clear and exact as any aggregate expressed in digits could be.

An indefinite number of parallel examples might be given here; but the intelligent reader needs no others.

### MULTIPLICATION.

This form of reasoning is identical in principle with addition. It is simply a short mode of finding the aggregate produced by a certain number of *repetitions* of any given quantity.

The distinctive trait of multiplication is that both its factors must be plural. If both or only one is singular we can have no change or increase. Ex.: $1 \times 1 = 1$ or $30 \times 1 = 30$.

One of the terms represents a force, mark, quality or "power." If it be only a single unit it is the mark of "one time" or equality; but when both the factors are plural the full force, mark, quality or power of the one is communicated to the other, so that all the units of the one enter into each of the units of the other; so that an increase takes place in each integer of the multiplicand equal to the full value of the multiplier.

Thus if I multiply ten pounds by three, each of the pounds becomes three pounds, and I have thirty pounds.

In logical multiplication the force, quality, or power though not numerated, is imparted in precisely the same manner. It must not only be a force, quality, mark or power as in arithmetic, but both factors must be plural as in arithmetic, and the one must be distributed to all the integers of the other—also as in arithmetic.

With this rule we can never have any difficulty in distinguishing a logical addition from a logical multiplication.

Man + Man = Men.
Accordant Wills × Mutual Promises = Contract.

Some factors appear to be in the singular number, but are really plural and capable of *distribution*. These are the nouns of multitude and many " absolute " or abstract names. When they are used in logical multiplication, though one or both of the factors *seem* to be in the singular, we should not overlook the plurality of their true meaning, the distribution intended by the expression.

Ex.: Animal + Reason = Man.
Animal × Reason = Man.

In the first of these two examples, we mean to consider a single individual endowed with reason; but in the second example, we consider a whole class or multitude of animals, among whom, and to each of whom, reason is distributed. The *sum* in one case is a single person; the *product* in the other is all mankind.

In our mental presence, this principle should ever be kept:

*Terms can be multiplied by each other only when they have a common measure, phenomena, property, or law.*

In arithmetic this rule is constantly kept in view, so that in adding we must place units under units, tens under tens; and in multiplying we cannot use integers of one denomination or standard as factors of those of another. Thus it is throughout the other stages.

A multiplier is, however, frequently given without any appellation to mark it as being of any denomination or standard, though one is always really implied. Take this example: John had 4 sacks of corn, but Tom had 3 times as many—how many had Tom? Answer: 4 sacks × 3 times = 12 sacks. It is evident that three times really means, *three-times-sacks;* for the product is, sacks; and if the number of times had been any thing else, we would not have known what name to give to the product. Hence, the question would have been ABSURD had it been: John had 4 sacks, but Tom *walked* 3 times as *far*—what distance did Tom walk? Even *pure* arithmetic is possible for no other reason than that certain pre-determined laws of change are imputed as common to numbers. If the laws of change are varied by a new convention, the new and the old cannot be computed together, unless by applying some process of transmutation. Thus a duodecimal cannot be multiplied by a decimal without *reduction.*

Ex.: 4 dimes × 3 reals, how many cents or reals?

Now, in ab-numeral mathematics or logic the rule,

though exactly the same, is of more extensive application. It is always requisite that two things be either, 1°, *commergable* into *one* term, or 2°, *interdistributable*, in order that they may be added or multiplied together; but in general logic the thinker who deals not with a question of precise numbers dispenses with arithmetical notation, without however departing from those primal laws of thought according to which numbers themselves have been framed.

I. Mergable into *one* term, is essential for addition.

II. Distributable into each other, is essential for multiplication.

III. But in multiplication, whether numeral or not, this interdistribution is never possible unless the factors contain some exchangeable force or property, common necessity or law.

Hence:

I. By addition. Ex.: Sheet of paper+written words+continued sense+personality addressed+personality addressing=a letter.

II. By multiplication: Book × repeated printing =Edition.

III. But if we have miscellaneous books though we might *add* them together to make a library, they would not be *factors* of each other.

Thus: when the terms are not interdistributable we cannot proceed by multiplication.

SUBTRACTION.

Now suppose that from a "Sale," I subtract the *price*.

The operation and result will be as follows:

Sale.
—*Price*.
=Donation.

A donation or gift contains all the elements of a sale, minus the price. A gift is without price.

Logical authors seem to agree, that reasoning may be considered as the putting of two ideas together; and comparing them to find their relation to a third. This is only another way of stating, that the difference or equality of two things may be ascertained by means of a common standard or measure, or, in other words, by Subtraction.

In deduction, the Syllogism is clearly a comparison of two things stated, so as to show that they are both identical with a third, or that both include the same lesser term or attribute.

In induction, the laws of Elimination are mere modes of comparing several phenomena, so as to isolate or discover their common and *residual elements*.

In Grammar, the prefixes E, EX, EXTRA, IR, IL, NE, UN, ab &c., import the exclusion of some element from a name.

The above and many others which might be mentioned, are assuredly examples of Subtraction.

### DIVISION.

Francœur, a mathematical writer, says: "In the same manner that multiplication is only the continued addition of the same number, we may consider division as a repeated subtraction, the quotient marking how often we can take the divisor from the dividend."

This is strictly true, but at the same time he should have added: "the quotient marks also the value of *one* of the parts subtracted, while the divisor marks how many of those parts are required to make up the dividend."

In numeral division and multiplication, it is essential that the multiplicand in one, and the quotient in the other, should represent *equal* parts of a sum total; and it is implied that each part being repeated a certain number of times indicated by the multiplier or divisor, the sum total will be produced.

The idea conveyed by the numeral quotient is not that it is alone, nor all that has been found, but is *one of several;* and that each of the several are exactly equal to the one written.

If I divide 12 dollars among 3 men, or 12 by 3, the quotient will be 4; but when I write the figure 4, I do not mean it as the whole answer. It is implied that I have found three sums of four dollars each, one of the sums for each man. The operation and quotient are really this:

```
Divisor 3) 12 Dividend.
     1st Man 4 ⎫
     2d  Man 4 ⎬ Quotient.
     3d  Man 4 ⎭
             ──
             12
```

Now, in the division of numbers by numbers, we take advantage of the real or supposed *equality* in amounts and of the identity in names, to abbreviate our answer by stating the quotient a single time.

This assumed equality is, however, very often, contrary to the real fact. If, for instance, instead of twelve dollars the division had been of twelve horses, the shares of three horses each might have been very unequal and grossly unjust.

In the division of *ab-numeral* facts—facts not resolvable into numbers—the theory is the same; but we find the abbreviation impracticable. We find the several quantities of the quotient to be *variables* bearing *different names*, so that we must write the result in detail. Nevertheless, each of the terms of the quotient must bear the impress of both the divisor and dividend.

Thus if we divide the "Ownership of Property" by "Modes of Acquisition" the quotient will be:

MODES OF ACQUISITION) OWNERSHIP OF PROPERTY.

Mode 1, by Prescription.
" 2, by Accession.
" 3, by Gift.
" 4, by Legacy.
" 5, by Inheritance.
" 6, by Wages.
" 7, by Usufructuary production.
" 8, by Manufacture.
" 8, by Interest.
" 10, by Damage recovered.
" 11, by Wager won.
" 12, by Sale.
" 13, by Exchange.
" 14, by Rents.
" 15, by Treasure trove.
" 16, by Preoccupancy.
" 17, by Capture.
" 18, by Salvage.

It is now time to remark that Division differs from Subtraction in this:

1. Division must be exhaustive, it must exhibit *all* the elements of the matter divided; but subtraction, after extracting a fact, or term, looks at the *remainder*. Whether this remainder, when found, be a simple unital fact, or term, or a complex and divisible one, may appear at once, or become the subject of further computation. Yet whatever it consists of, or whatever is done with it, still it represents only a portion of the subject first stated, and does not, like the quotient, contain or imply all the original matter.

2. Division also differs from subtraction in this:

subtraction may proceed to eliminate arbitrarily any distinct or separable portion or element, without regard to the question, whether the remainder has or has not any measure in common with the portion deducted—while, on the other hand, in division 1°, the parts given by the quotient must *all* bear the mark of the divisor, as being their common modus, function, or law; and hence 2°, the divisor cannot be arbitrarily selected, but must be phenomena, property, or law of the *whole* dividend.

All classifications which do not conform to these laws of division, are necessarily wrongly computed, or mere enumerations of direct facts. They may be arranged with more or less skill in grouping, but are wanting in the essentials of a true and fruitful ordination.

Thus, for instance, in the French and Louisiana codes, 1°, the contracts of Mandate, Deposit, and Suretyship, are set down as modes of acquiring property; 2°, several well-known modes are omitted; and 3°, acquisition by accession is placed under another title.

### REDUCTION.

In addition and multiplication, in subtraction and division, our aim is, either to compute the sum total of several facts, or to separate those sums into their elements; but when we deal with *several sum totals*, if we try to add them together we may find them, in their present form, not to be *homogeneous*, and thus to resist our addition or multiplication—while subtraction or division would only give us a greater multiplicity of separate and incommeasurable terms.

Reduction, or generalization, which enables us to obtain a common denominator or term, within which our distinct sum totals may be comprised, is the mental process which overcomes this confusion.

The reduction of compound numbers, of vulgar and decimal fractions, &c., are in numeral mathematics the types of this mental process.

Such a reduction was performed by Franklin, agreeably to this type applied to ab-numeral facts, when he found the common properties of the flying clouds and Leyden jar.

By a like process the framers of the Civil Code, after resolving Sale, Exchange, Loan, Hiring, Wager, Deposit, &c., into their elements, found them all to contain two essentials: viz., Accordant Wills and Mutual Promises, and to be thereby reducible to the same denominator: Contract. Hence the book of Conventional Obligations was deduced to set forth, under a general head, a vast number of principles common to all contracts.

Reduction consists in finding, by enumeration, and the other processes, already described, what phenomena, force, law, &c., separate facts have in common.

The term which attaches to all the facts taken in

connection is the common denominator, or the reduction.

All things in nature are interfused or interlinked. If it be otherwise, then each thing is isolated from every thing else; but we know by experience that such isolation is not the fact. If no connections nor interweaving existed there could be no such thing as reason; for reason is conversant only with the agreement or disagreement of things compared to each other, or with the production of one thing by another. Without points of communion with that which is not itself, mind itself would remain consigned to absolute solitude, ignorance, and silence. Hence, since there are conformities and contrasts inter-distributed among all things, and since something in common is implied by this accord and interpenetration, it is this common something, whether Phenomena, Forces or Laws, which forms the ground-work of all reductions; and thus the elements of a possible reduction to some common measure is contained in the things themselves.

It remains to be seen how these elements are to be detected.

In pure mathematics, these elements are given beforehand by definition. The definition and consequent axioms are the facts and laws of the case. Definitions=facts. Axioms=laws. Every *term* in pure mathematics has a precise sense and value positively fixed at the beginning, so that nothing remains but to reason upon the given, precise, and certain data; and by combining them, to develop the successive phases through which, agreeably to the original definitions, they may be carried.

In concrete mathematics the initial step is not so easy. *Real* quantities must be first found as *direct facts.* It is only when immediate sensation or enumeration has furnished two or more of these facts, as stated terms, that a process of computation may begin and progress. Yet we operate with the real quantities in the same way as with the assumed and abstract. The type is in our mental nature itself; there is an innate rule, and we must conform to it, even after we have left the ideal and nominal for the real and denominate.

Thus no sooner was the *decimal* scale arbitrarily assumed, than it became subjected to the typical forms of addition, subtraction, multiplication, division, reduction, and ratio pre-existing in the mind ; and thus, too, when no real concrete units exist they are created by virtue of the same innate laws : Space is cut up into leagues, miles, &c., and Time is severed into hours, minutes ; and thus, too, so absolute and immutable are the laws of thought, that when the necessary elements of an argument are not apparent in the object thought of, they are artificially collocated with it, and standards purely conventional are made to serve the purposes of the thinker ; but they serve that purpose because, at the same time, they are themselves moulded into the sole matrix of thought nature has herself deposited within the mind of man.

Hence, it is not to be imagined that these laws of numbers do not also prevail in ab-numeral mathematics or general logic.

To make a generalization or reduction the operation is always the same, whether we deal with numerals or with non-numerated terms, facts, or symbols.

First, the facts must be furnished by direct enumeration, aided by subtraction and division; and secondly, search must be made throughout these facts for their COMMON *divisor*.

The process of finding this common divisor begins, even in arithmetic by *experiment*, guided by our knowledge of certain pre-ascertained properties of numbers. Each of the several items are separately tried by every prime number which may divide them without a remainder, and then the different sets of prime quotients are compared to see if there is any *common* to all the sets.

In the reduction or generalization of non-numerated facts and names, the process is the same.

1°. The facts or names are enumerated or stated.

2°. They are tried or tested by separate divisions to make them disclose their common divisor.

3°. When all the members of a set of terms are found to be divisible, each by one-same term, a REDUCTION is accomplished.

Referring to what has been said under the head of multiplication on the subject of inter-distribution of factors, I proceed in addition to call attention to the fact of correspondence between multiplication and division. This correspondence is well known to be this :

    Dividend with Product.
    Divisor with Multiplier.
    Quotient with Multiplicand.

So that, since the divisor and multiplier are similar in principle, and may exchange functions—since one of the main objects of ab-numeral reduction is to find common forces and generic laws—and since two terms cannot be factors of each other unless they have properties in common, or unless there exist between them some law of mutual adaptation—it is evident, that multiplication may be as good a *trier* as division ; and that should we find a single factor with this common adaptation, &c., to each and all of a set of several terms, it will disclose either.

1. A *common divisor;* or
2. The *general law* which governs all the terms.

This last result is by far the most desirable ; for a general law is a light to the eye of thought, and enables the mind from a single glance or point of view, to understand a multiplicity of Phenomena.

It is by means of the process of reduction that many laws, once scattered, when found all bearing the characteristic of prohibition against the violation of right through fraud or force, were placed under the head of Criminal Laws. It is by the same process, repeated upon all the laws, that we have found *common denominators* for a till-then-confused mass of other laws. Thus the whole law is now classified as follows:

>Constitutional.
>International.
>Administrative.
>Civil.
>Commercial.
>Maritime.
>Martial.
>Ecclesiastical.
>Local.
>Private.
>Penal.
>Justicial, (or Procedure.)

Each category of facts possesses within itself the properties of its reductibility.

All common nouns are examples of reduction.

### RATIO.

We have now reached the last step in the process of thought—the point of progress from whence philosophy is evolved.

Philosophy seeks universal truths—truths which pervade all other truths—which enter into the others as attraction enters and controls every material thing. This movement and aim of philosophy is dictated and moved by the intellectual faculty of knowing and computing *Ratio*.

Ratio is the property of the intellect which is conscious of *proportion*. Ratio is the mental act which computes the laws of *gradation,* beginning at the mathematical point, and spreading in wave-circles of regular progression till lost in the infinite.

Addition and Subtraction detects mere sums and differences; but Ratio detects *resemblances between differences* whether of sums or remainders.

Multiplication, Division, and Reduction find single results of combination, partition, and adaptation; but Ratio finds *a series.*

Ratio compares Products with Products, Quotients with Quotients, to find a fourth term, or *a scale* of harmonies and differences; and thence through accords of common denominators, progresses to exhaust the finite and frame an index to the infinite.

In numerical science Ratio gives us the laws of arithmetical and geometrical progression, roots, powers, rule of three, proportion, &c.

In physical science perfect models of Ratio are afforded by the works of Newton and Dalton.

"A proportion is a comparison between two equal ratios."

"Every RATIO is divided into two terms: the first is called the *antecedent,* and the second the *consequent,* and the two, taken together, are called a *couplet.* The antecedent is regarded as the *standard.*"

"Every PROPORTION is composed of two EQUAL ratios; and the 1st and 4th terms of a proportion are called the *extremes:* the 2d and 3d terms of the proportion are called the *means.*"

## A PROPORTION.

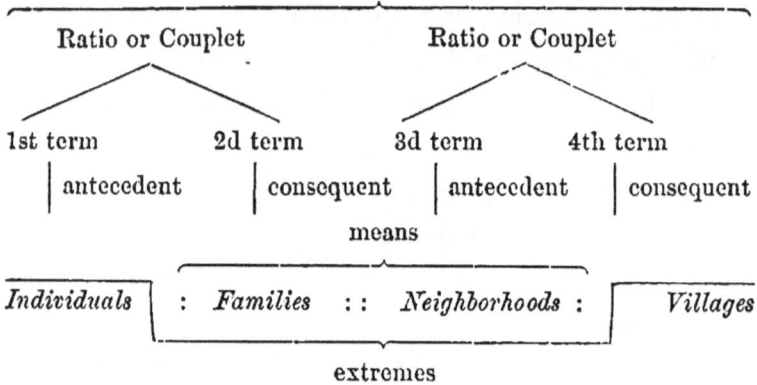

"In every proportion the product of the extremes is equal to the product of the means." And in every proportion, the 4th term is equal to the product of the 2d and 3d terms, divided by the 1st. Example:

Individuals : Families :: Neighborhoods : *x*

$$\frac{\textit{Families} \text{ multiplied by } \textit{Neighborhoods}}{= \text{Many Families of Neighborhoods}}$$

Divided into unities or individuals, thus:

$$\frac{\text{Individuals} ) \text{M\textsc{any} Families of Neighborhoods}}{= \text{Village or Villages}}$$

viz.: a unit, a Sum, single collection or assemblage of Families, of Neighborhoods; *or*, several units, or sums of Families of Neighborhoods.

It remains to be decided whether the 4th term found is singular or plural.

This can be determined by the *laws* which regulate proportion or ratio, viz. : the Ratios must *be equal ;* and in every proportion the two couplets must increase or decrease, directly or inversely, *alike*—so that when the proportion is direct, their ratio is always the same, and when inverse, their product is always the same.

Now in the above example the *consequent* of the first couplets or ratio *increases directly :* plurally to a plural antecedent or standard ; and so (according to the rule) the consequent of the other ratio must be plural also. Hence—

Individuals : Families :: Neighborhoods : Villages.

If the first consequent had been singular, it is plain the second would have been of the same grammatical number.

Individuals : *Family* :: Neighborhoods : *Village.*

Referring to the elementary text-books on arithmetic for the *laws* of Arithmetical and Geometrical *Progression,* I have only to add that these *laws* are in force among ab-numerals, as well as numerals. In every science things or facts are found to exist in *series* (whether of equidifferences or ratios) of *progression*. A little investigation will be apparent to every one ; and therefore I content myself with a couple of instances.

1°. Example: ARITHMETICAL PROGRESSION.

HOMICIDE.

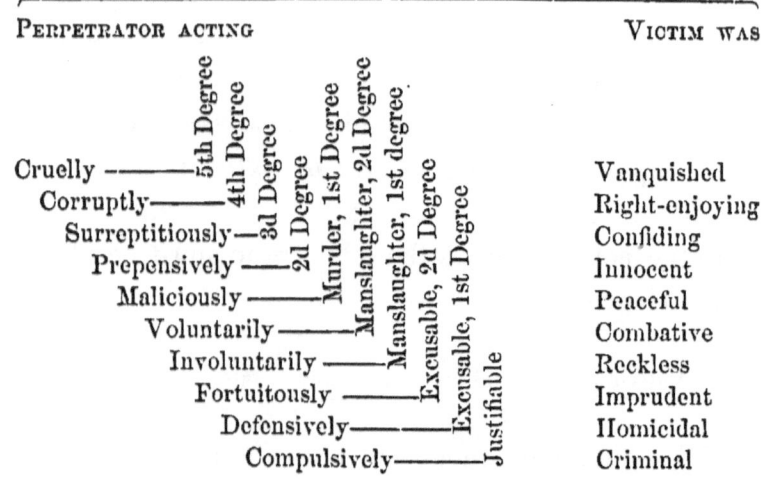

| PERPETRATOR ACTING | | VICTIM WAS |

Cruelly —————— 5th Degree
Corruptly ————— 4th Degree
Surreptitiously — 3d Degree —— Murder, 1st Degree
Prepensively ——— 2d Degree —— Manslaughter, 2d Degree
Maliciously ———————————— Manslaughter, 1st degree
Voluntarily ————————————— Excusable, 2d Degree
Involuntarily ———————————— Excusable, 1st Degree
Fortuitously ————————————— Justifiable
Defensively —————
Compulsively —————

Vanquished
Right-enjoying
Confiding
Innocent
Peaceful
Combative
Reckless
Imprudent
Homicidal
Criminal

2°. Example: GEOMETRICAL PROGRESSION.

Let us take the series familiar to political economy:

Labor × Labor = Production
Production × Production = Exchange
Exchange × Exchange = Commerce
Commerce × Commerce = Distribution
Distribution × Distribution = Consumption
Consumption × Consumption = Demand
Demand × Demand = Labor.

The result is a circulating series of ab-numerals, in which the same terms return ad infinitum; but dispensing with the difficulties which might be suggested by this illustration, here is another of plainer construction:

Individuals:
: Families:
: Associations:
: Villages or Communes:
: Cities or Townships:
: Shires:
: Provinces:
Nations.

The progression of these things in multiplying or geometrical ratio is positively certain, yet it is also impossible to apply any numeration to the terms, or to frame for them a table of determinate values.

We have now noted the primary acts sufficiently to be prepared to turn our attention to the operation of the properties, and process of thought upon its CONTENTS: viz., upon

## PHENOMENA.

Were the human mind limited to simple consciousness of sensation and emotion—were it left unaided by numeration, it would, I contend, (and hope to show,) have contented itself with objective nature in its direct and unanalyzed aspect and power. But our mind does not stop at the immediate deliverings and memories due to direct sensation. Our mind is capable of subjective deliverings and memories, which react as it were upon consciousness, and cast its contents into a measured or formal matrix and fashioner.

Apart from number and its postulate measure, suppose we were to consider nature as presenting phenomena only—phenomena which could be, as proposed by the idealists, considered "in themselves," or "absolutely." They would then remain, for us, as indeterminate and irrational qualities and powers, as mere changes of chaos, tossing us about, upon its accidental and conflicting movements.

But the human mind must do itself violence, to place itself, even for an instant, in a condition to consider nature in this aspect—an aspect familiar to the brutes, who have no concern with nature but to feel and obey its direct action upon their organism.

While the brutes are conscious of nature only as a moving panorama, of irreducible and absolute attractions and repulsions, pleasing and displeasing influences, *we* at the same time ideate nature, and all its qualities and powers, as simultaneously and continuously answering those quantitative notions known as time and space, force and law.

The world of *pure* quality and impression, or as the metaphysicians express it, the world of the absolute and unconditioned, is the world abstracted from all our ideas of thinkable quantity, all concept of numeration and mensuration; and is therefore the world of the brute.

In their efforts to imagine nature from this point of view, the idealists have deluded themselves into a belief of success; but they have unconsciously allowed, for it was impossible to prevent it, the concept of the unit to impose itself upon their meditations; and made them produce extensive entities, which they defined and named as vaguely as possible.

If by an effort of thought we consider quality "in itself," apart from all relative ideas—if we take each quality as wholly disconnected and isolated, we may fairly admit *the existence* of Substance, Gravitation, Heat, Light, Electricity, *the existence* of Colors, Sounds, Tastes, Odors, and Feels, severally—the *existence* of Hunger, Thirst, Excretive-habitude, Genital-desire, and Motor-vitality—AS FACTS. That they *are*, is all that consciousness, unaided by the conception of quantity, can feel; but consciousness without quantity could not even (as I have just done) pronounce or articulate the fact of this existence; for they must be conceived as distinct units before language can name them; every noun being a unit or sum. Hence the brutes having only the "pure," the "absolute," the "unconditioned" idea of fact, and being incapable of ideating the unit, have no language but that of interjections; and express the state of their consciousness by simple emotional cries and notions, only. Without the mechanism of instinct to move them, they would be lost in the midst of nature, as in chaos.

Thus all we can say of Phenomena in themselves, is that they constitute the world of existent and unrationalized *fact*.

*Phenomenon* IN ITSELF *is* EXRATIONATE *fact.*

But human language does not afford terms and phrases to discourse intelligibly of the absolute or supra quantitative. Let us therefore hasten to take up the subject of time and space, force and law.

## TIME AND SPACE.

For the human *mind* there is no such thing as ab-quantitative phenomena. The archeus or primary principle of thought, works with *constant* diligence throughout human consciousness, in disclosing the quantitative elements of the cosmos. Hence we may set it down as a direct and immediate fact, that we are conscious of nothing, otherwise than as being contained *in* time and *in* space; or, in other words, as having limit or measure. Every *definition* of a word, thing, or idea, is the statement of its components or parts, and therefore of limits and extension, affirmatively or negatively. Even the idea of God becomes pantheistic, that is to say null, unless we separate it from phenomena, limit it by excluding all materiality, and thus distinguish God himself from those manifestations of his own creative omnipotence we behold in the universe.

Infinite time and space are no doubt existent, but to imagine them we must begin by a unit of one or the other; and after convincing ourselves that there is *no* end, *no* boundary to arithmetical or geometrical progression, we stop at last, with the certainty that there could not have been a time when there was no time, nor can there be a space where there is no space.

Most of the philosophers who have sought for the primary ideas of the human mind, begin with Space and Time; and think in doing so that they start from the deepest core of thought. Number is treated as a mere auxiliary; and yet in spite of all attempts to assume ideas of time and space, as the beginning and basis of thought, number constantly obtrudes itself and takes her precedence, though the philosopher may be unconscious that such is the case. This is apparent in the works of Kant and Whewell, who begin with Space and Time, and do not perceive that number stands first; that space and time are undefinable, are nothing, without the precedent idea of number to give value and proportion to time, quantity, and dimension to space. Space or time, placed before the primary idea of the unit, are utterly null and unthinkable. Hence the obscurity and contradictions of Kant, all due to his impossible germ-point: space, independent of number, and without an idea of units of measure. Yet it is strange to see how often he steps over the true ground, without being conscious of standing upon the pivot around which all thought revolves, and from which all thought proceeds.

The process of mind which thus adduces all phenomena as limited units, and as contained in time and in space, displays itself in the act of forming *rational* IMAGES of the contents of consciousness; and we may call it—

IDEATION.

Regarded as a faculty, in its undefined sense, it is known as "ideality," and its work as that of "imagination;" but its functions are much more important and precise than the meaning of these names would imply. It is the arena on which all the battles of the idealists and presentationists have been fought; battles in which at every moment the combatants seem to forget that they have any organs of sense, but those of sight. Ideation not only produces the flowers of romance and poesy, but it is the field wherein doth grow those sciences which are concerned with time and space; and particularly it is the field of Geology and Geometry.

Indeed, the functions of our faculty of Ideation are used in every science; for no science can dispense with considerations of time and space; and no appliance of science *to art*, can take place without its aid.

Do we not all, when any statement or thought which may be figured or located, immediately draw a mental sketch? Do we not give each thing or fact its proper room and shape in an ideal picture? Do we not trace in this picture the course and scope of every law, force, and motion; and assign a time and place for every quality or property? Few will deny the fact. However vague the lines, however undetermined their length and course; yet they assuredly make up an image, fixed or changeable, definite or obscure, of spaces, places, forms, limits, &c. The lawyer who discusses circumstantial evidence, the sociologist who studies the evolution of human progress, the chemist who seeks the elements of matter, the philosopher who analyzes the movement of mind, all naturally give their thoughts a frame-work and body-form *in space*.

Every syllabus, synopsis, table of contents, &c., having the least pretence to logical arrangement, placed at the head or end of any work, is nothing but a localization and arrangement in space and time of the writer's thoughts: an outline of the image formed, a map of distribution. Blackstone gives an admirable example of one of these at the beginning of each of his volumes. The best system of mnemonics known in our day, yet as old as Cicero, is the system of localization, in the shape of appropriate symbols.

When we think of any event or thing, or even draw inferences from one state of facts to another, do we not put successive images before the *mind's eye*, thus as it were to *see* whether the visions the mind evokes are geometrically adapted or concurrent, and do not obstruct or exclude one another. Even the course of time is subjected to this delineation in space; and historians depict on paper, as rivers, the parallel and commingling vicissitudes of empires.

Errors in the process of ideation, whether in Philosophy or Ethics, physical science or concrete art,—errors such as mismeasurement of distances, misdirection of lines, misplacement of contents, misdrawing of figures, nondetection of discrepancies, will mar the truth and deceive the judgment. In fact, the judgment we form is itself an image—fictitious, imperfect, or faithful.

For instance, suppose we behold a dead body, with a death-wound upon it: thought at once conjures up a terrible scene of mishap or of murder. As the circumstances become known, now one then another, new tableaux arise, with increasing distinctness, till one plain and certain drama appears to the mind. Till this is done we waver in doubt and fix no opinion.

The scene beheld by the *physical* eye is the disclosure of perception—it is direct fact; but this immediate image is only one of a series of other tableaux which present themselves to the *mental* eye. We know that as there is a *present* reality, so there must be precedent and subsequent realities, *at* times, *in* places, and *by* forces. Thus the known evinces the unknown. The body, the wound, the knife, lying now here and thus, are not limitable to *this* moment, *this* spot, or to *this* condition; but (as subject to many forces and laws, in successive times and different places) have been and will be figures in other events and phenomena. Certain marks in the *present* state of things are recognized as the *traces* of antecedent or the *omens* of future forces, places, and times; and thus suggest the previous and posterior phenomena.

The assassin plunging his weapon into the victim's side—the struggle which preceded the blow—the attack which preceded the struggle—the resolve which preceded the attack—the motive which preceded the resolve, &c. Or subsequently, we foresee and imagine the assassin's arrest, his trial, execution, &c.

If we consider this course of thought merely as a series of inductions and deductions, our conception of what has taken place is imperfect; for the terms induction, deduction, inference, are inadequate to the enunciation of the whole fact. Something would remain unexpressed, and that is the formation of the images—images evoked in phases—images mentally seen—images distinct in space, time, and movement, as a drama with its scenery, impassioned actors, and successive events.

In the same way when we behold any object, though we see *only one of its sides*, we mentally image the others; and in fact we cannot have any satisfactory idea of the object (whether it be a building, a tree, an animal, or any thing else) till we have formed a *complete* image (however true or false the mental picture may be) of the unseen parts.

Thus it may be safely said, that *thought is the intellectual formation of images of the unknown and unperceived.*

  Mensuration more or less determinate—
  Enumeration, numeral or ab-numeral—

are acts of thought, primarily necessary in the formation images of the unseen, . . . past, present, or future.

1. That this necessity of mensuration exists, is apparent from the fact that these images involve form, place, order, adaptation, &c.; and that to compose a picture due regard must be had to size, distance, perspective, proportion, &c., in all the figures and scenery. Hence, *ideation is innate* GEOMETRY.

2. That this necessity of enumeration exists, is apparent from the fact that mensuration or geometry is impossible without number and its modes: *id est*, units, addition, subtraction, reduction, ratio. Measure relies upon number. Hence, *the distributer and framer of " image " is Arithmetic.*

So, it is doubtless already perceived, that the laws and methods of number and measure, operate in ideation as in every other process of the mind. Were it otherwise the images would be all disorder—they would be even more confused and incongruous than our wildest *dreams;* for in our most absurd dreams, there are some traces of connection and adaptation of times, places, forces, &c. Without the processes of number and measure, all would be chaos; but by means of number and measure, a due succession and fitness arises. Indeed, the test of the rationality of each image, is its being possible to *place it* and all its parts, without disturbing the other pictures of the series, to *time it* without anachronism in the succession of events, to *evoke it* as the effect or resultant of sufficient forces and laws. The existence of these possibilities we ascertain by number and measure. We *count* the hours, &c., we *measure* the distances, &c., we *compute* powers, physical and moral, which act and react; and compose the image, placing its personages and movements in conformity with the requirements of *applied* mathematics. When the measures are found proportionate or coincident, when the forces are ascertained to be adequate, and when the numbers of the measures and the forces are found harmonious and orderly among themselves and the surrounding facts, the image is a true one.

For example, a man is accused of murder. The time and place of the homicide are made certain. On the other hand, the presence of the accused in another place, *but at another time,* is made equally certain. Now, the measurement or counting of distance, time, and motion, enables us to find whether it was possible for the man, with his strength, &c., to pass over the intervening space in the intervening time, so as to have been present at the homicide. If the computation gives *minus*, an *alibi* is proved; and no image showing the accused in the scene of murder, can be framed without disturbing the truthful image of his presence elsewhere; but, if the computation gives *plus* ( *id est*, time, space, and force to spare) the two images may co-exist without interference or anachronism.

In the preceding example it is self-evident that

Arithmetic furnishes the mode of reasoning on the question of the guilt or innocence of the person accused; but there are cases where the arithmetical process is not so apparent, though equally active. For example: take the homicide of * * *. He was killed by a gunshot. Near his body was found a piece of paper—the fragment of a letter—which had served as the wadding of a gun. Afterwards the remnant of a torn letter was found on the person of the man suspected of the murder. The two pieces of paper were placed together, and not only the tearing, but the writing of the two pieces were found correspondent and adapted.

The question in this case being one of *form*, is therefore of Geometry. The adaptation of the two pieces to each other, shown when juxtaposited, is the demonstration "by application." It is here direct and practical; but the principle is the same as that used to prove "by application" that the diameter divides a circle into two equal parts. [Prof. I. Davies' Legendre.] The two pieces would not answer the definition of one letter, if they could not be co-adapted.

Let it not, however, be assumed that arithmetical ideas and processes can be excluded in the rationale of this case. The total absence of numbers might create this impression; but a moment's consideration will show that in this instance (as in every act of reasoning) Arithmetic furnishes the rule of ratiocination. The operation of putting the two pieces together was a practical or tangible *addition of fractions of the same denominator*. The two "pieces" were ab-numeral; but nevertheless they were the numerators of fractions, of which "a letter" was the common denominator, and as really so as if they (the numerators) had been expressed in numbers. If it had been found impracticable to unite (add) them together, the conclusion would have been (according to arithmetical rules) that they were not of the same denominator.

The subject of Time and Space, necessarily calls our attention to the science of measurement.

#### GEOMETRY.

The idea of Measure imposes itself in all our notions of Space, Time, Law, Force, and Phenomena. These cannot be conceived apart from measure. "*Absolute* Space and Time" are often spoken of, but I doubt the ability of any man to form a clear conception of the reality sought to be represented by the words. As Hamilton has it, absolute space and time are "unthinkable." We might as well try to think of a rainbow without colors, as of time and space without measure. As to "infinite" space, time, or force, it is only thinkable as the boundless, or endless, or everlasting *repetition of measures* of extension, duration, or motion. To convey our ideas of infinity, eternity, or omnipotence, we are obliged firstly to state *units* of space, time, or force, and secondly to imagine an unlimited repetition, proceeding from "*the where,*" at which we are placed in all directions, or from "*the when,*" into the past, without finding a beginning, and into the future, without reaching an end, or from "*the why,*" "*the how,*" and "*the what,*" into the power, wisdom, and will of God.

Hence the first concern of Geometry is to give, by means of definitions, certain units of form and extension, square, triangle, circle, cube, cone, sphere; and to fix the relative *values* of these units, and of their several elements. The units once fixed, are used in computing the abstract sums, differences, and ratios of one element of a figure with regard to another element, and one figure with regard to another figure; and though this be done, a *practical* application will also require the numerals of arithmetic, thus proving that the rational formula of geometry is in reality the arithmetical formula.

Indeed Geometry, though apparently ab-numeral, employs the symbols of arithmetic. These symbols, $+$, $-$, $\times$, $\div$, $:$, $>$, $<$, $=$, &c., are of constant and necessary use in geometry—yea, even in abstract and ab-numeral geometry. Thus we see that arithmetic finds application independently of numbers; and if we are attentive we will see, over and over again, that these *signs* are the true MARKS *of all the acts and re-*

*sults of thought,* whether in abstract, moral, physical, or concrete Science. Geometry, like every other branch of knowledge, is a science of units, quantities, differences, equalities, and ratios, whether of phenomena, force, law, time, or space.

Most all the facts or theorems of elementary Geometry are ab-numeral. They are the laws of the measurement of magnitude—not the measurement itself; and though ab-numeral, they are units, as positive and determinate as if they were expressed in numbers. Yet they are nothing till subjected to the *five* processes of arithmetic, whether numeral or ab-numeral. 1°, Enumeration; 2°, Addition and Multiplication; 3°, Subtraction and Division; 4°, Reduction; and 5°, Ratio, must lend their light to resolve the problems contained in the points, the lines, the surfaces, and the forms. Of the many kinds of pure units known to Geometry, under distinct names and definitions—centre, intersection, perpendicular, diagonal, square, circle, cone, sphere, &c.,—no reasoning can be framed till the laws of numerical computation helps. Number, with her standards, her axioms, and her signs, must help Measure; Number must come forward, with her formulas and laws, to enable Measure to distinguish the greater from the less; identify the equal with the equal; give the common elements of various figures and magnitudes, and show the ratios of force and law which exist in the entire synthesis and its parts.

Then it is that Geometry becomes a science. Though her quantities have no digital numbers, they are defined units of computation, (enumeration;) they are elements to distinguish one line or form from another, (subtraction;) they are sums by joining one line or form to another, (addition;) they are denominate by the applicability of the same theorems to the same forms, regardless of size, (reduction;) and they are proportional by the very fact that they are the rational, not concrete, parts of a totality, (Ratio.) This totality is *Space*, or Extension, which *thought* has dissected not merely according to tangible and direct phenomena, but according to the laws of thought itself, or what is the same thing, according to the laws of arithmetic.

Hence Geometry is, after all, purely a physical science; a knowledge of space acquired by the aid of number; for, geometry begins by ideating portions of space as units or integers, and then seeks for *proportions* of lines composing each figure, for the *ratios* of the contents or of the distances from point to point.

In fact, Geometry ought not strictly to be considered as a part of Mathematics, but as Space analyzed by means of the laws of number; and we may apply the same remark to Mechanics, which treats of the mathematical analysis of Force.

Thus as we proceed, logic is more and more identified with mathematics; for Mathematics is, as Davies defines it, "the science of *quantity;* that is, the science which treats of the *measures* of quantities, and their relations to each other;" and all the logicians declare that their science Logic, is also a science of "quantity;" and that it all turns upon the *measured* relation between the major and minor terms of the syllogism.

It is fashionable to consider all the indirect facts in Geometry as being "*deduced*" from the smaller number of direct facts; and hence Geometry has been called a "deductive science." The definitions and axioms are given as the major premises from which every subsequent proposition is deduced by successive demonstrations.

This theory looks very plausible, but it is liable to obvious objections.

In Geometry we rarely meet with a proposition which is immediately deducible from any *single* previous definition or axiom. Now, if there is any difference between deductive and inductive reasoning, it is that in the first consequences are extracted from a *single* premiss, on the principle that the major includes the minor; but in the second, the consequence is necessarily determined from *several* surrounding circumstances, cotemporaneous forces, and co-existent laws; and this last is no other than the method employed for geometrical demonstration. The truths of the propositions are made apparent by calling attention to a multiplicity of facts, which concur in pointing to the necessary existence of a certain state of things, but each of which is insufficient, *per se*, to authorize the conclusion. Herein we recognize the mark of the inductive method, or the process of *ideation* I have described above. Open Euclid at any page, and the correctness of this remark will be verified.

True it is, Geometry proceeds step by step; and, as it were, by "sorties;" but why? Simply because the fabric of the science has been thoroughly surveyed, its order of elevation discovered, and its most comprehensive facts or laws set down at the foundation of the edifice. The propositions now *seem* to grow out of one another; but centuries of study were required for the evolution of this classification; and as yet no continuous and unbroken, regular and *real* sorites has been found linking the propositions of Geometry as in a chain. No such chain is possible. What has been constructed is a beautiful temple of truth, with its principal walls, its several columns, its span of arches, its towers, and its dome, all dependent upon each other; but no one piece includes or supports the whole.

If we want to prove the truth of any geometrical proposition, the proposition immediately preceding it is seldom sufficient, notwithstanding the artful manner in which the science is arrayed. We must call to our aid other propositions, and hedge up the fact we wish to appropriate—we must erect barriers on every side, and occupy every point of surrounding space. When thus encompassed, the hunted truth cannot escape, and is found in its proper place; but a straight chase, by syllogisms and sorites, would not have found it on the track, and could not have secured it.

Take, for instance, the theorem: " In every triangle the sum of the three angles is equal to two right angles," and see how many different facts must be brought to bear, and how many distinct definitions, axioms, corollaries, and scholiums must be noted and stationed before the demonstration can be completed. No such thing as a chain of deductions is here displayed, but as in the spider's web the many threads of a net-work of facts converge to a common centre. This is induction, not deduction. It is like the circumstantial evidence of the courts; it is the ideation of which we have spoken—the forming of the picture of a previously unknown condition of things, out of parts of those already known and fixed.

To teach geometry by deduction alone, it would be necessary to find one (and only one) self-evident fact, including or effusing all other instances of the laws and phenomena of magnitude.

## FORCE AND LAW.

The same reason which prevented us from discoursing on Phenomena, apart from Time and Space, prevents also any rational separation of the ideas of Force and Law.

Force may be regarded as being "in itself" *a fact;* but man ideates it as implying degrees of strength; and these degrees as implying Laws of cause and effect.

The nearest notion science has formed of absolute Force is: Inertia, but Inertia itself as involving laws.

The mathematic nature of the human mind compels us to conceive all force as measured and seriated; as having *value* as a cause, and as producing effects *adequate* to that valued causation.

The origin of our ideas of causation is fourfold; for they find a starting point—

1°. In the *feeling* of vitality itself, or of the innate power of action we instinctively use.

2°. In the *consensibility* of primary impulses and motives.

3°. In the *consciousness* of the activity and influence of the forces of objective nature.

4°. In the internal knowledge we have of the creative and formative operations of thought; and of the dominion reason exercises over our conduct.

Force and Law are those two essential co-ordinates of phenomena, which the logicians of the syllogistic school have found it impossible to work into their fragment of the art of thinking. The logic of Aristotle makes a good appearance as long as it deals with real or figurative *extension;* but when called to assist the thinker in the world of Mechanics, Hydrostatics, Hydraulics, Pneumatics, Ceraunics, Optics, Calorics, Meteorology, Chemistry, and Physiology, the queen Syllogism is forced to give precedence to king Reckoning.

Having evolved the unit, our archeus of thought proceeds to posit other units with the first; and having said one, one, one, . . . . . . it is able to say one, two, three, four, . . . . . . and having said four, &c., it finds that two and two *make* four—*create* four—are the *cause* of four; and thus the true and primary idea of causation is evolved, and runs all through mathematics, gathering complexity as the science progresses. In no other way than on *this basis* of mathematical reckoning, can we have any rational idea or initial standard of Cause and Effect. It is out of and from that first principle of thought, the ideation of the unit, that all science proceeds. Hence the mind seeks for numbers in every thing; nor is it disappointed, for since, in modern time, number and measure have been sought for in God's works, all the wonderful sciences and arts which are the glory of humanity have arisen; for God has created all things in numeral proportion and measured harmony.

No person who has a distinct knowledge of any branch of natural science, can deny the proposition just stated; and therefore I will not stop to cite examples; but I simply appeal to the facts, and refer the reader to my witnesses: the text-books on **any and every branch of Physics.**

All the great originators of science were mathematicians, who carried into the investigation of nature the primary principles and axioms and methods of mathematics—men who understood the spirit of mathematics enough to know that until they had found the numeral units the Grand Archeus of the Universe had formed for the phenomena they were studying, they could work by undeterminate quantities, signs of greater, less, equal, &c., applied to names of various phenomena, that could seek for common denominators by means of direct and experimental reduction: that they could at once begin—1°, to add *one* phenomenon to another, to find *sums* of force adequate to given effects; 2°, to subtract one phenomenon from another, to find residual elements as ultimate terms of computation; 3°, to multiply and divide phenomena and phenomena, for classes and orders; 4°, to rate the progressive and proportional processes of phenomena, in order to find the laws of nature, the connection of forces and entities, the movement of cause and effect.

Thus, all discoverers have viewed every phenomenon, at any moment of time, as an effect and as a cause. As long as it was reducible by any means into parts, or convertible into other forms or aspects, they have never been willing to conceive it as beginning with itself, and invariably seek for its initial unit—a something of adequate power as an antecedent; and as long as they find a complex sum of forces as the immediate cause, they continue their work of research and reckoning. This is the law of science, and being the law of thought itself it is even the warrant of superstition, for superstition is only the ignorant supposition of an adequate cause.

Thus, too, have discoverers always been unable to admit of an eternal permanency of present effects; for having found that forces, properties have VALUES of *constant* persistency in volume and modus, sum and proportion, they predicate that effects must necessarily be also causes; and that changes produced by causes, to which consecutive and everlasting quantities can be assigned, will continue to produce equal and proportionate changes.

Hence it is that any reasoning upon cause and effect is a computation of forces, and the ideation of their measurable power and action, course and relation, in any given event, or phenomenon.

The preceding remarks on Ideation may be summed up in this proposition:

The pivotal function of thought is—

### THE IDEATION OF THE UNIT.

The tendency of the mind to frame the unit is so essentially its primal and universal law, that it does not stop short of *all nature*.

In the beginning of human consciousness, the facts it

noted were necessarily without apparent links, and stood therefore isolated and disconnected in memory; but every instant of experience in the history of the race or the life of the individual must have, does now, and ever will furnish new points of contact and homogeneity in all things.

In the beginning, for instance, no unity was known to exist between the gushing fountain, the broad ocean, the wind-wafted clouds, and the falling rain; but these facts which at present to us are mentally inseparable, were once so disunited in thought, were each considered as so circumscribed in their scope, that they were personified as distinct deities, entitled each to a special worship: Naïdes, Neptune, Eolus, Pluvius, &c. Still more disconnected were the lightnings of the clouds and terrestrial electricity.

Yet the human mind, by virtue of its syncretical function, could not stop short of these scattered units; but ideated all facts as *one*, and called the whole Nature —the Universe, &c.

So rapid was this summing up of all consciousness as a single entity, that it was in fact the starting point of philosophy, as the traditions we have of Thales, Pythagoras, &c., abundantly show. So immediate must have been the unital conception of nature, that the rudest languages of primitive men have words to express the ideal totality of nature, however incoherent its contents may have seemed at first.

In fact, as each of us progresses from infancy towards age, every impression on consciousness is added to its predecessors, and conceived as increasing the sum of all things, as augmenting our capital of experience, as a mere fraction of that entirety we call self, or as an extension of the ever-spreading circle we call the Kosmos.

But while, on the one hand, first the law of mind induces the formation of this great unit, or *macrocosm*, the same law of unity prompts us to frame other and minor units, whenever it is possible either *de facto* or conceptually. Whenever two or more facts are found together, or to fit each other, or to be homogeneous, in time, place, force, or law, they are *ideated* as one or as a sum. Of such units all our knowledge of Nature is composed.

Thus *adding* forever one perception to another we obtain the great unit of the "*one and all*," with the myriads of integers of which it is composed.

But *subtracting*, dividing, commeasuring, &c., we never cease to combine and invent new units and integers, denominators and ratios, of motion and mechanism, fact and art.

In these data the processes of abtraction, association, suggestion, imagination, comparison, analysis, generalization and the like, display themselves with a light so clear that it is hardly necessary to enter into illustrative details.

Every idea considered as a unit is but a fraction of the all-embracing denominator, the Universe. An idea may be conceived as A POINT *to* which a multitude of other ideas send their rays of light, and *from* which at once new rays arise, to increase the general illumination, and generate other centres.

I present this comparison of the intellectual with the physical—this analogy between thought and light—not as a direct and tangible fact, but only as a figure or image serving to aid the reader instantly to understand my meaning, when asserting the simultaneous unity and multiplicity, division and community, which the numeral function of the mind finds in consciousness.

Hence association and suggestion develop themselves intelligibly, and in their legitimate connection with analysis and synthesis; and as arising simply from the interconnection of one and all in the process of ideation.

Thus suppose we should, as an example of ideation, suggest " *an atom.*" Instantly, from the units of number, space, time, form, color, weight, order, substance—beauty, motion, place, force, law, cause, effect, &c., &c., converge, and, as it were, offer themselves to co-operate in the construction of the idea of this atom; and the fractions or contributions we accept and put into our conception of the unit thus formed, ever retain their connection and identity with their several sources, so that one cannot be present to the mind without the others being also present; and the mental phenomena of suggestion, association, and endless re-suggestion, necessarily take place.

In proportion to the scope of the macrocosm known to an individual, in proportion to the multiplicity of distinct units, of which his sum of knowledge is composed, does any one of the units of thought suggest a greater number of others. Thus the fall of an apple presented many associate facts to the people of the middle ages, but now it presents many more, for by Newton's great discovery this fact also suggests all the wonders of astronomy, even to the boys and girls of our common schools.

Over this process number and its laws necessarily preside, else all would be confusion; would be consciousness and memory, without reflection and invention, without unity and construction of units.

Hence we may now say that Ideation is in fact *consciousness, aided by Thought*—consciousness of sensations and emotions past and present, assisted and enlightened by the mathematical powers.

But, says the reader to me, Where are these mathematical powers to be placed? located? to what assigned? matter or spirit? You refuse to the phrenological organ of number, the power of counting—and condescend to admit only its faculty of perceiving plurality. You push back Comparison and Causality to a place among the perceptive organs of men and beasts. You treat them as mere perceptions and memories of direct differences and connections. Where shall we seek for the mathematical powers of man—where shall we find Thought?

Postponing my answer to this question until I have more fully prepared the ground, I therefore proceed to a BRIEF REVIEW OF LOGIC.

It is now well settled, practically at least, that the Aristotelian system of logic does not embrace the most important processes or acts of the mind in reasoning. It treats only the laws of the final and easiest evolution of thought, immediately subsequent to the finding of the main truth, whereas it was all important to determine the laws by which the main truth itself might be sought and demonstrated. Few disputes arise about the consequences to be deduced from admitted principles and facts. The debates between philosophers, politicians, theologians, physicians, &c., turn generally upon the premises major or minor. The moment the facts are ascertained and generalized beyond cavil, there is always an end of disputation; for the immediate consequences which the third term of a premiss might serve to express, are at once apparent to all. Hence it is that the logic of Aristotle was so sterile; hence its exclusive use retarded human progress; hence it was finally considered as futile, and its study is now generally abandoned; while, on the other hand, the fruitfulness and progressive powers of the Baconian system of induction has gained it not only the admiration of every great mind, but also entitles its first expounder to the gratitude of the human race.

Logic is the *science* of the laws of thought; it includes Method, which is the *art* of applying those laws to the discovery or demonstration of Truth.

If, therefore, Induction be one of the grand laws of the process of thought, it ought to be carefully and amply exposited in every treatise on Logic or Method. In fact, the logicians of the present century have shown their full appreciation of this necessity, and have conceded a place to investigation, analysis, analogy, and elimination alongside of grandmother Syllogism. The Aristotelians have striven to show that their system really contains the elements of Induction, and that Bacon owes his merit to the Stagyrite; while the Baconians treat this pretension with ridicule and contempt. Certain it is that the world of practical reasoners not only are fast forgetting many of the terms, but pay no regard to the formulas of the Antique school.

These extremes are unjustifiable on both sides; and I. S. Mill, in his admirable "System of Logic," has shown how they may be made to meet and work together, as the essential parts of one science.

Let him, therefore, be our guide in this review of the science, for which he has so ably reconstructed a single temple, out of the parts of two distinct shrines intolerant votaries had erected, one to the generator Induction, and the other to the parturitive Deduction.

Our guide begins his system by an examination of Language.

"LANGUAGE," says he, "is evidently, and by the admission of all philosophers, one of the principal instruments or helps of thought;" and he might have added expressly, as it is evident he tacitly held, that *a human language* (words and grammar) *bear the impress of the laws and processes of* THE MIND, *which has produced that language.*

What is the *object* of Language? Is it not the expression of Emotion, Sensation, and Thought? Does not language, therefore, necessarily reflect the feelings, impressions, and ideas of the mind, as exactly as it is possible for the expression to do so? Does not the speaker strive to convey to the hearer, to reproduce his own sentiments and reflections in the mind of the hearer?

What is the *origin* of language? Is it a divine revelation, or a natural gift? What matters it whether it is the one or the other? for in both cases would it not be from God? and as being the gift of a first cause, must it not bear within itself the primary laws of an intellectual origin? In fine, must not the instrument of thought be conformable to the thought that created it, as well as to the thought it was made to serve?

The works of De Bonald, Des Brosses, Herder, Gebilin, and Degerand, directly, and those of Leibnitz, De Biran, Reid, Stewart, and Locke, incidentally show the absolute connection between the development of language and that of thought; the dependency of the form of language upon the mental matrix.

Thus:

1. In the history of language we find man beginning, in order to express his primary sensations and emotions, by giving utterance to rude interjections, and making pantomimic gestures.

2. Then we hear him give utterance to these sensations and emotions, by means of *imitative* sounds. He strives to reproduce to the ear, the impressions of his consciousness; and when, as in the case of emotions, this is impossible, he does it by analogy and personification. Our English word "Spit" is imitative; "Hate" is derived by analogy from *heat;* "Hope" originally meant *reaching forward;* and I might give hundreds of examples; but I think it suffices to refer to the authors above mentioned, and to that wonderful work of human industry and science, Webster's Introduction, wherein the symbolic formation of words, expressive of emotions, &c., is fully illustrated.

3. Next to this we may trace the process of forming words declarative of a reasoning power; and we will generally detect in them an arithmetical or geometrical type. Thus, says Webster, "for example, all nations, as far as my researches extend, agree in expressing the sense of *justice* and *right* by *straightness;* and *sin, iniquity,* and *wrong,* by a *deviation* from a straight line or course." He adds many other examples.

What was, after the first cry of feeling, the first thing man had to communicate to his fellow-man? Was it the names of objects? Assuredly not; for, if man never had had any wants to satisfy, or desires to gratify, the names of objects would have been indifferent to him. If objects had not been the mediums among which and by which *events* occurred to man, he would have neglected to name any object. Webster, in his Introduction, sustains this view; he says: "it is demonstrated that the verb is the radix or stock from which have sprung most of the nouns, adjectives, and other parts of speech belonging to each family." Indeed, speech would not exist at all, were it not for the purpose of 1, affirming; 2, questioning; 3, petitioning; 4, commanding; and 5, discussing. Hence the verb was first required; and nouns, adjectives, &c., grew immediately from them, and took the features of their parent. Things were named from the actions or movements of mind or body with which they had become associated.

The intervention of the rational element induced man to convert the terms given by emotion, and it was not till they had been fashioned to suit the laws of number, that they became thinkable.

Thus, it was necessary—

1. To obtain *units;* and hence the article, demonstrative pronoun, proper noun, and words of like import.

2. To add and multiply; and hence the collective nouns, cardinal adjectives, conjunctions, plurals, &c.

3. To subtract and divide, state fractional parts; and hence the adjective, abstract substantive, &c.

4. To reduce or classify, according to a common measure; and hence the distinctions of gender, common substantive, &c.

5. To determine ratio or relation; and hence ordinal and comparative adjectives and adverbs, tense, mode, case, auxiliary verbs, adverbs, prepositions, &c.

At the centre of all is the verb—the germ and life of all assertion, declaration, &c. Even in the spontaneous interjection the verb is implied. No expression of existence, sensation, emotion, consciousness, action, or thought, can be pronounced without it. It is the pivot or fulcrum of every proposition or argument—the motor power of the machinery of thought.

Words are so evidently the units and integers of thought, that even the scholastic logicians seem to have perceived the fact. Witness the earnestness they display at the outset, in urging the use of words in their exact signification; the necessity of selecting words of precise import; the advantage of ascertaining the connotation or contents of words; the dangers of vague and ambiguous terms. They complain emphatically of the perversion of language, as preventing the philosopher from classing and demonstrating truth, and as enabling the sophist, by means of equivocal "names" and metaphors, to obtain the triumph of error. Now, what does all this amount to? When properly interpreted, it turns out to be a periphrase of the first law of arithmetic, which requires us to determine the *value* of the unit of computation. We must have, says Davies, "a clear apprehension of the single thing which forms the basis of number." Thus, at the threshold, we find logic to be really ab-numeral Arithmetic. Logic hypocritically disguises her true personality, by using a different nomenclature. If she had said *unit* instead of "name," she would not have lost sight of her parentage, and might have proved herself worthy of her legitimate filiation.

NAMES are distinguished by logicians into several kinds or classes.

1. The distinction of names into GENERAL and PARTICULAR, is more clearly understood by the definitions of *general terms* and *particular integrals,* or of *composite* and *prime* numbers, in mathematics. The simple distinction of common and proper nouns given in Grammar, comes much nearer to the real meaning of the logicians, in defining general and particular names; and by frankly adopting these they might have avoided much perplexity, for the syllogism is useless and impossible, whenever the matter to be reasoned does not afford a divisible common noun for a major premiss.

2. The distinction of names into CONCRETE and ABSTRACT, is taken from Arithmetic, which defines these two kinds of units or quantities; and in accordance thereto, the grammarians have found that in the formation of language, mankind, under the direction of their faculty of *subtracting,* have been able to adopt "abstract nouns" for ideas and qualities; and to separate

this class of nouns from the common, proper, and collective.

3. The distinction of CONNOTATIVE and NON-CONNOTATIVE names, was necessarily suggested by that of concrete and denominate units on the one hand, and "indeterminate" and "independent" quantities on the other: the one being suggestive of *attributes* or standard parts; and the other being a quantity without a known value or relative measure.

4. The distinction of POSITIVE and NEGATIVE names is also derived from the arithmetical and geometrical nature of thought, which furnishes the idea of *plus, equal*, and *minus*. Plus is positive, minus is negative. In algebra they are so recognized and treated, and the sign of addition, +, is applied to the one; the sign of subtraction, —, to the other. In grammar the *prefixes* and *suffixes* are given in lieu of these signs. As to "privitive" names, they are the expression of remainders.

> Thus: Activity—Activity=*in*activity.
> Sight—Sight=Sight*less* or Blind.
> Lady+Beauty=Beauti*ful* Lady.

5. The distinction between Absolute and Relative names, is also noted by authors on logic; but it would be very difficult for them to carry out any such division practically. In mathematics there are absolute terms; but they are only so accidentally, as being complete though present in the problem under solution.

Such a distinction might be admitted in ab-numeral arithmetic or logic, and denoting conceded data or points needing no discussion. To carry the idea of absolute terms as distinguished from relative any further than this, does not appear possible, and must be vain and serve no useful purpose. Even single and isolated words have rarely if ever an "absolute" meaning; that is to say, a meaning independent of any relation; for it is only by relations that any term can be defined. Hence in grammar the absolute substantive is unknown, and in mathematics it is synonymous with "complete."

Thus it is evident that the distinction of names, as established in the logic of the schools, is, as far as it goes, borrowed from mathematics and grammar, but that the appropriation has not been thorough or well adapted. Had the logicians applied the formulas of mathematics to grammar and philology, I am confident they would have been much more successful in finding a good classification of names. The simple division of substantives into—1, proper; 2, common; 3, collective; 4, abstract, as given by grammarians, is unobjectionable and sufficient.

GRAMMAR shows, by its analysis, that language was framed by the mathematical attributes of mind.

1. THE VERB is, as we have already proved, the *motive* power of language; and therefore verbs are subjected to the laws of quantity, in time and force, in space and direction, by virtue of which motion itself is thinkable. A movement must have place where, time

when: it must have a force, a figure, a beginning, a course, and an end; and a verb to be a verb, must imply all these elements of number and measure. Our inability to compute by numeric values, or delineate by exact lines, every action expressed by a verb, does not affect the mathematical nature of the conception they declare. If we have not found a *standard* of value for the intensity or velocity of the act, we supply the want of the exact measure by the use of approximate and graduated terms: thus we say creep, crawl, hobble, limp, linger, loiter, trudge, saunter, walk, march, haste, hurry, canter, trot, rush, gallop, run, fly, &c., &c. "To love," is an act of emotion; and even in its infinitive mood this verb implies a degree of intensity; and it may be ranked in the scale of affection thus: to fancy, to admire, to like, to cherish, to *love*, to adore. But the workings of computation in the creation of verbs is not confined to its root; for all the variations of the verb are due to the same influence.

Thus:

—One of the termini of the act is always indicated by the agreement of the verb with its Nominative.

—If the end or object of the act is first given, this inversion of order is indicated by the Passive Voice.

—Variations and gradations of time are marked into periods by the Tenses.

—The intensity of the act as positive, hypothetical, possible, probable or necessary, is rated by an Auxiliary verb or a change of Mode: will, may, can, might, must.

—And even the acting unit is exhibited in the verb itself; for it varies with the Person and Number of the subject.

A Noun, we have already seen, is an ab-numeral unit or sum: 1, proper or concrete; 2, common or standard; 3, collective or composite; 4, abstract or pure. Whatever may be individualized, and thus become an object of numeration, may be represented by a noun. Whatever cannot be counted cannot be expressed by this part of speech. Hence the verbs "to be," "to have," "to do," cannot become substantive without personification or integration, so that naming is unquestionably quantitative—the determination of a whole, a sum, an integer; and quantity is of the essence of nouns; they are the objects of every mathematical process; they may be increased, diminished, or limited by other words implying something plus, minus, equal, or proportional. Not only is the given noun thus augmented, reduced, or determined by the article, adjective, pronoun, but a super-addition or sub-elimination is made by other words appended to the adjective itself. Moreover, by means of changes in the signs, or modifications of the noun or of its representative the pronoun, it is made to exhibit not only the plurality of *Number*, but also *divisions* and *classes* in Gender and Person, or the relations of Case, of exclusion and inclusion; distribution, identity, and generalization. A glance at the *personal, demonstrative, distributive, indefinite,* and *relative* pronouns, will satisfy the read er how man, in giving names, was applying to practice those primary types of thought, number and measure, was presenting notations of identity and equality, difference and multiplicity, order and relation.

But verbs and nouns could not supply all the necessary symbols of that branch of ab-numeral mathematics treated of in Grammar. Hence the other parts of speech, Adjectives, Adverbs, Articles, Participles, Prepositions, and Conjunctions.

3. ADJECTIVES, ARTICLES, PRONOMINAL-ADJECTIVES, ADVERBS, and PARTICIPLES, indicate that the unit of thought, whether verb or noun, has some *plus* or *minus* value which must be computed, included or excluded. Thus: a good man, is Man+good; a lifeless body, is Body—Life. This class of words can be arranged in positive and relative categories of Number, Order, Place, Time, Quantity, Force, Form, Course, and Value. We find this or a like classification of the Adverbs already made in every grammar, and it is therefore unnecessary to give examples.

4. PREPOSITIONS supply the place of geometrical lines and diagrams of movement or position, the direction, course, or circumscription of units of action or of phenomena.

"Of" marks the source, author, initial, or agent: it represents a line directed *back* from a principal to the element or object.

"To" marks the end, object, or recipient: it represents a line directed *forwards* towards the element or object.

"For" sometimes means "in the *place* of:" it represents an algebraic or geometrical substitution, or the movement of something into a place and of another out of it. "For," sometimes means "towards." It has other meanings, but they all delineate some reciprocal or opposite motion in the double sense of "of" and "to."

"By" points out the line, the guide, the route, the standard, or measure, which was, is, or to be conformed to.

As to the other prepositions I need only say, they have evidently no other function than to fix a point or trace a line. It suffices to glance at the list of this class of words in order to verify this fact.

5. Conjunctions.—Conjunctions have no other function than that of noting some mathematical process.

"And" requires adding together.

"Although" implies a plus force overcoming a minus; and so does "but," "notwithstanding," &c.

"Because" or "For" indicates value *adequate* to the cause or effect stated; and so does "as," "since," "therefore," &c.

"Or" announces division, substitution, and the separation of quantities.

And so I might continue to the end of the list.

The values of words are not only defined by their isolated meaning, but also by auxiliary signs or notations. I have already shown the use of etymological modifications in determining the value of words; but there are other variations which should not be overlooked.

Thus we have—

THE PREFIXES, which generally declare a total subduction or a diminution.

THE SUFFIXES, which generally declare an accretion or equivalence.

The curious student may, by looking over the definitions in "Town's Analysis," satisfy himself that the office of all these particles is to note some operation of which the type is in mathematics.

THE SIGNS OF COMPARISON exhibit at once their arithmetical origin. Good, *better*, *best*, is a Ratio.

SYNONYMS are often terms of *equal value;* yet their main use is to state, with greater nicety, variations *of value* in similar conceptions. There is generally graduation, degree, *progression*, *ratio*, in any group of synonyms. Ex.: Feel, perceive, heed, notice, view; imagine, suppose, conjecture, surmise, guess, assume, presume, believe, cognize, observe, consider, examine, collate, investigate, scrutinize, analyze, compare, test, identify, verify, know, discriminate, deliberate, calculate, think, ponder, muse, meditate, reflect, cogitate, speculate, reason, generalize, infer, theorize, synthetize, apprehend, deem, conceive, comprehend, understand, deduce, value, grant, admit, concede, assent, concur, conclude, decide, resolve. Similar groups to this might be formed of other classes of words, thus showing how the entire language is made up in the same way; how the mathematical element of mind is always afferent in the creation of words; and how when numbers cannot be used, for want of an exact standard of unity, *scales* of approximate values are provisionally invented.

SYNTAX and PROSODY teach us how to state the *problems* we have to work out, or the solutions we have found. They teach us how to set forth *propositions, demonstrations, theorems, lemmas, corollaries, scholiums, hypothesis,* and *postulates*, with correctness, precision, and perspicuity. In the narratives and descriptions, discourses and orations, of ab-numeral thought, the object is either the disclosure of facts or the enforcement of argument, and to accomplish this properly the methods of mathematics must be observed, or a medley will be produced. Hence in RHETORIC, the care with which we are taught to divide and arrange every discourse, according to the best plan of demonstration. Methinks the study of mathematics, and the application of its laws of exposition, would remove many impediments, and aid the cause of truth. It would lead me too far from my direct object, if I entered into details in order to sustain this remark; and I must be content with alluding to the construction of SENTENCES. First the verb is posited as the soul of the sentence, (its quantum of existence or force;) and then, rules are given—for *placing* the subject and object; for regulating the *concord* of the different words, so that their *functions* may be apparent; for positing the adjectives, adverbs, &c., in connexity with the terms they serve to *limit*, augment, or diminish; for employing and varying the *equivalent* signs, such as personal pronouns; for making *a sum* of several terms by means of conjunctions; for exhibiting with precision all the *relations*, and adjusting the unity of the sentence.

What else is done by mathematicians with the digits and diagrams of their language, when they use it to give or demonstrate a fact reducible to exact number or figure? The signs, digits, &c., or mathematics, are really *words*, simple instruments used by thought in noting its own operations. Hence, as the words treated of in grammar fulfil the same office as those treated of in mathematics, there is no essential difference between them. In mathematics the words and syntax are more definite, as standards of exact value exist for every term or phrase; but as science advances, even this difference may disappear. For instance, if phrenology be grounded in fact, the language even of Ethics, like that of Chemistry, or that of Mechanics, may admit of numbers.

In time, Pythagoras will be understood; and it will be seen that his mystic adepts have concealed and travestied the profound truths their master taught. So it has been with the moral philosophy of Jesus. For ages it was distorted by superstition and priestcraft; but it may yet cease to be the password of idolatry, to become a criterion of Science.

Having discoursed of Language, Logic turns its attention to the "THINGS *denoted by names;*" but becomes at once embarrassed to frame categories, and the like. Aristotle, Kant, and others, have vainly tried to classify things in general, but their work could not be perfect, because they had not exact terms at their disposal. Their attempts, nevertheless, show they were fully impressed with the utility of subjecting the objects of thought to a process of DIRECT DIVISION.

Their list of the quotients of this direct division, is identical with the matters upon which mathematics performs her operations: 1, Substance; 2, Quantity; 3, Quality; 4, Relation; 5, Acts; 6, Passions; 7, Space; 8, Time; 9, Epoch; and 10, Place; all of which are thinkable only by virtue of one of them, viz.: Quantity; for, what rational import could Substance, Quality, &c., have, unless they be referable to some standard of quantity—some process of computation, however imperfect it may be?

Thus, again, are we forced to conclude that Quantity is the basis of thought, and Mathematics is the law of thought.

DEFINITIONS and PROPOSITIONS naturally follow the consideration of words and things.

1. *A definition* should describe a unit of thought by stating *all* its parts or constituents; but most generally it is found so difficult to gather and state *all*, that we are content with those indicia which serve to

distinguish the unit from any other. This is convenient, but it is dangerous; for it leads to the habitual omission of values, which may be important to correct computations and solutions. Hence the defining terms should, when added together, be equal to the defined integer. Brevity is, however, always desirable; and therefore the most comprehensive constituents or fractions of the object of the definition should be used, whenever the problem can be solved without a minuter analysis. Logicians give an excellent method of framing a definition, with a view to comprehensiveness and brevity; they say: "*A correct definition must state the next higher genus* (i. e. term of progression or ratio) *within the extent of which the given definable lies, and then* ADD *the essential attributes* (i. e. subtractable term) *by which it is accurately distinguished from all collaterals or subordinates.*" The collaterals or subordinates must not contain the stated subtractable term. This method is evidently borrowed from the mathematical process of forming denominate quantities and scales.

Hence logicians, in order to frame definitions by this rule, must comply with the true and only laws of thought, viz.: the formulas of mathematics. Their rule for defining requires divisions into class, order, genus, species, variety, and individual, disposed in due progression and ratio. Without this recourse and subjection to mathematics, they could not have given a rule for definition, answering to the requisites of Manifestness, Adequacy, Unity, and Brevity. Hence it is unnecessary to follow them in their classification of definitions, into—1, thorough; 2, complete; 3, descriptive; 4, explicative; and 5, locative definitions; for, by a single view of this classification, as it stands in the books, it may be seen that these distinctions amount merely to another way of saying that definitions may proceed by integers, additions, remainders, or may be based upon the lowest and other proportionate divisors or quotients.

2. *Propositions* come next. Logicians consider them to be " assertions of a phenomena, as being always accompanied by another; " or the declaration of a judgment " affirming a relation between two objects of thought; " and out of this an endless and complicated system of nominal differences among propositions is devised. Having attached themselves more to the concept of words, than to the realities words are made to represent, the logicians were greatly embarrassed when they attempted to classify propositions; for language presents myriads of intricate combinations of meaning in words and sentences; and the labors of logicians to parcel them out was of necessity limited to what GRAMMAR had done for them. Unfortunately the real ownership of the analysis is disguised and lost under another nomenclature. A Verb is the copula; Mood is Modality; Inversion and Transposition of Sentences is Mood; the several grammatical moods are not the Indicative, &c., but Assertive, Problematic,

Apoditic, &c.; Common or Multiple Nouns are "Universals;" Proper and Abstract Nouns are "Particulars;" Adjectives and Adverbs are Exposita or Modals. Thus might we go through all the details. True it is that many of the terms of Grammar are preserved; and indeed sometimes the nomenclature the logicians apply to propositions, might be advantageously adopted by grammarians; but after all, the analysis of propositions given in Logic, belongs to Etymology and Syntax, and should be frankly surrendered to those branches of learning.

Now, if we accept without reservation the definition of Propositions as given in Mathematics, the true course of procedure will at once appear. The logicians call their propositions "judgments;" and seem to think that judgments depend more upon the framework of exposition or of expression than upon facts; but in Mathematics a proposition "is a *proposal* TO PROVE *something;* it is a theorem to be verified or demonstrated." This points at once to the business on hand, and demands a fruit-bearing analysis. Attending to *the fact* that nothing is thinkable, that no reasoning can take place in any category unless QUANTITY (absolute or indefinite, moral or physical, positive or negative, concrete or abstract) be considered, that all ratiocination depends upon computation, that even *quality* does not escape this necessity—it follows that it is not BArBArA or BArOkO, but the formula of Number and Measure, *as found* in works on Mathematics, which should be applied to propositions. Thus would the battles between deduction and induction cease, to give place to the generation and summation of increasing and decreasing series.

THE SYLLOGISM or DEDUCTION is an illustration of the correctness of my position. The logicians admit that reasoning " is the *comparison* of two or more conceptions with each other." This should have instantly suggested that reasoning had its type in number and measure; and that since its object was to ascertain equality or difference, its laws were of necessity given by mathematics. Neglecting this truth, which was so apparent from the very definition of reasoning, Aristotle went on and invented the syllogism as the type of thought; but the syllogism itself, though Aristotle may not have been conscious of the fact, imposed itself (as a model for thinking) by virtue of its mathematical nature. It is a mere periphrase of the axiom: " An equal to one of several equals is equal to the other equals," or " the equals of equals are equal."

Aristotle's dictum is: " Whatever is predicated *universally* of any class of things, may be predicated in like manner of any thing comprehended in that class." This is what the logicians call the *dictum de omni et nullo*, which Mr. John S. Mill has already converted very nearly into its true signification, by remarking that " if we generalize this process, (the syllogism,) and look out for the principle or law involved in every such inference, and presupposed in every syllogism, we find not the unmeaning *dictum de omni et nullo,* but a fundamental principle, or rather two principles *strikingly resembling* the axioms of mathematics; the first which is the principle of affirmative syllogisms, and is to the effect that things which co-exist with the same thing, co-exist with one another," &c.

When we have proceeded a little further, it will be seen why Mr. Mill failed to perceive that Mathematics is the only logic. He certainly was on the right track for discovering that Logic, instead of being the governor was a mere parasite of Mathematics. So, too, Professor Davies, of West Point, was on the road, and if, instead of attempting to write the " Logic of Mathematics," he had reversed the problem, and shown the *Mathematics of Logic,* he would have produced a work of incalculable importance; for his great knowledge of the first of sciences, would have enabled him to strip Logic of all its borrowed plumes.

Aristotle's dictum is really a self-evident truth; but it was turned into a sophism by the use of the word " universally," instead of " *every* unit or part."

The proposition should have been thus: "Whatever is predicable of every unit or part of any class, may be predicated of any one of the units or parts comprehended in that class." Or, in other words, the great dictum, stripped of all its useless and vague words, and boldly stated, amounts to this trivial tautology: What is true of *every* one of a class, is true of *each* one of the class.

If any logician contests the accuracy of my restoration of "every one" to the place of "universally," I will ask him to adduce any valid syllogism in which "*all*" cannot be properly changed into "every," or "each." Indeed, this is *ex necessitate rei;* for we learn that the major term is the "principle," the minor is "the case," "instance," or "example," coming under it; and that the minor or middle term must be *distributed* or included in the premises. The major is a *class*, the minor a *genus*, the conclusion an *individual*. Now, how can there be cases, instances, examples, genus, and individuals, in principles and classes, unless these be composed of separable or divisible units? Indeed, the whole doctrine of the syllogism depends upon certain laws of what the logicians call "DISTRIBUTABLE *quantity*," which presuppose the divisibility of the subject into units or integers, and necessarily comport "every" and "each." Yet the students of logic have been so blinded by the words "all" and "universal," that they have even gone further than Aristotle. I have a work on logic before me, which puts the dictum thus: "Whatever may be predicated of the *whole* may be predicated of the parts." The master was too wise and cunning to have uttered such a proposition. The earth, for instance, may be termed "a whole;" could we reason thus: the earth is globular, America is a part of the earth, therefore America is globular? Evidently the term whole will not do here, and the fact that it does not fit the syllogism, shows clearly that the major *must* comprise two equal parts, each equal to a third posited by the minor.

The eternal example of a syllogism given in every book on logic is:

*All* men are mortal,
Socrates is a man,
Therefore: Socrates is mortal.

Is it not plain that "all" men really means every man; and that the argument may be symbolized by:

$$a = x$$
$$b = a$$
$$\text{Therefore}: b = x.$$

What then was it that estopped Mr. John S. Mill from at once adopting mathematics *as* logic, in lieu of trying to unite the scholastic syllogism with the Baconian organon? It was the apparent obstacle presented by "QUALITY." Mr. Mill thus states the difficulty he encountered: "These truths, though affirmable of all things whatever, of course apply to them ONLY in respect to their QUANTITY;" and further down he says: "In these various transformations the propositions of the science of number *do not* fulfil the functions proper to all propositions forming a train of reasoning: "viz., that of enabling us to arrive in an indirect method by marks at each of the *properties* (qualities) of objects as we cannot directly ascertain (or not so conveniently) by experiment."

The fact, however, is, that if any of the objects of thought be more than the rest dependent upon mathematics, its axioms and rules, in order to become thinkable, it is *quality*. No reasoning can take place with regard to properties and qualities, till they become quantitative, whether they become so directly, indirectly, or arbitrarily. Every logician is bound to admit this, as deducible from the primary definitions of the reasoning process itself. It is therefore of the quantity of quality, the quantity of *force* in properties or qualities, the quantitative ratios of the *laws* of properties and qualities, the quantity of duration in *time* of properties and qualities, the quantitative dimensions or *space* occupied by properties and qualities, that we may reason. It is only through quantity that we can understand quality in itself, or can argue and conclude upon any quality. If it were otherwise, we could never go beyond such propositions as these: white is white, or black is black; but the moment we say, black is not white, we begin to determine those units which are reducible to the common denominator known as color, and then may proceed to value and seriate according to the formula of ratio, &c.; thus, by means of the laws of number, disclosing the science of optics. Without this quantitative process of determining units of *value*, this subsequent *reduction*, &c., we never could have drawn a single inference about colors, &c. Hence when we say: "Snow *is* white," we assign a *value*, a computable value, to snow, determining not only its proportionality with the color of other things, but also include all the subsidiary values and ratios of whiteness itself. Rationality is therefore in quantity alone, and logic, which professes to teach the laws of rationality, is a science of quantity, and has nothing to do with quality apart from quantity.

Let us look at all the sciences which are concerned with quality or properties. They all owe their very existence to the mathematical elements of thought. Every student must be aware of this. Chemistry since Dalton, Optics since Newton, Mechanics since Archimedes, Acoustics since Sauveur, have become strictly mathematical; and every other science concerning quality, even ethics, is tending that way. Phrenology even attempts to settle the partnership accounts among propensities, sentiments, and faculties. Statistics is daily furnishing data for moralists to reason upon; and Jesus, centuries ago, gave the great practical equation, by which every application of these data may be determined: "Love thy neighbor as thyself."

Whenever and whereinever exact numbers and measures cannot be used, ab-numeral quantity is applied, according to the axioms. The terms commonly used for the purposes of argument, show how impossible it is to think, that is to say, put two things together so as to extract or compose a third, without the aid of number. For instance, the words based, dependent, arising, adequate, included, parallel, equivalent, position, hence, therefore, because, possible, contradictory, and a thousand others, refer to mathematics for the key of their meaning. The fact is there is not a word in the dictionary which is not indebted to quantity for its rational value; and in order to test this, let us take the most absolute imaginable, and then see whether its meaning does not suggest a variety of units: differences and adequacies of phenomena, force, law, time, and space?

Take, for instance, even the moral qualities. Have they not each their degree? Do not their powers act and react, according to values of intensity? Are they not influenced by attractions and repulsions, intercompensable? Are not our motives weak or strong; and do they not alternately yield, overpower, or become balanced?

INDUCTION is the last branch of logic which it is necessary to notice. The logicians, since the days of Bacon and Descartes, have endeavored to ignore it; but it has invaded every department of science, and has conquered so many mysteries, that the logicians have at last condescended to give it a place in their books, but only a secondary place, in what is called "Method," thus trying to make it pass for the servant of deduction and of the syllogism. But the effort is vain, for the verdict of mankind is rendered; and if it were possible to dispense with either deduction or induction, the world would prefer surrendering the former. Why? Because induction has borrowed all the rules and axioms of mathematics, except the *one* previously taken for a model to the syllogism; and hence induction has for its share all the instruments which serve to discover the unknown, while deduction can only exposit the known.

"Invention," says Mill, "though it can be cultivated, *cannot* be reduced to a rule; there is no science which will enable a man to *bethink himself* of that which will suit his purpose." I quote this sentence because it is illustrative of the consequences which flowed from the failure to see that, for all purposes of thinking, quality is secondary to and dependent upon quantity.

If Mr. Mill means that to perceive *direct* facts, *immediate* facts, as a dog, a horse, an elephant, we must depend upon our senses, so that if we have never seen or heard of a horse, we would never "bethink" ourselves of riding one, he is right. But there is an immense gap between this bethinking and the bethinking of invention. The one depends upon the accidents of sensation, which are, at every instant, casting precious but too often unnoticed means in our way. The other obeys the *laws* of thought; for there is unquestionably a code which ordains how we are to bethink ourselves of what will suit our purpose. This code is in the rules of number and measure, governed by that archeus which commands us to numerate, add, subtract, reduce, and *rate*. Thus whenever we want to bethink ourselves of what will suit our purpose, we begin at once to number and compute, weigh and measure, equate and seriate, the things within our previous experience or standing before us.

It was obedience to this code of bethinking, that enabled Copernicus and the long train of discoverers and inventors who descended from him, to change the status of the world. A detailed review of the history of science would show that the world owes its progress of the last three hundred years to mathematical bethinking. Before Bacon published any thing, Kepler, Tycho Brahe, and Galileo were continuing the work of Copernicus; and before the Novum Organon had obtained any celebrity, Harvey and Torricelli were announcing the result of their investigations. The good ground of science had been found; for from the moment the Copernican system was published, the splendid results of mathematical science astonished the world; and the number of votaries and adepts of that science were increased. We have the fruits. The glory of Bacon is in the fact that he was the first to show that every science, as well as Astronomy, might proceed from particulars to generals. Bacon, though not conscious of it, really introduced ab-numeral numeration, addition, subtraction, and reduction, to aid the isolated, and therefore inoperative, equation of Aristotle.

The canons of induction, as stated by Mr. Mill, and which are similar to those found in other books on this subject, bear witness to this proposition.

### 1. *Method of Agreement.*

FIRST CANON.—If *two* or more *instances* of the phenomenon under investigation, have only *one* circumstance *in common*, THE circumstance in which *alone* all the instances agree, is the cause (or effect) of the given phenomenon.

### 2. *Method of Difference.*

SECOND CANON.—If *an instance* in which *the* phenomenon under investigation occurs, and *an instance* in which it does not occur, have every circumstance, *save* ONE, IN COMMON, *that* ONE occurring only in the former; *the* circumstance in which alone the *two* instances differ, is *the* effect or cause, or a necessary *part* of the cause of the phenomenon.

### 3. *Joint Method of Agreement and Difference.*

THIRD CANON.—If *two* or more *instances*, in which the phenomenon occurs, have only *one* circumstance IN COMMON, while *two* or more *instances*, in which it does not occur, have nothing in common *save* the absence of that circumstance; *the* circumstance in which alone the two sets of instances differ, is the effect or cause, or a necessary part of the cause of the phenomenon.

### 4. *Method of Residues.*

FOURTH CANON.—*Subduct* from any phenomenon, such part as is known by previous inductions to be the effect of certain antecedents, and the residue of the phenomenon is the effect of the remaining antecedents.

## *Method of Concomitant Variations.*

FIFTH CANON.—Whatever phenomenon varies in any manner, whenever *another* phenomenon varies in some (one) particular manner, it is either a cause or an effect of *that* other phenomenon, or is connected with it through some fact of causation.

That these few rules of inductive investigation are borrowed from mathematics, is too plain to need any comment. They are the mere SYNONYMS of *some* of the Axioms or rules of Arithmetic or Algebra; and, as this is apparent as soon as the parity is suggested, it would be idle to dwell upon details. Let me, however, suggest that if he had simply taken the axioms and rules of arithmetic, geometry, and algebra, as they are, and in their original succession, and had extended their phraseology without altering their sense, he would have succeeded a great deal better, and might have given *all* the laws and canons of both deductive and inductive reasoning, instead of the few instances he has been able to hit upon. In a subsequent work I shall endeavor to supply this desideratum.

A great number of other instances might be adduced to show how entirely both deduction and induction are derived from number and its laws; and I am confident that in time some abler mind than mine will frame a new logic, based upon the application of *the whole* of mathematics to ab-numeral quantity.

In the mean time the progressive neglect into which the logic of the schools is falling, will allow more time for the study of the logic of nature, the science of number and measure.

I now resume the task of connecting

### THOUGHT AND THE SOUL.

Vainly have the sensationalists endeavored to explain thought, by the effect of objects upon the senses. Vainly have they tried to reduce reason to objectivity; and to explain all the phases of analysis and synthesis by impressions, upon a *tabula rasa*. The ingenious explanations of Hume and Condillac, in the effort to show how *a statue*, by being endowed with organs of sense, imparted to it in a certain supposed natural succession, would, by the acquisition of sense alone, and the mere necessary action and reaction, and consequent transformation of impressions, dependent upon outward pressure, would evolve and use, not only language, but also induction and deduction. The example of the imaginary statue owes whatever plausibility it seems to contain, to the incidental and unauthorized assumption of *computation*, as the matter of course *effect* of the impressions of direct identity and variety, direct connection and severance, made upon sensation. How and why, *passive* sensation, by its own laws, can *actively* transform itself into computation, invent the abstract unit and make it the standard of mental operations, is a question the sensualists have left entirely untouched. They use their assumption without even marking when and where it comes into their argument; so that having thus unconsciously assumed it as tacitly conceded to them, they proceeded onward, and the rest was easy. It happens, however, that the objections to sensationalism begin precisely at this point, thus taken for granted. Man does compute; but by virtue of what does he do so? To what principle or force, laws or properties, does the mind owe the power of positing the abstract and arbitrary unit, and of calculating by it and with it? It is said that the statue after receiving this, that and the other impression, will do so and so. But that is the very matter in dispute, and it has not been shown how the *statue* could do any thing more with the impressions, than a daguerreotype plate could have done. In vain are various sensations detailed, and the assertion made, that different impressions must produce different states of consciousness, and that these states being present in memory, are necessarily compared with each other. It is precisely this necessity which cannot be made evident, without the aid of an initial and specific power of the mind to perform the operation.

True it is that *man's* mind instantly, upon any sensation, connects an idea of quantity, intensity, degree, proportion, or distribution, with that sensation; but the idea thus annexed can only be due to some property or power in the man himself, for *if* IDEAS *were only* COPIES of pictures and of feelings perceived, as they must be if produced by sensation only, how could they be divided into parts, and new ideas be built up with the severed materials; how could ideas ever be conventional or arbitrary, as often they are? Assuredly sensationalism never answered this objection, without evoking some innate archeus to do the work.

It is very certain that there is nothing in the objective or sensational pictures themselves, to divulge the mathematical unit. Nature does not furnish us with a ready-made multiplication table, or with fore-settled common divisors. The *real* is one thing, the standard of measure is another; one is given *to* consciousness, the other is the product of an operation of the mind. How often is reality exhibited to consciousness without any mark of divisibility, as, for instance, time and space; but the mind will not tolerate this, and arbitrarily supplies the conditions of computation.

If sensations were sufficient to impress ideas of value or quantity, whether absolute or relative, then all other animals would necessarily be as wise as man is, in the science of numbers; for brutes also have the five senses. Sensation in brutes is as perfect, and often more active and intense than in man; but it is, at the same time, certain that brutes are totally destitute of mathematical ideas. Now, that the unit not only evolves, but *presupposes* all mathematics, no one who understands the rationale of numbers will deny. Hence if we were to grant, for an instant, that any sub-human animal numerates, we would be obliged to concede that they do perform every subsidiary process. It is impossible to separate the act of positing and counting the unit, from any part or from the whole of the science of numbers; for, let me repeat it, the conception of the unit imports the conception of addition, subtraction, &c. Prof. Davies says: " Since all numbers, whether integer or fractional, must *come* FROM, and hence be connected WITH, the unit one, it follows: that there is but one purely elementary idea in the science of numbers; that the idea of every number, regarded as made up of units, is necessarily complex; that all numbers, except one, must be so regarded when we analyze them; that since the number arises from the *addition* of ones, the apprehension of it is incomplete until we understand how those additions are made," &c.

I now put a simple and indubitable fact before the reader—a fact which, with all its simplicity, is fraught with consequences of the utmost value.

It is this:

PHYSICALLY, *the inferior animals have every organ or faculty possessed by man.*

Every thing that matter, vitality, and sensation can impart, they have in a degree sometimes even superior to man. Brutes are *materially* equal to man. They are made of the same materials, have the same osseous, fleshy, vascular, and nervous organs. In vain have anatomists labored to find a single fibre of the brain, in man, which is not to be found in other mammals.

The Mathematical Potentiality *or attribute is the only essential thing which man can assert as belonging exclusively to him; as his alone; as not held in common with brutes; and therefore it cannot be due to any physiological property or organ.*

This must be so, for otherwise the axioms and laws of induction (the canons of which I have quoted above) would be lies; but they are imperturbable truths, and they imperatively sanction my argument.

The residual or distinctive circumstance in which man differs from brutes, is that of having the idea or archeus of number and measure, and of being able to apply it to substance and quality, form and force, time and space, action and passion, motion and law.

Hence it is to this "residual circumstance" that man owes all his ideations of Truth, Utility, Morality, Beauty, and Art.

What is Truth? It is the *ratio* of Substantive Reality; the adaptation of number and measure to fact.

What is Utility? It is the *ratio* of Action; the adaptation of means to ends, by the measure of physical laws.

What is Morality? It is the *ratio* of Reason and Passion—of flesh and spirit, individual and society.

What is Beauty? It is the *ratio* of Quality: form, dimension, distribution, color, sound, &c., proportionate and complete, in variegated unity.

What is Art? It is the adaptation of number and measure to the reproduction, by man, of Truth, Utility, Morality, and Beauty: it is realized Thought.

Thus, it seems, truth, utility, morality, beauty, art, arise from number; and hence if brutes could ideate the unit, they would—

1°. Have with it the ability to add, subtract, &c., for the unit presupposes mathematics.

2°. Have with it languages as copious as those of human kind; for speech is made up of words expressive of integers of quantity.

3°. Have with it arts of their own invention; for computation is the bethinking instrument which enables man to invent.

But to be certain that thought (which I have now identified with man's power to numerate and measure) is NOT *physical*, let us cast a glance upon objective nature.

THE ELEMENTS of matter (as every student knows) are governed by mathematical laws. These laws are applied to a multitude of substances and properties, and display themselves in an infinite variety of forms, so that there evidently exists a computer, distributor, or artist. The Grand Archeus of the Universe, therefore, necessarily exists; for mathematics is thought, not substance. *Variety* of adaptation implies—a *selection* of appropriate materials, a *modification* of the materials themselves, to suit the work; and that this must be done, and each adaptation be realized, in the midst of countless substances, qualities, and properties, of which only a portion are fit and the rest unfit, in each instance of formation; and therefore rationality and design must preside over nature. A choosing and determining Thought must exist.

PLANTS, though they possess vitality, have not in themselves any power of thought; but since their *acts* are rationally ordained, (as I have abundantly proved,) those acts must be determined by a rational archeus *out of themselves.*

BRUTES (as I have shown) possess mere physical sensation and consciousness; their impressions are *passive*, and their action instinctive or though*tless;* but since the acts are rationally ordained, while the actors are themselves incapable of thought, the power that thinks for them and predetermines their instinct, is not only rational but *out of them.*

MAN (as I have also shown in the preceding parts of this study) is endowed with Thought; and hence the archeus which did not dwell in the brute, dwells in man; becomes a part of man, identifies itself with, or adopts his organism; and thus, according to the declaration of Jesus, human beings are the children of God, for his seed (which is Thought) is sown in our body;

and while in that body may bear fruits of Thought. Truly has it been said: "Man is an intellect making use of an organism."

Thus we have also found the link of

### CONSCIOUSNESS AND THE SOUL.

Consciousness is physiological; but it is the surface upon which thought or the soul operates from its zenith within. It is upon the objective world, as given in consciousness, through sensation, that Thought or the soul throws *its light;* and creates, by the union of the outer with the inner light, that intellectual consciousness of which man alone on earth is the depositary.

We may now easily understand how man may know himself, and perceive the connection of

### SELF-KNOWLEDGE AND THE SOUL.

All ethics are based upon the assumption that man may know himself; and therefore the precept "Know thyself,"—or the proposition, "The proper study of mankind is man," is the initial point of wisdom and virtue.

To know himself man must have the faculty of self-examination. This is so self-evident that it looks trivial. Cooks say that the first thing necessary to make a dish of baked turbot is to have a turbot; and we say that in order to know ourselves we must possess the inherent power or faculty of self examination. In this truism, however, we find matter for serious meditation; and ground for important deductions.

A *machine* may be extremely complicated, the steam engine for instance—it may operate with the greatest precision, and seem to be gifted with volition—move as a thing of life; but with all its co-ordinate complication, and moving forces, it is dead to itself, and though doing the work of mind it has no mind.

A *beast* is endowed with life, but all its actions are passive or fatal, being dictated by that class of motives with which reflection and judgment have no concern. Their acts are determined, like the movements of a machine, by a sort of propelling power known as "*instinct.*" Whatever variability or versatility we may observe in brutes must be attributed to outward pressure alone. A complex and circumstantial coercion, determines the acts; and a careful study of the facts has always shown it to be so.

*Man* alone observes himself, attends to the processes of his own mind and feelings, reviews and corrects his own reasonings, examines and defines his own motives, puts himself as it were on trial before himself—he the accused and he the judge. This is or can be done by no other animal. All the labored arguments of materialists to show that dogs, horses, elephants, or monkeys have ever evinced even the semblance of this faculty, are clear failures.

In this distinctive trait we find the *first* mark of man's separation from brute creation, the *first* link which connects him with divinity; and it is because this capacity of self-examination is a *pre-requisite* of all moral and mental science, that it is placed immediately after those in which man 1st, becomes conscious of life, and of material good and evil; 2d, learns the necessity of labor and principle; 3d, witnesses death and conceives the hope of regeneration.

Yes, man is capable of knowing himself; and now let us mark the consequences of this primary truth. It is pregnant with evidence of the *duality* of man—proves that man is body and soul. The observed and the observer are necessarily *two*. The eye cannot see itself—a mirror cannot reflect itself.

These two examples are sufficient to show the necessity of there being *two* to do the act of self-observation. Mechanics, chemistry, &c., might furnish us with other examples, but the detail would require more space than we can afford. The seen requires a seer—the heard, a hearer—the reflected, a reflector; and thus, man must possess, within and distinct from himself, the *image* of himself in which he may recognize and *commune* with himself.

Remove that other self, and all power of "reflection" must immediately cease. If any man says the contrary, let me see him lift himself and carry himself upon his own shoulders.

Instead of cavilling with, resisting or wilfully closing our eyes to the undeniable fact of the duality of man, we had better receive this truth at once, with cordiality, and proceed sincerely to find its harmony with all other truth. It is suicidal to struggle against truth, for she is powerful and must prevail. To deny a truth is to concede that its demonstration would impeach our religion and philosophy. Let us rather accept it with frankness, and having, once for all, posited the fact that man is double—let us see if this duality is not the body and the soul—the animal body and the spiritual body—the flesh and the spirit—the beast and the angel?

The moment we concede as we are bound to do the duality of man, we may clearly understand *how* the mind may look upon itself for all the purposes of recognition, revision, and correction. Then we may comprehend how man *does* hold intercourse with himself, and improve in self-knowledge. Then, too, we may realize a rational and consistent idea of the real differentia between men and beasts; for observation, comparison, and reason will show that the reflector, the other self, the internal mirror—*must be the soul.*

Call it by any other name if you choose—the thing itself will not, thereby, be changed; for what *we* call the soul is the distinct type of the mortal man—a type which has a *superior* and specific existence of its own.

You may ask why we accord, not only a specific and distinct, but also a "superior" existence to this type. We answer simply: that because they are two there must be a differentia to distinguish them; that because they are two, they must be either equal, or one must be superior and the other inferior, but their equality would require us to admit that we have two equal bodies, which we know is not the fact; that because they are two, one must be the animal nature we hold in common with brutes, and that therefore the other contains the differentia which distinguishes us from them; that because they are two, and one must be the animal which cannot reflect, the other is therefore our intellectual element—the spirit of Love and Truth; that because they are two, and one being animal, the other, from the necessity of differentia, must have some property not animal; and finally, that because all the works of God are seriated and progressive, he has when he added unto man that which entitled him to a higher place in the scale of being, necessarily added some *superior* element or essence.

Thus, by means of the palpable truism with which we commenced this argument, the existence of the *soul of man* is demonstrated.

So also is the fact that there must be an affinity—common properties of union—and reciprocity of action between the mortal body and thinking soul; for how else could the soul become, even temporarily, identified with the body, feel and suffer with it, think and act congenially to it, and bear, as it does, the penalties of its conduct; and how could the body be affected, as it is at all times, by the merits and demerits of the soul?

It is therefore certain that the soul is the type of the body, as God is the archetype of the soul; and the text is verified: "God created man in his own image." And another truth becomes also apparent. It is that man has a *real* conscience, subject, as every other manifestation of Divine wisdom, to fixed laws. Hence when the animal creature infringes any of those laws, the soul must suffer; and revolt against every feeling or act not congenial to its own essence.

We may now proceed to a study of the

### EXISTENCE AND ATTRIBUTES OF GOD.

I. In the early days of History there appeared men of Wisdom and Inspiration, Philosophers and Apostles, who, contemplating nature—the Stars, the planets, the course of the Sun, and the changes of the seasons—dimly perceived the first of causes, and the destiny of man beyond the grave.

' Since those days, many pages of the book of nature, to the ancient sages unknown, have been unrolled to the eyes of mankind. In each successive generation, great men of science and genius have appeared and lighted new beacons to guide mankind to a knowledge of God.

Yet, with all the lights of science, with all the efforts of theorists, God is now proved by the same process of reasoning as in the first days of history. The philosopher who discovers the most hidden secrets of nature, only brings new witnesses—new *facts*, to illustrate and fortify the first dictates of natural reason.

The savage and the sage, both reason alike; and viewing the mysteries of creation—struck with wonder at the order, beauty, and wise combination of minute atoms and stupendous worlds, they exclaim—Behold! can it be true that there is no God?

The Materialist answers—" abandon matter and choose God, and you only exchange one mystery for another. You put back by one degree the great cause, but creation is not thereby rendered intelligible. Like the world of the idolater, supported by a mighty tortoise, it remains for him to learn the foothold of the supporter. Is it not as easy to believe that the universe itself is eternal, as that God, the all wise, the all powerful, existeth uncreated from all eternity?"

And now behold, Skepticism arises, and laughs with scorn at the presumption of all who pretend to divine the undiscoverable secrets of nature.

"In these theories," says she, " our reason is confounded by equal mysteries; and the finite mind, when at last it counts the real riches of this treasury, finds itself the owner of three *words ;* invented by itself, yet beyond its own comprehension: Eternity, Infinity, God! Who *knows*, says the skeptic, that matter had, or had not, a beginning? Who *knows* that there is a God, or that no God existeth? There may be one God, or three Gods, or tens, or hundreds, or thousands of Gods, or *no* God; but of all this we *know* nothing, and must remain content with our ignorance."

Let it be then, that I must choose between three

things—the Eternity of God—the Eternity of material order—and the blind, the deaf, the mute, the death-like mystery of Skepticism. How, between these, can I hesitate?

Shall I suspend or smother thought, and be satisfied with ignorant Skepticism? Shall my mind be as the bird of the deluge, ever on the wing, without a resting place, over the boundless waters of a world submerged? Shall I be content that the waves of doubt shall cover all the works of nature? Shall I be content not to infer and judge, or not even to guess? Nay, Skepticism is contrary to the nature of man. We all feel the necessity of believing something; and the most radical doubter has always a cosmogony of his own, and is not satisfied until he has, in his own way, built up the universe. If man thinks of his own existence, his mind will ever be asking, How? Why? Whence? Nor will it ever let him rest or sleep until an answer is found, plausible at least to itself.

We are therefore, all, either believers in God or materialists; and he who in argument asserts that he is a pure skeptic, content with ignorance, or without a theory of creation, is a liar or an idiot.

Materialism is unsatisfactory to me. That word is almost as cold, as dead and as dark as skepticism. It lacks the sanction of ages, it smothers the first promptings of natural reason, it speaks not to the soul; and leaves man, in the midst of Chaos . . . . ignorant of the materials, and ignorant of their laws . . to build the universe. Materialism allows no communion of thought among men; for, every materialist has a system of his own, understood by none but himself. He affects to despise the dreams of the Theist; and yet, none more than himself yields to the allurements of imagination; for, all his theories of matter, and of the formation of worlds, are pure inventions of a mind which will not brook ignorance of the birth of nature, and which strains its ideal powers to invent the laws of an unknown necessity.

And, now, since our nature pushes us to imagine; and, in the absence of demonstration, to divine—since we must find a word for the enigma, or live unhappy—let that word be . . . . "God;" and in that word let us rejoice.

Who can shake off the thought that word conveys—who will consent to forget its meaning—who does not understand it—to whom does it not express a sublime idea? Grandeur, perfection, infinity, power, wisdom, justice, unbounded benevolence, charity, foresight, and knowledge . . . . the author of creation, the preserver of all, from the insect to the sun. If that word fell not upon our soul, as well as upon our ear, eloquence would lose its warmth, history become a blank, truth lack her holiest witness, and poetry weep her brightest inspiration.

If Theism is but a theory—it is the most sublime and the most perfect, the most pleasing and the most moral—it is not inconsistent with any positive knowledge—but indeed it adorns and crowns all knowledge. It points science to a great and glorious origin and end—gives a soul and a voice to nature—and tells the traveller on the way of time, that there is a goal to his path, and a hope for his journey. If among theories I must choose, I will adopt the most beautiful; and if the mind seeks a point of immensity, for a resting place, let that point, for me, be a belief in the existence of God.

Let me illustrate this.

II. A traveller is cast upon an unknown coast, and after scrambling in darkness, along the shore, at the dawn of the day he finds himself suddenly on a broad and winding highway, where everchanging prospects meet his eye at every step, and where he sees thousands of travellers journeying along like himself, all in the same direction. Will he ask none where that road doth lead? and if he meets no one who can answer that question, will he then content himself with passive and absolute ignorance, and frame no supposition, the most plausible and probable he can, as to the object and termination of that road? If the road is well paved and bridged, if each stage is marked, if every mile-post points onward, if well-ordered grounds and symmetrical palaces present themselves at every turn, will he not admit the presence of intellect and power? and if he is made like a man, and has a mind like that of his fellow creatures, will he not look forward to an end analogous to the means employed to enable him to reach it? Will he not picture to himself a magnificent palace, or a great city; for why this road, whence all these tokens of design? Yes, the picture of that great city or palace will grow upon his imagination, and each step will confirm its existence, until, convinced of its reality, he will walk forward with more alacrity, more hope and confidence. The narrow-minded reasoner may think himself extremely wise, and laugh at what he calls the phantasies and dreams of this traveller who expects an adequate term to such a beginning; but while the doubter scoffs and loiters amidst present and unfruitful enjoyments, the child of nature, he who listens to the free promptings of his reason (and believes the eternal production of intellectual effects, must depend upon the eternal existence of an intellectual cause)—would go on, with a glad heart, cheered by brilliant hopes; and when the darkness of night would descend upon both the travellers, one would lie down in despair, while the other would yet look forward to the City of Immortality.

III. The idea of a God is so natural, and so conformable to the plainest reason, that it suggests itself early to the human mind—it is so forcible, so irresistible, that it takes hold of and commands all the intellectual faculties of man—so clear and satisfactory, that it produces more than conviction, and assumes the character of enthusiasm and religion. By the proper use of his faculties man with difficulty reached the arts and sciences of civilization, while the ignorant savage already for ages had possessed a full conception of the divinity. It required the sublimest efforts of genius and study, by men of superior minds and deep investigation, to discover the order of the Solar System, the rotundity of the earth, the principles of Gravitation, the laws of electricity—while the aboriginal, of the great prairies of the West, not possessing sufficient perfection of intellect to discover the hidden laws of matter, had conceived, in the spirit of nature, a pure and correct idea of the Deity.

Yet let us not contend that the idea of a God is simply innate, independent of and unsupported by our reason, apart from our feeling.

Innate ideas are inherent feelings of the mind which develop themselves, by their own force, in a certain and invariable form. These are different from the *faculties* of the mind, which are those qualities or properties of the cerebral mass, that appear when acted upon through the senses. The first are the spontaneous combustion brought on by the natural changes of matter; the latter are the latent sparks of the flint which dwell quiescent, till stricken by a steel-armed hand. The instinct is like the natural whisper of the conch-shell; but the faculties are like the strings of a harp, pregnant with music, yet silent, till played upon by the proper musician. They are the instrument, nature the performer, our senses the hand, and reason the Music.

To maintain, then, that we have merely an innate idea of God, is to degrade a sublime thought and discovery of the human mind into the mere operation of instinct. It would then be, indeed, not a compound, but a simple sensation which would require no reflection, no combination, no reasoning (however plain) to bring it forth.

Let us cherish a more elevated opinion of the source of our ideas of divinity; and contend that the experience of all—the *books* of the sage and the *talk* of the savage—prove that humanity's belief in God is deduction, and not the mere growth of instinct; for it is only by the combination and computation of preceptions we call " reasoning," that both the philosopher and the simplest child of nature have been impressed with a faith in the Divine Existence.

IV. It matters not if we fail to find the rigorous mathematical demonstration required by the atheist, who does not admit the *belief* which is based upon strong rational deductions. There is a medium between absolute knowledge and total denial. It suffices that Deism responds, with thrilling harmony, to the most melodious tones of that music of thought . . . . the Reason of Man.

To test this accordance, the first thing necessary is to define the idea or subject we seek to examine.

What is " God " ?

The answer requires an example.

A mathematical philosopher observed the falling of bodies, the laws of weight, the attraction of all things, to a common centre, and the revolutions of the planets around the sun ; and finding that all these things were governed by a single and invariable principle, he gave that principle (though itself impalpable and invisible) a name, and called it Gravitation. The Theist does the same—he observes the perfect *order*, immense *life*, and infinite *intellect*, which fills the universe ; and seeing that these are governed by certain immutable rules, which indicate a common origin or cause,—he calls it " God ! " In fact, to the mind, the word God is nothing more than the unit expression of the attributes of a great essence, (in itself unknown ;) but which acts everywhere, from the centre of the Sun to the utmost travels of the Comet, with the force of omnipotent wisdom.

As of Gravitation, men know nothing of this essence except by the Phenomena it produces. These phenomena proclaim its presence everywhere, and appear in modes so multiple and varied, as to equal infinity. Man observes them by the sensation they create within him, through the senses ; and thus it seems, that the preceptions and sentiments by which man becomes acquainted with matter and its laws, are also his means of knowing God ; for, ask the theologian how he knows, or rather why he believes there is a God, and he will appeal to the material world, to the wonderful *order* and *life* which pervade it, and to the operations of *intellect* which we *see* around us, and *feel* within us.

Behold order in every formation of matter from the crystal to revolving worlds—behold life in the reed and the oak, in the crawling insect and in man—behold intellect in every operation of nature's laws, behold it in our own souls, and in the wonderful design which governs all planets and suns, and pervades the immensity of space.

The presence of God is necessarily connected with the Phenomena of order, life, and intellect. They are only modes in which he appears, and is made evident to man—the only means by which man is conscious of him, has proof of him, and finds authority to believe in his existence. These Phenomena are produced by his presence as inevitably as Electricity by Friction, Weight by Gravitation, Expansion by Heat, and Light by the Sun.

I may therefore conclude that God is the principle of Order, Life and Intellect, in the universe. In other words, there is a principle which pervades all nature, the essence of which is order, life, and intellect; and that principle I call God.

V. These attributes may be considered as only one which may be called, and which necessarily is the *organizing power;* that is to say, the power which arranges, combines, and regulates all things, so as to produce harmony and all its consequences. Order, life, and intellect may be considered as modes, effects, or higher grades of one great and all-pervading *principle.*

Stones possess order, plants order and life, man order, life, and intellect. The order possessed by the plants is more perfect and complicated than that possessed by stones, and the order which appears in the organization of man is still more complete and wonderful than that of plants and stones.

Life, when combined with order, seems to depend upon it, and appears (in the vegetable world for example) to be nothing more than the operation or action of a more perfect arrangement of the particles of matter.

To this combination add a set of nerves, unite them together in the brain—develop that brain with ventricles and cincritious matter and intellect appears. So that it would seem that in intellect, as well as life, we have but a more perfect phenomenon of the *principle* of order.

I do not stop here to show (as I might) how this apparent dependence of intellect upon a more perfect order is a mere illusion, how this illusion arises by mistaking effect for cause, and how organic order and life are subordinate to the causative force of a powerful, independent, and designing *will*. This theme is reserved for another place; and as it does not directly affect the present argument, I refrain from the tempting digression.

VI. *Order, life, and intellect are the trinity of nature, one and indivisible.*

Air may be decomposed into original elements,

hydrogen, oxygen &c, which are often found totally separate from each other. These elements of air have no necessary connection with each other, they may exist isolated, they may combine, separately or jointly, with other substances—they are therefore recognized as distinct gases or original atoms of matter. On the other hand, light is known as a single element, though it may affect our senses in different ways, though its rays may produce different colors to the eye, yet they are all *rays of light;* for notwithstanding their different colors which melt into, and combine with each other, in shades of infinite gradation and mixture, still all these grades possess the one characteristic, a degree of whiteness, or transparency, which is properly called *light.* The different rays are merely regarded as different kinds, or rather grades of light; and these either combined or separated (whatever be the proportion) always produce . . . . *light;* or rather, always appear to be the light. They are therefore considered as one and the same element. If order, life, and intellect, like the elements of the air, were different essences or principles, we would sometimes find them separate—sometimes entirely isolated from each other; but their union (as I will show) is, like that of colors and light, inseparable and co-existent: and they may well be designated by the single appellation I have already used, to wit: " the *organizing* power."

VII. In the Physical world, when atoms of matter

can no longer be divided into others of a simpler nature, the atoms so found to defy all further analysis, are considered as elements of matter. In the spiritual world, when attributes cannot be conceived as distinct from each other, but absolutely require a simultaneous presence to constitute a unity, these attributes must be considered as manifestations of the same entity.

1. I am not unconscious of the fact that the house we live in, the furniture it contains, the clothes which cover us—and in fact every work of art, (viewed apart,) possesses order without life and intellect, that the vegetable kingdom possesses order and life without intellect; but it is this apparent contradiction of fact with my theory, which, when explained and conciliated, will form its clearest demonstration and insure its triumph.

Take the palace we live in as an example. How does it exist, with its beautiful proportions and judicious divisions? Was it not intellect that planned, and life that executed the work? Without the living intellectual man who did the work, where would be these walls, these chambers, these columns? This order could not exist without the life and intellect which devised and arranged it; nor could it be preserved without the action of the same principles which brought it into existence. Let life and intellect cease to inhabit this dome, how soon will it rot, how soon crumble into dust. The moment life and intellect completed their work, it commenced the process of decay; and its total ruin is only retarded by the care of the keepers. The separatior of life and intellect from the order they created was the first step towards total decomposition. This building now rots like the body of a dead man. The work of destruction may be sometimes slow, but it is always certain.

But I do not speak with sufficient precision. There is a distinction to be drawn between Material and tangible order, and the principle or essence of order. This last is evidently a cause, the other is nothing but an effect. The material order of this palace did not exist of itself or by chance; it had, therefore, a cause, which (*judging from its* EFFECTS) we may properly name the principle of order, or the organizing power. Now we know that the palace was built by an architect possessing life and intellect, which he applied to the materials—we know also from experience that decay is going on in every part of the building—however slow the operation, however apparent the duration. While the architect performed his labor, order was produced; now that he has left, the formation of order has ceased, and ruin has commenced. Is it not evident, therefore, that though material order appears to continue, yet the principle of order is gone;—that this principle was contained in the man who formed the work; that is to say in a being endowed with life and intellect? In fact, what else than these could it be? Do we not all know from experience that life and intellect are the only powers within us which enable us to produce order?

2. Is not intellect in man the principle of the material order he produces? Experience answers, yea. Can there exist in nature *two* principles or essences of the same things? Experience and Philosophy answer, nay! I therefore conclude, there cannot exist *two* principles of order; and that the organizing cause which brings forth the material order of stones and plants, is the same as that cause, in the mind of man, which when it acts, creates the order of art, literature, and science.

In proportion to the excellence of the exertion of his intellect, does man produce that which is excellent in his works. If the mental operation be a perfectly intellectual one, useful plans are executed, beautiful designs are embodied, and sublime discoveries are made. Such is the action of intellect, such are the indications by which the presence of mind is known. We are conscious of no other cause, we can conceive of no other origin of material order, than an intellectual cause; for we see that order is only an intellectual effect produced upon matter. But we know that life cannot exist without this intellectual effect, this order, which is heaven's first law; and without which the vital force, if it were distinct, and did not necessarily comprise the organizing and intellectual forces, would forever float inertly and uselessly in the midst of chaos.

3. If we contend that it is the vital principle that develops by its force the beatiful symmetry of vegetable and animal nature, we give to it the same function as

intellect, and acknowledge it as an intellectual power. If we assume that order or arrangement determines life —still, as intellect is the essential principle of order, no arrangement, adapted to the design of receiving and sustaining life, can exist without mind, to conceive and determine the form it shall assume as well as the modes and means of its duration.

VIII. I have shown the identity of order, life, and intellect. I have shown that they are qualities, phenomena, or modes of one great principle or essence—let me now demonstrate that this principle or essence is GOD!

IX. Let us recapitulate.
1°. We have endeavored to show the existence of a universal organizing power.
2°. We have argued that this power is single—though it appears in three modes to the organs of sense.

X. It remains for us to meet the objection of materialism; and then, to demonstrate this organizing power to be the Divinity.

XI. *The materialists contend* :
That order is necessity :
That life and intellect are phenomena produced by the action of the component parts of matter upon each other:
That order, life, and intellect are effects of many

causes, and that these causes are certain qualities or properties of material elements.

Let them give the utmost range to imagination, and call up the whole arcana of supposition, and they will find only two alternatives consistent with materialism.

The first: that order, life, and intellect have no distinct existence of their own, but are mere chemical results produced by the combination of matter with matter.

The second: that order, life, and intellect are one or more *distinct* SUBSTANCES acting chemically upon other SUBSTANCES, and producing certain effects.

Both these suppositions can be shown to be erroneous.

XII. I argue thus:

I. If we treated the assertion of the sufficiency of mere chemical action to produce order, life, and intellect in the same spirit as the materialist treats a belief in God—if we examined the doctrines of the materialist with the same rigor—what would become of his philosophy? Let us call upon him for proof. How does he know that the mere combination of various particles of matter, arranged in a certain way, will produce order, life, and intellect? How does he know it I say? Does he not deal in mere hypothesis? I ask.

Reasoning from analogy does not satisfy him—it leads to mere probabilities or possibilities—the materialist does not admit evidence which tends to mere belief—he contends for absolute mathematical proof—otherwise he would be forced to admit the beauty, the force, the plausibility of the arguments of Theistical sages, poets, and orators; and confess that, if mere probability or analogy were sufficient, he would be forced to admit the existence of God. No, says he, when the order of the heavens and the earth are shown—it does not suffice that you should conclude, because man makes a watch, that the heavens and the earth were made also; for if all order must have a maker, who made the maker? Well, then, mere analogy, mere approximative evidence, is not enough, proof positive must be given, so that man inay say—"*I know.*"

Where is there such proof as this in favor of the proposition, that order, life, and intellect are merely combinations of matter? Such is the proof the materialist requires from the Theist; and such is the proof materialism, to be consistent with itself, is bound to produce. Thus would the advocate of the self-sufficiency of matter—thus would he who asserts the eternity and necessity of order, resulting from the properties of matter alone, be silenced by his own favorite phrase—"How do you *know?*"

II. The premises upon which the materialist builds his theory, are his ignorance. He has *no knowledge* of any thing but matter—therefore he concludes there is in nature nothing but matter. What logic! to derive from ignorance a theory which presumes to explain the profoundest secret of nature: a theory which pretends to explain eternal and universal order. As well might the chief of some savage isle—ignorant of lands beyond the ocean that surrounds his narrow dominion—assert the title of—"King of the World." Ignorance is proof of nothing: it can only hope to learn, but never to teach.

III. And can it be pretended that we know enough of the chemical properties of matter to say that a chemical combination, apart from an organizing power or essence, suffices to produce order, life, and intellect? If the materialist denies his ignorance, and presumes to say that he reasons affirmatively from affirmative facts, then let him tell us the ingredients wherewith an organized being may be formed, and endowed with the faculties of mind. If he possesses the knowledge let him show us the creature his science has produced, without the use of agents to him mysterious, intangible, and unknown; but if he cannot tell, not only the component parts, but the proportions and process of the chemical composition to which he attributes such wonderful effects, then let him *stand mute* when the organizing, vivifying, and thinking action, in nature, is sought to be explained.

IV. The materialist, when he undertakes to demonstrate his propositions, must prove them by our knowledge of matter, its properties and laws. Indeed, from the very nature of materialism, these are the only evidences its followers have a right to advance. To them the phenomena of order, life, and intellect can only present questions purely chemical, involving the analyses and synthesis of mineral and vegetable substances. Within this circle they must solve the problem of organization, vitality, and thought. Science (for in science alone they have faith) will admit of no chanceful hypothesis which cannot be tested by experiment; and science refuses to grant them a favorable solution. But let us deal with liberality; let us take the theories of materialism as they are, and see if (apart from exact demonstration) they even command the secondary tribute of belief. I say they do not; and all nature is my witness.

V. From the innumerable facts to be found in natural history, and which rebut entirely the opinion that a mere combination of matter is sufficient to explain the trine phenomena—order, life, and intellect, let us take one or two examples:

1. The egg, when in its natural state, is composed of certain elements. The quality and character of each of these are exactly ascertained by chemistry; and it is known that the analysis of the body of any bird will produce precisely the same elements, without any difference in the proportionate quantities, as an egg of the same species before incubation.

2. Nothing is more certain that if an egg is cut across into two equal parts the analysis of each half will produce precisely the same chemical result; and yet, when incubation takes place, it will be found that

one of the halves has been formed into the head and neck and breast and wings, while the other has been transformed into legs, abdomen, and tail; and this is accomplished without the addition of materials different from those composing the egg, or even a change of their proportions; for, as I have already said, the analysis of the flesh, blood, fibres, and feathers of the bird show their component parts to be the same as the yolk and albumen of the egg.

3. In the human body, notwithstanding the difference of the shape of the several parts—head, breast, abdomen, arms, legs, hands, and feet, it is found that these parts are composed of precisely the same elementary particles of matter, without difference of proportions.

4. It is also observed that the flesh, blood, and fibres of the beast of the field, are made of the same gaseous compounds as in man. That the egg of the domestic fowl is composed of the same chemical atoms as the body of a human being; and, finally, that blood is the same, in material, as flesh; and all the fibres and other tissues of the body have the same basis as the flesh and blood. Form and adaptation vary infinitely, but the elements of construction are ever the same; and, what is more extraordinary, always in substantially the same proportion throughout.

5. In fact, this uniformity of material continues even into the vegetable kingdoms. A great proportion of the plants and fruit which supply animal nature with

food, are of the same composition as the bodies which they nourish; and yet, in other forms, these same compounds are sometimes fatal to life.

6. The basis of all *organic* nature consists of four gases, well known to chemists as the material out of which all things (vegetable and animal) endowed with life, are formed: yet these elements may be combined in every imaginable proportion (in the same proportion in which they are found in the living animal or vegetable) without developing the phenomena of vitality. The boiled egg, the cooked meat, the plucked grain or fruit, the dead man who expired yesterday, all contain the same elements of matter as when throbbing with life.

7. The absence of life, however, it seems, leaves these materials without any formative power. Decomposition and disorganization (the separation and dispersement of the elementary particles) follow, as if the power which had bound them and arranged them, had departed.

Now take these facts and ponder upon them.

VI. It is a law of the material world that like causes always produce like effects. This is the principle which is at the foundation of all physical science; and if it did not hold good, there could be no such things as knowledge and reason. Without this principle no one, on seeing an act or phenomenon, could attribute it to any definite cause. All would be confusion and doubt; and man could never have trusted to, or have been served by, that inductive philosophy, which judging of cause by effect, and reposing confidence in the uniformity and consistency of nature, has been so useful and so sure a guide to natural science and physical art. If, then, the mere combination of matter be the cause of organization and life, whence such varied effects so totally dissimilar, from so definite and single a cause as the union of four elements in one certain proportion? The plants of the earth, the birds of the air, the brute and the man, in all their infinite varieties of form and character, from the mushroom to the oak, from the worm to the eagle, from the polypus to man, all possess the same *organic* elements. Thus teaches philosophy; and therefore philosophy must also teach that these manifold and different effects cannot be *produced* by the same identical composition of matter. The matter may serve as the material; but the appearance of the same material shaped into frames so totally unlike one another, must be attributed to something else than the mere chemical affinity; for the same chemical affinities, independent of other operative causes, would always produce the same result.

VII. Two or more chemical ingredients mixed together, in precisely the same proportions, are frequently found to compose substances totally different, in color, form, taste, and other properties: in one form poisonous and in another perfectly innoxious. What then is the cause of these different characters in these identical mixtures? The inherent properties of the compound are certainly not sufficient to explain why it takes now one action and then another. To say that the power resides in the material, is to assert that matter may determine its own form and modify its own properties; and thus to award it a power of volition and choice, which no knowledge will allow us to admit; and which if acknowledged would, at any rate, lead to consequences entirely inconsistent with the doctrines of materialism; for if we admitted this power of volition in matter, we would have to say that the substances at one end of an egg *choose* to form themselves into head, wings, &c., and at the other end they *choose* to take the shape of legs, tail, &c., and that the *choices* of these several parts were so connected and prescient, so adapted to useful purposes, that they conceived and organized a living body, wisely adapted to the great fabric of nature, and to the observance of nature's laws. Thus would the materialist be compelled to endow a composition of matter, with that sublime power and design, superior to the intellect of man, which the Theist acknowledges to belong to God alone.

VIII. If the material itself were endowed with this power, then man by putting the same combination together would produce the same result as nature; but he finds the compounds he arranges totally inert so far as the production of organization, life, and intellect are concerned. Pure physical effects are all that he can attain, combustion by the union of such and such things, an electric current by this and that fermentation, moisture, &c., but never life and intellect, where they did not already exist; and even if he could create or develop these by an artful arrangement and mixture of matter, still would it be the intellect within himself using the properties of bodies as the instrument of knowledge and reason. If with the crucible, the alembic, certain parts of matter, and the electric current, man may bring forth an organism, (though I deny his ability to do it,) we would still have to credit his *mind* with the result, and consider the elements and other means employed as the passive instrument of a power not belonging to them, but to a being capable of exercising an action similar to the infinite wisdom which controls the universe.

IX. But as if to show how completely matter is only the instrument of some great cause, it appears that life, in the vegetable kingdom, acts in a form totally different from the animal. Vegetables generate oxygen and animals consume it; and it seems that this generating on one hand, and this consumption on the other, are necessary to the maintenance of life in the respective organisms. The action which maintains life in the vegetable would destroy it in the animal; the fish and the beast require different elements; other animals exist indifferently in air or water; some feed on grass alone, others devour only flesh; while many eat flesh and grass together:—so that organization and life do not depend upon any peculiar process of action; for, the process varies, and yet organization and life are produced.

Nor does any one process always develop the same form of action or existence; for, aquatic animals differ as in the crab and whale; those that require the aërial fluid differ, as the bird, the beast, the man; and these again when every process and condition of life seems to be identical, differ in their form and mode of existence—among the herbivora we find the sheep and the horse—the carnivora include the eagle and the tiger—the omnivora, the swine and the man.

X. Indeed, physics and chemistry do not afford, by the compounds, combinations, or processes of matter, any solution to the phenomena of life. The same ingredients and proportions of matter are found to compose inanimate as well as animate bodies. The same process and conditions of *matter* are found to belong to different forms and modes of life.

XI. To show how utterly absurd it is to suppose that all physical order or organization might be the blind and unintelligent action of matter upon matter, I will adduce one more instance. I find it in the *distinction of the sexes*, and in THE ADAPTATION OF THE SEXES TO EACH OTHER. What formative force is there in matter itself to produce not only *two* sexes, but to adapt one to the other, so beautifully and wondrously? The materialists in this case would vainly urge their favorite examples: showing, for instance, that, by dint of use and in the course of time, organs and members adapt themselves to the things and influences by which they are surrounded—the reindeer, they say, gradually becomes adapted to the arctic cold and moss food—the camel's foot and his ability to resist thirst, they say, is not produced by divine intention, but by the continued action of desert sands and heat—one moulding itself (ex necessitate rei) to the influence of the other. But how would their absurd argument apply to the combined difference and accord of the sexes? Two individuals are born at different times, and from different wombs: there they are, separate and independent organisms, never before in contact, and yet when they do meet, it becomes evident that one is made for the other, and that the two (though so distinct) are but the components of *one* idea—the harmonious instruments of a preconceived and unital design. \* \* \*

The laws of matter are, therefore, not the laws of life; but the vivifying principle evidently acts upon and governs matter, imparting properties and power unpossessed before. The elements of matter do not produce organization, for they are passive to organization.

XII. If, therefore, the living organization is not the effect of a combination of matter, we may conclude that it belongs to an *independent* cause or principle; but before inquiring into the nature of this cause or principle, I will again revert to the laws of physics to support this conclusion.

*a.* When the Naturalist sees the same phenomena appearing within dissimilar bodies, he attributes (for reasons already alluded to) differences to distinct causes, and similarities to similar causes. Light, heat, gravitation, electricity, appear in bodies which seem to have, in other respects, nothing else but these phenomena in common. Light shines in the Sun, in the lamp, in the flame of gas, in the volcanic lava, in the heated metal; yet no philosopher presumes for an instant to suppose that the light which appears in one form is different from that which appears in another. Heat is found in a thousand forms and in bodies having no affinities with each other—fire, water, sunshine, friction, chemical mixtures, iron, wood, gas,—all contain heat; and none will seek in compounds having no elements in common, the cause of an identical effect produced within them all; but will rather attribute the common phenomena to a common principle, having properties of its own, and imparting these properties to all bodies simple and compound without distinction. The same may be said of gravitation and electricity; for who will pretend that these do not exist independently of the atoms upon which they act? Electricity can be conveyed from one substance to the other—from the clouds to the earth, with instantaneous rapidity; and gravitation throws her eternal chain from suns to planets, through the immensity of space. If, then, we are guided by the rules of natural philosophy we are bound to conclude that organization, life, and intellect (which do not appear to belong more than light, heat, gravitation, and electricity, to the substances, combinations, forms, or processes in which they act) are a distinct substance or spirit, having an action and properties of its own.

*b.* Substance or spirit? Here is the difficulty. The materialist will find, after all, no great obstacle in attributing organization, life, and intellect to the operations of a single *substance;* but the word *spirit*, has for him no meaning—it shocks his understanding. Reconcile him with this word, and the difficulty between him and religion is settled. Show him the *word* spirit to be the most appropriate to describe the principle of order, life, and intellect, and he is converted. Substance or matter implies something corporeal, and *directly* perceptible to the *senses* or to any one of them. To affect the senses is not enough; the thing must be also *corporeal* to be entitled to the appellation of matter. For instance, *sound* is a thing which affects the senses, and it certainly is not itself matter, but an effect produced by a certain action upon matter. It also remains doubtful if *attraction* is a material cause; for its being perceptible merely by the weight of all things, is not of itself sufficient to stamp it with that corporeal quality which distinguishes matter. The weight produced by gravitation is not gravitation itself, no more than sound is the body from whence it proceeds. If, then, we cannot with propriety call gravitation a substance, how then shall we call it? We cannot say that it is an effect, for we perceive it always *acting as a cause;* and therefore we may class it among the primitive essences or spirits of nature. In fact, the word spirit is understood even in a more extended sense than this. It is frequently applied to things which are volatile, and active. In religion it is only used in a negative sense, to describe the nature of God as *not* partaking of the known qualities of matter; and to express how imperceptible the divinity must be to our senses of sight, hearing, taste, odor, and touch. In this acception, the gas called nitrogen might be called a *spirit;* for it is not cognizable by any of the senses; and its presence is only known by induction. When we say that God is an immaterial being we only express a negative idea, which is that the qualities of matter are not embraced in his being. He exists—he *is* a being—but his *mode* of existence we do not, we cannot know. We speak of him as a blind man does speak of light, as the deaf of sound. The blind know that something exists which is called light; which serves to guide those who lead the blind. The blind experience daily this important difference between them and other men, and they are forced to acknowledge that there exists a means of perceiving, of which they can form no conception. The deaf know nothing of sound, yet they constantly see its powers exerted: they see only effects; and though they cannot define the cause, and though it is beyond the direct powers of their sensorium, they must admit its existence. In the same way, persons may be born without the sense of smell and taste, and ascertain clearly by induction, that others have natural means, which they have not, to discover certain qualities and existences. They find that others can tell, not only that unseen flowers are near; but also they find that the name of those flowers, by some mysterious agency, is divulged. Wine is distinguished from water, though darkness pervades around; and the man who has never been endowed with the faculty of taste must acknowledge, in his fellow-being, the presence of a faculty to him refused by nature. In these examples, colors or light, the aroma of plants or the pestilential exhalations of dead bodies, the flavor of rich viands or the bitter properties of gall, might be looked upon as having no material existence with regard to those thus deprived of all power to perceive them, as parts or properties of matter. Now in the same way, if we give the most extensive sense to the word "*immaterial*," and define it to embrace all things, not corporeal, beyond the direct cognizance of the five senses of man, and all things which he knows to exist only by induction, then we will no longer be shocked at the idea conveyed by the word *spirit*, in contradistinction with substance or matter as explained above.

*c.* But if aught immaterial can exist, may there not be a spirit, an entity, existing as a being, and endowed with faculties even greater than those of man? May we not call this being God; and by observing the operations of this being upon nature, may we not ascertain what attributes to him appertain? A *sixth* sense, if given to us, for that purpose, might enable us to behold the beauty and glory of the divine existence, spreading its ethereal essence throughout the universe, and working the celestial machinery of heaven; but until this sixth sense is imparted, or until it disencumbers itself of the thick veil of earth which obscures it, we must content ourselves with the inductions afforded by our present powers of observation; and bless the faculty of *reason* which enables us to infer a God, and which connects us with HIS nature.

*d.* If, however, these *words*—mere *words* are they—" immaterial," " spiritual," &c., are still offensive to the ears of the materialist, let us for a moment argue without them; and see what conclusion we may reach, from the facts ascertained. We have already shown that neither combination, form, nor process of matter are sufficient to explain the existence of organization, vitality, and mind. We have concluded that these must depend upon a separate cause, acting upon the materials used, and determinating their form and action. Well, for the sake of argument, let the separate cause be considered as material; and then let us inquire what consequences will follow?

1. The cause of order must be universal, it must pervade immensity; the unbounded regions which are filled with myriads upon myriads of suns and planets, rolling harmoniously in tracks assigned to each, and wisely combined to prevent collision and confusion, proclaim the presence of the principle of order throughout all space.

2. The cause of order must be *a unit;* for, its operations are not diverse, as the operations of separate units. It tends to a single object, and produces a sin-

gle effect:—*order*. Different and separate agents of order would probably clash in their operations, unless we suppose them to consult and concert with each other, as so many distinct divinities, always agreeing, never dissenting, and having one purpose in view. This, in fact, would constitute a mental unity. We could not know of its parts, or apportion each to itself, no more than conceive of the existence and life of a man's head apart from his body; and we thus find, after all, that it would not aid the cause of materialism, to admit a theory which would constitute a physical organizing cause, acting by a union of many parts, as essential to each other as the heart, the lungs, the sensorium of the human body, are to the individual they compose. The forms of order are infinite; but the idea of order is one. We might rather separate gravitation into separate entities, than divide order (the first law or principle of nature) into more existences than one. We see a single effect and a single purpose—we therefore infer a single cause.

3. The cause of order must be powerful. And here need I stop to observe that the agent which governs the circuit of worlds, organizes the insect, and illumines the sun, must be infinitely powerful?

4. The cause of order must be intellectual. This is the plainest and most important part of my argument. It seems almost self-evident that none but an intellectual agent or power could arrange, adapt, and move the universe, in all its immensity, in all its details. But

let us follow the method we have hitherto pursued, and see if the fair inference and the inductive reasoning of natural philosophy, do not establish the proposition I advance. Like causes produce like effects. Intellect in man, when it acts, produces order. Here, then, is a positive cause, within our certain knowledge, producing certain definite effects: adaptation and useful arrangement—effects indicating a rational plan in the operator. A house, an engine, a book are produced from conception and design in man. Why then should we look for a different cause, in the works of nature, as producing results essentially similar to these? Do they not equally appear to arise from conception and design? Not only it is a correct principle of natural philosophy to say that like causes produce like results; but it is also correct and philosophical to hold that nature does not employ different powers to produce similar effects, and that she does not capriciously use now one power, now another, for identical purposes, but that she is economical and constant in the agent she employs. This is established by experience, and is proved by the known consistency and simplicity of the laws of nature; and therefore, when we know that the intellect within us is the conceiver and disposer of order, we may fairly contend that intellect is the universal principle of order, wherever order appears. Is intellect confined to the animal organism—to the brain of man? Let each of us ask himself if intellect is confined to his *own* brain? we all answer no; as regards ourselves, each of us has long ago ascertained (however great and wise he may be) that he is not alone the depository of the intellectual power. How do we judge our fellow-creatures possess thought? Other men perform the same acts that we do, the effects they produce are applied to similar uses, we understand them when they reason and base conclusion upon facts. We see plainly that their acts are determined from mental operations, and that when they do any thing they observe, they think, they form a design, and in the ratio of the perfection of their observations, thoughts, and plans, so is the perfection of their work—this we observe to be the case with ourselves; and we conclude, that all men are endowed with the same intellectual faculties which govern us. And why not carry this inductive process further; and if we see intellectual effects throughout nature, what reason can we allege for not attributing those effects to an intellectual cause? But when we find in nature a cause or power that observes better than we do, that foresees better than we do, how can we (frail and transient depositories of the limited and obscure spark of human reason) strut with pride as the sole possessors of mind, and assign the infinitely superior operations we behold around us, to blind combinations of matter? In the power which governs the formation of the animal organism, the wonders of earth, water, air, and fire—in the equilibrium and motion of planetary systems, can we refuse to behold the action and purposes of infinite reason? We allow reason to the inventor of the bow, to the discoverer of alphabetic writing, how can we deny it to the formative power of worlds—to the principle or spirit of universal order?

XIII. Thus do we see that even if the cause of order, life, and intellect, be material, that cause is
    1°. Universal.
    2°. Single.
    3°. Powerful.
    4°. Intellectual.

Infinity, unity, omnipotence, and wisdom—these are the attributes of God, be he spirit or matter; and now, presumptuous materialist, bow down thy head with humiliation while I raise my hands and voice in adoration. Let this being be for you a material essence or principle, yet remember that it is the fountain of thought—*the* MIND which governs all. Such a being I prefer to distinguish from the grovelling creatures and things perceptible to sense; and I call it or HIM a spirit; and thus shall I name him, and adore him, until he can be bottled like gas, or decomposed like air.

XIV. But let us suppose that the atheist or materialist is right in asserting that order, life, and intellect are but the *effects* of matter—the result of certain combinations which occur of *necessity*, and act in a certain rotation—*still* would I contend that such combinations (if they exist to produce the phenomena of organization, vitality, and thought) must necessarily constitute a SINGLE, infinite, eternal, intellectual, and powerful *existence* or BODY; and that, therefore, he who rejects a spiritual God is compelled to accept a material one.

1. Is it single and infinite? If the order of the universe be the effect of a material compound, that compound must either be co-extensive with nature, *or* spread its influence (by some medium or other) throughout the universe. The materialist cannot himself suppose more than one great *physical* motor of the universe, more than one universal compound controlling all others; for, if there existed many such combinations or motors capable of producing and moving worlds, then accident or necessity might develop new systems, in the midst of the present infinite harmony of nature, so as to destroy the existing order of things—new and disturbing effects might be indefinitely multiplied; and confusion, collision, and chaos would take place. The concordance of all things to one great plan or design displays the action of a single power, superior to all others, and preventing all others from interrupting, changing, or destroying its course. That its influence is not limited by space, but extends to the most distant of stars and embraces all nature, is evident when we consider that the physical power which (controls the fixed stars, shining millions and millions of distances beyond the reach of human vision or telescope) exists in an absolute and continued agreement, not only with the physical power of the planet we inhabit, but also

with the power acting upon all other systems and planets, so as to produce the most beautiful and complete harmony. To apportion these effects among various and distinct powers, is to suppose that which cannot be proved; is to admit that which is contrary to philosophical experience and to the plainest laws of reason and consistency. We might with as much plausibility suppose that the movements of the different parts and members of the human body are each under the influence and regulation of a different and distinct brain.

2. Is this combination of matter which the materialist assumes, *eternal?* It is; for it may be traced back by geology and astronomy to countless ages, and naught seems to threaten its continued duration. The geologists have hardly pierced the rind of the earth, and yet counting the formation, one above the other, of the few strata as yet discovered, they may count ages upon ages of past duration; but they remain conscious that they have plunged only the tips of their fingers into the fathomless depth of time; and that countless periods of the history of suns and stars must ever remain unnumbered, and beyond the scope of human conception. Nor can the materialist conceive *an end* to the compound of elements which he supposes to have done this work. He cannot suppose that the cause which has operated so uniformly and continually for millions of centuries, without derangement, and which has followed in all its changes a progressive chain of cause and effect, should have been the result

of *accident*—of *accident* which in its nature is transient, versatile, incongruous, and unconnected. The materialist supposes, on the contrary, that the order of the universe is the *necessary* effect of the elements of matter; and therefore, to suppose an end of this order, is to suppose a cessation of the *necessary* consequences of the essential properties of matter—or the annihilation of matter itself—neither of which hypotheses any atheist or materialist can possibly admit. The eternity, therefore, of the cause of order (be it matter, combination, action, or spirit) must remain undisputed, by men of all colors and shades of opinion.

3. That the cause of order, though it be a material compound, must be *intellectual* and *powerful*, may be demonstrated by the reason, already given, to show that a *spiritual* cause of order must be endowed with the properties of mind.

\* If I call the building of an engine an intellectual operation, performed through physical means, I must, from the very nature of things, call the formation of a planetary system an intellectual work. The works of man and the works of nature bear, both of them, unequivocal signs of derivation from a similar origin.

\* The presence of mind is known by the phenomena its action produces. We possess mind within ourselves, we see its operation around us, in the action and words of other men; and in the same way that we recognize its presence in men, do we recognize its presence in nature.

\* We know that mind possesses certain properties, which belong to no other process or thing. These properties are, principally, computation and design. It is by the appearance of these properties that we ascertain the presence of mind, just as we discover the presence of Heat, Electricity, or Gravitation, by the peculiar nature of its action.

\* Mind is the *only* cause, *within our experience*, which we know is capable of conceiving and producing continued links of intelligent and useful order and design; and therefore, when we perceive this conception and these effects to be universal, we must admit the existence of the mind of nature, just as we admit the existence of the mind of man.

\* Reason can commune with, and understand only, that which is reasonable; . . . that which acts by rules and motors similar to its own; and therefore, if an act or effect be produced by other laws, it appears to reason only as creative of disorder and destruction; if language is spoken otherwise than according to the laws of reason, it is unintelligible to the reason of all men, and appears to be confused and erroneous. The course of nature appears to reason to be consistent, orderly, and correct: it therefore acts according to, and is administered by, the laws of reason.

\* The madman seems governed by an incorrect knowledge of things—false impression, defective power of comparison, and a consequent inability to form a design of action consistent with nature and experience:

we say, therefore, that he is bereft of reason. If thus we conclude that the madman is divested of intellect, in the same way must we argue that nature *is not* deprived of reason.

* If the works of reason alone appear rational to reason, it follows that the works of nature are performed by a rational power; for, if it were not so, it is evident, from the nature of things, that these works would be unintelligible to the human mind: unless we suppose that that which is reasonable may continuously and forever be performed by a reasonless power.

* If the works of nature are not rational works, then they are irrational; but if they are irrational, we could not comprehend them; yet we *do* comprehend them, therefore they are not irrational—therefore they are rational—therefore they are derived from a reasoning power.

* Though the materialist considers thought, *in man*, not to be a distinct thing like heat, electricity, or gravitation; though he contends that the mind of man is but an effect of a compound of elements; still the *existence* of that mind, as an entity in each individual, must be admitted; and, therefore, by an analogous and consistent reason, must he admit (though as a result of a composition of matter) *the existence of the mind of nature*—which must last, as a unit, as long as its elements remain together and continue their healthy action.

* But we have shown, even according to the dogmas

of atheism or materialism, the order of nature to be *eternal* and infinite—that the materialist cannot suppose the harmony of the universe to be dissolved, unless he admits the annihilation of matter or its properties. We therefore say that the mind of nature, though it be an effect of matter, *is immortal*, and cannot disappear, like the limited mind of an individual, by a separation of atoms; for matter, according to the materialists, *doth fill all space*, and its action upon itself cannot cease, unless these chemical affinities, of which materialism doth boast so much, doth also cease to exist.

\* If the properties of matter were distinct from the substance itself, then the materialist or atheist could no more deny that REASON (which he considers the property of a certain compound of matter) would also be distinct from that compound of which it would be a property; so he contends not only that matter or the compound of matter fills all space, but that the properties of matter are not distinct, but identical with the material particles themselves. It follows that the action of the properties of matter must continue as long as matter exists, and that no separation can ever take place; for, if matter or its effect fills all space, where will one portion go to escape the influence of the other? And thus, though *infinite* reason be but a property or effect, it cannot die until the *infinity* of matter endeth also.

\* The materialist may seek if he chooses the component elements of this infinite reason which is co-equal with infinite *time, space,* and *matter,* and show how it is produced. We bid him speed in his work; but while he labors, the Theist remains satisfied with *the fact* that the mind of nature doth live. The *form* and *mode* of that life is a mystery, which the heated and distorted imagination of atheism may attempt to solve; but this very attempt is an admission of ITS EXISTENCE.

XV. 1. Not being able to deny the existence of this all-pervading and rational power, it remains for the consistent materialist to explain, how the power which controls all matter was produced by matter— how the effect can govern and control its cause—how, before reason existed, (for if reason be but an effect, it once did not exist, for its cause must have produced it,) how, before reason existed, I say, blind and reasonless matter could have produced so perfect and rational an existence as the governing power of the universe must be—how rational effects could precede a rational cause —how the force was created by the object it directs and moves—how a rational existence, bearing all the outward marks of design which a physical God must bear, could have been before reason itself existed; and how the most wonderful results of design may be produced by the blind constituents of matter, and how a power inferior to the intellect of man (mere minerals and gases) may act according to the most perfect dictates of reason?

2. The Theist has nothing to do with all these difficulties, or with the other objections, already mentioned, which meet the doctrines of materialism at every step. The Theist considers that things which are evidently effects, that is to say, passive to some force or action, must have a cause; he considers that there is a vital force in nature; that the vital force is "a peculiar force, because it exhibits manifestations which are formed in no other known force;"\* that the vivifying and organizing principle are identical; that they produce effects indicating design and a concordance with the infinite and unital design of the universe, and are consequently endowed with an intellectual principle; that matter and mind, the material and the organizing power, the substance and its vivifyer, have existed in all eternity—one active, the other passive, one neutralizing, the other moving. The past eternity of God proves the past eternity of his manifestation, however varied may have been the modes and forms of those manifestations; for God is cause, and cause implies effect, and hence at no time has God been other than manifest and acting. A *specific* display of his power and wisdom, such as this solar system, those stars, suns &c., may have had a beginning, but no starting point of time can in the abstract be assigned to the glorious and phenomenal deeds of the ETERNAL ARCHEUS. In this ORGANIZING POWER, which he studies and

\* See Liebig's Animal Chemistry—last paragraph of Chapter I. of Part III.

contemplates, with all the lights of science and reason, the Theist beholds all the attributes of Divinity; and he exhults with joy when he finds that he knows his GOD. In vain does the obdurate, the infatuated materialist, pushed to the last resort, endeavor to degrade the idea of this organizing power, by calling it the "Formative Instinct of nature." If it is instinct, then the intellect of man is lower than instinct. No! it is not instinct—it is infinite Wisdom. It is a perversion of words to call it instinct—it is the power and will of the ruler of all, lighting suns, driving worlds through space, building the minute fabrics of the invisible animalculæ, it is the intellect that understandeth (for it fills) immensity and eternity.

XVI. Now that we know our God, let us endeavor to perceive his purpose: the object of his design.

Behold the lessons of geology and astronomy.

The earth was once an ignited mass,—it cooled—strata upon strata of inorganic matter was deposited—water and air were then formed, and vegetation made its appearance—then gross aquatic and amphibious animals came forth; but as layer upon layer was added to the shell of the globe, organization, both animal and vegetable, became more complex and perfect, until man, the most admirable of all, was created. These strata of the earth, as they rise from the depth below, each new strata adding new and more perfect organization to those which precede, present almost the same progressive chain of beings, as the natural history of the present surface would give. The zoophite, the shell, the fish, the reptile, the bird, the mammalia, the man, each made their appearance, in turn, and when the earth was prepared to receive them, by a similar improvement of mineral and vegetable nature. The sandy and marshy plains rose through the gradual work of ages into green and irrigated hills and dales; the soft reed, scanty bush, yielded a place to the bread-tree and the oak; and a fit habitation was prepared for a superior order of beings. And has this progress been stopped forever? No, unless the great motor has also ceased to act.

Look at the planets that course around the sun. They increase in perfection as they rise from the source or primitive elements from which they come. The first and second planets have atmospheres suited only to aquatic and amphibious animals; they present the same features as the earth must have presented when naught but fish and reptiles inhabited its surface. The clouds which totally cover the first planet, and which form a ragged veil over the second, proclaim the one to be a watery globe, while the land of the other hardly emerges from the deep. Our earth as next in order, presents clearer skies, higher lands, more complicated phenomena, seasons more temperate, and a moon whose influence is immense. The fourth planet shows its fair face undimmed by watery vapors, and wrapped in a lighter and purer atmosphere. The fifth, sixth, and seventh show wants and conditions still more active and complete. Though stupendous in size, they whirl around their axes in ten hours' time; and though their nights are so short, luminous rings and moons shine upon them with a constant light, and produce the most admirable effects. Of the gradation of the planets we possess with certainty the first links; those beyond the earth have received improvements and modifications, of which we can form no idea; but the certainty we have, that there is a regular scale of improvement in the three first planets, gives us the glimpse of a law of nature which indictates improvement to continue to the utmost bounds of the planetary group. If the earth came from the sun, it must have been once a molten and blazing ball; if the earth were put in the place of the first planet, its waters would rise at once into a deluge; if put in the place of the second, the waters would partially subside, and humid lands, reed-covered plains and rocks, and amphibious animals, would appear beneath cloudy skies and superabundant rains. If advanced a link further, the habitation of man would be formed. What need we go further into the depths of time and space to know what has been, and divine what will be? Does not geology show that the very changes this advance of the earth, flight by flight from the sun, would produce, have actually taken place? First a comet, the seed of worlds, catches the generating flame of the sun, and forms by combustion a fiery globe; then, consolidated and cooled, it is covered by water;

then ascending, it becomes the fit dominion of the lower order of animals; then, behold it rises again, and man takes possession of the garden prepared (through ages) for his use.

Is not, thus, the eternal purpose of the spirit of nature made manifest to all? Blessed sciences of geology and astronomy, what a magnificent lesson do you teach! You divulge the advances of the works of the great artificer of heaven and earth. You show that his task and his pleasure is to act upon matter with a view to improvement and perfection. In this chain of progressive beings which dwell on earth, and advance with the planetary scale, we find new evidence of the existence of an organizing power which gradually overcomes the inert and rebellious properties of matter, moulds and modifies the material to serve the high purposes of intellectual life and pleasure; and at last, emboldened by the glorious promise all nature seems to make,—our soul, that vivifying spark of the divine essence, *hopes*—nay looks with confidence, for those successive periods and transitions of happiness and bliss, which mount to the regions of transcendent Wisdom and Joy.

We may now easily solve the question of

### LIBERTY AND NECESSITY.

The following proposition will of itself suggest a direct and conclusive solution of the supposed dilemma of liberty and necessity: Humanity is subject to that necessity God has ordained as the Code of physical and vital animal Nature; but Humanity is at liberty, by means of thought, to apply those laws in modes of infinite *variety*.

Let it be noted that *there is an* INTERVAL OF TIME *between temptation and choice; and that this interval is made by the action of thought*, in considering the various and contradictory motives, ideas, &c., which occur to or are evoked by the mind. During this interval man, it must be admitted, is undoubtedly free.

The use of the term "free-*will*" for this subject-matter, misdirects the mind; for the word "*will*" in itself implies a determination brought about by affection and thought; implies a *cause*, which is either feeling or judgment. The will is not the *arena* of free agency, for it is only the voice proclaiming the victor in the contest of ideas; the will is the expression of a conclusion delivered by sentiment or reason. It is the solution of a question, apart from the process by which it was revolved.

To put the question fairly, we should ask: Does man possess a free mind, a liberty to choose? That he has this faculty is apparent from *the fact* itself; he exercises it. Nor is he under a delusion, when he recognizes this fact; for while he is conscious of the interval of reflection between suggestion and determination, he also finds that one of the attributes of reason in itself is freedom.

Hence it is erroneous to consider judgment as similar to motive. A judgment is the will itself; and, as such, is an end, not a motive—the deliverance of thought, not its generation and parturition. It is the finality (not the activity) of the mind; the fulcrum or dead point at which thought and motives terminate, and the action of body begins.

But while the will may be the expression in one instance of pure feeling, or in another instance of pure reason, or more frequently of the two united, yet it is only as a rational being that man is free. If he does not stop to weigh and measure motives, compute experience, study the present state of things, and ideate the future, he is the mere instrument of impulse, instinct, habit, or prejudice, and has no right to consider himself as actually enjoying the only free element of his nature.

Reason is the only area of freedom. The rational mind in itself does not obey; it deliberates and commands. Reason cannot be a slave. If not free, it ceases to act at all; for if not free, it would not be reason, but something else, a kind of instinct. Hence Kant lucidly says: "The very existence of reason depends upon its freedom." So that, if we are ever able to demonstrate free agency, it will be out of the attributes of reason, considered as a human power, distinguishable from affection; and importing impartiality, investigation, choice, &c.

When those who argue against free agency say that

man acts from motive, and when they show that he is the puppet of passions, desires, education, and the like, they are in one view right. Man may be entirely subject to such influences, and in that condition may cease to be a free agent; but if he ever falls into such a state, he also ceases to be truly man; since, to be thus controlled by feeling only, he must have abdicated the essential attribute of humanity, and retained the characteristics of animality alone.

It is vain to say that, on the other hand, he would become the instrument of reason—that reason would control him just as motives, affections, &c., sometimes do. This objection could not stand for an instant, for reason, in itself, is freedom, and man is therefore a free agent to the full extent of his exercise of the reasoning power or spiritus.

Thus, by reason, he often divorces with characteristics imparted by birth, habit, or prejudice, and puts on a new personality of opinions, conduct, &c.

You may say, if you please, that man is the *slave* of his *judgments;* but a judgment is the terminus of deliberation, reflection, &c. While the judgment is forming, and until the mind's internal debate is ended, we are in a state of equilibration or freedom, and so we continue till our mind is "made up." Even then we may, at any time, reconsider the vote, and seek a new design. Hence, when reason sinks the scale on one side or the other, and will is evolved, the act that follows is the act of a slave to judgment, indeed; but the judgment itself is the fiat of a free agent, for it is the fiat of that reason which is man's spiritual self, and which, because it is reason, is essentially free.

Taking the magnet of thought as his guide, he may find his way all over the physical world; study it by measuring rule and graduated compass, and instruct himself.

Taking the scales of thought, he may weigh and calculate the equation of right and duty, justice and love, and control himself.

Sitting in judgment upon his own emotions, motives, and powers, upon the things, forces, and laws surrounding him, man is at every instant of existence left to select among innumerable possibilities of action, as well as among a multiplicity of realizable hopes. Far from submitting to the first direct motive, knowing that he may study the value and bearings of every motive, conscious that he may subject it to the jurisdiction of thought, and that the secret master within bears the light of Truth, he checks himself, examines, and decides. Often, in fact, by investigation and thought, he bethinks himself of new and better motives, rejects the one and adopts the other. Indeed, out of the materials of intellectual consciousness, he designs and fashions a state of mind of his own invention, so that man makes his own motives out of the materials over which his intellectual nature has given him authority or jurisdiction. Just in proportion as he observes and thinks, instead of blindly obeying the crude impetus of feeling, in that proportion does he rise above the brute, and widen the area of his own liberty.

## V.

### ACTION.

Having thus far satisfied ourselves of two great truths: 1°, that God exists, and that his essential attribute is what man recognizes as the eternal and infinite power and manifestation of Thought; 2°, that every man's soul is an image or iota of the divine Archeus of Thought, we come now to consider the application of these demonstrated propositions, in the sphere of Human Action.

#### I.

##### NATURE AND ART.

These terms, (nature and art,) in this connection, serve to mislead the mind. The word "nature" would seem to imply a fatal necessity; moving, uncontrolled by any volition; operating by virtue of inherent qualities, or working without the interference of mind. The nature of a thing we habitually consider to be its integral constitution, which *of itself* must display certain manifestations. This view would relieve us from considering the universe and its phenomena, as a product of Supreme Thought; and would, by accustoming us to the idea of a natural law, having its germ in matter itself, lead us into materialism.

The idea of nature, which begins with the properties of matter, is atheistical; for it assumes the natural law as primarily arising by and in the material substance itself, and ignores the necessity of a will to impart and of a thought to invent.

Short-sighted is he who remains satisfied with the sufficiency of a concept of nature, having for its prime ratio the properties of matter alone, to explain the evidences of elective design in the universe.

They who are disabled by this mental short-sightedness, from perceiving the marks of free thought in the cosmos, may most frequently lay their infirmity to that undefinable word: "nature." It implies every thing, while it means nothing. It includes not only the general view of all phenomena, but also implies in every thing the indefinite inherence of a something—its nature, equivalent to no clear idea whatever.

The time is past when *savans* could impudently explain nature by nature, and confound mind with matter.

It has now become plain, that to explain nature by nature, we must recognize supreme thought as an intimate property of matter itself, and thus concede the truth of Pantheism.

Hence, to avoid vagueness and confusion, we should endeavor to find expressions in which the definition is not confounded with the term—in which cause and effect are not posited as one.

Let " nature," if you please, mean the aspect of the universe; but let the mechanism and motion which the universe exhibits, be the operation of *Divine* ART.

Who confounds man with his works—who confounds the instrument with the mind which contrives it? Yet some would have it that nature is both universal matter and universal mind; or, still worse, that nature (the aspect) shows the indicea of thought, without there being an existence (ens realissimum) of thought, either as property or actor.

As meaning force or law, property or action, the term nature should be discarded, but we should confine it to the *bodily* aspect of the universe, while the force which moves it should be the "Divine WILL," and the *laws* which control it, the "Divine ART." Let the aspect alone be "nature."

This distinction is also appropriate to Human Nature, in which there is a visible and tangible *body*—a *will* to resolve, and *reflection* to design.

I am instinctively conscious that within me dwells an inherent FORCE.

Independently of all observation of external things, I feel the potency of an innate energy for volition and action.

This energy is my own.

In me and to me it declares the fact of causation; for *force* cannot be felt as a positive fact, without imparting the immediate and simultaneous certitude of causality.

This is the SUBSTANTIVE beginning of philosophy; for, in the certitude of force and causation, the lever of thought obtains a fixed point on which its fulcrum may positively rest.

The new-born infant *feels* the possession of a causative force. It stretches forth its hand to grasp; and, though it has not yet learned *how* to use its limbs and do, it feels the power to catch and to hold.

On this immutable centre the mythologist and idolater places the personifications he is wont to worship and propitiate as Gods.

On this positive basis the naturalist relies as the substratum of the laws of Matter.

On this indubitable reality the materialist builds his theories of necessary order.

And from this pivotal truth the theist lifts his mental vision, to behold the Grand Archeus of the Universe.

The origin of our idea of *cause* is twofold:

1°. The direct feeling or consensibility we have of internal instincts and emotions, as having power to determine the will, and, through the impulse of will, to evolve action;

2°. The self-knowledge of thought; for thought knows its own operations; knows them to be energetic processes and a succession of acts, of which the past have produced the present, and of which the present serve to determine the future.

In the first category, man feels himself as *passive ;* as the passive instrument of forces within himself.

In the second category, man feels himself as *active ;* as the master to do or not to do, according to his idea of what *ought to be ;* and as constantly achieving independence of that which *is*, through the creative and progressive changes wrought by his own inventive genius.

In both these categories the idea of energy, power, force, cause, is primary, and starts from the centre of self; and the idea of causative force thus delivered by self to self, must be taken as one of those *initial facts* at which reasoning begins, and behind which reasoning cannot go without suicide, simply because there is no higher, deeper, or wider fact from which it might be deduced, other than the idea of the Supreme One, who reigneth in all space and time.

Looking out of self we cannot fail to recognize that the causative force (as felt in us and evolved by ourselves) pervades all nature, and presents itself a direct external fact.

If we were (as the brutes are) only capable of the passive instinct or consensibility of a causative force, the aspect of nature would never awaken in us aught but feelings of immediate necessity; the full idea of causality (as understood in philosophy) could never have arisen.

But while we possess this consciousness of *passiveness* to force, and while our *animal* impressions and instincts could not go beyond the mere feeling, and would directly obey its impulses, we also carry within ourselves the archeus or principle of number and measure. This Archeus is not only self-active, not only imposes itself as a supreme power, but imparts notions of distinct units of force, of values, and purviews of force, ratios, and adequacies of force, with which it performs operations of mathematical computation.

Thus, while instinct posits the simple idea of an unintelligent force, thought posits, in and by its own properties, the idea of an intelligent force, and the two derive their title to be considered as forces, from the fact that they both answer to the definitions of force, which is dynamical energy, producing motion, and known to exist by its accomplishing changes. Both move and do, both are exerted externally and internally, and both accomplish acts and changes. The one is the property and movement of the elements of matter, producing organic and inorganic effects; and the other is the property and movement of thought upon itself, computing the data of consciousness and influencing the will.

Without this double element springing from the

*germ-cell* of his animal nature, on the one hand, and the *focal-light* of thought on the other, the senses of man, like a mirror, might have reflected for ages the changes of nature; but he would never have ideated the principle of causality, the laws of connection between successive phenomena, or the mutual and measured dependency of all things in time and space.

Hence, by virtue of our self-nature, we conceive the universe as subject, in its parts and totality, to Causative Force.

Hence, too, we ideate this force, 1°, as a *reality*, (real existence;) 2°, as enforcing and fulfilling *laws*.

Hence, moreover, (recurring to our previous study of the existence and attributes of God,) it is clear that we must regard the works of Deity and the works of man from a same point of view, to wit: as the products of mind:

1°, of the mind of God, the universal unit of thought;

2°, of the mind of man, the atomic particle of thought.

Hence, further, if we regard the works of nature as well as those of man, as due to a thinking cause, identical in esse, but differing from man to God as a spark would differ from a boundless light, we at once have an index to a true theory of the Arts; for then Human Art would look to Divine Art for methods and models.

When we consider Divine Art, we recognize certain

facts, which language adduces by the adjectives—True, Good, Beautiful.

In the *True*, we find the immutability of laws—the necessity of adequate causes—the consistency of all in all—the economy and identity of means—the harmony of things with ideas—we find that truth is the adaptation of Reality to Design.

In the *Good* we find a plan and a use, the plan being recognized as such only so far as it has a purpose, consistent with the enjoyment and perpetuation of universal harmony—we find that the good is the adaptation of Use to Design.

In the *Beautiful* we find multiplicity woven into unity, and hence wherever we meet with variety seriated, proportioned, combined under one idea, it is beauty, of which there are many grades more and more perfect in the ratio of the number of minor phenomena as necessarily enter into the grand unit, without effacing it. Beauty is the adaptation of Variety to Design.

Variety of substance and causes, converging to unity, adduces the True.

Variety of processes and effects, operating in unity, adduces the Good.

Variety of aspects and impressions radiating from unity, adduces the Beautiful.

But these three synthetical unities, as we have heretofore shown, are necessarily merged in a still higher unity, which is Design—the Divine Mind—the Divine Will—the Divine Art.

And hence, Human Art must be this same Design, in a limited sphere, seeking to reduce varieties of Cause, Movement, and Impression to *units;* such as Systems of Science, Schemes of Invention, and Groupings of Taste.

But here I check myself, deeming it unnecessary to bring forward proofs to show that the works of Human Art are determined by the same economical and æsthetical principles as appear in the Works of Divine Art. The illustrations of this fact present themselves on every side, and are so palpable and numerous that no intelligent reader needs a cicerone to point them out. In a future work I may, however, in an artistic mood, endeavor to institute the analogy of Human and Divine Art; but in a work like the present one, a mere mention of that analogy should suffice.

## II.

### SELF-SCIENCE AND ECONOMY.

Some conceive the precept, "Know thyself," as meaning that they should, by self-examination, discover their own vices and virtues, defects of knowledge and disposition, qualities of feeling and of mind, with a view to correction and improvement.

True, this is self-knowledge, but it is of an inferior

and imperfect kind. True, this kind of self-knowledge has its uses and benefits, but only in a limited and empirical way.

Real or integral self-knowledge is found only in the study of human nature—of the instincts, faculties, emotions, and reason of man; of his physical, social, and spiritual destiny. When we clearly understand these things, we may then posit terms of comparison, first principles, and standards of perfection, by which individuals and communities, ourselves and others, may be tested and judged.

Nor is this self-science exclusively applicable to moral and intellectual relations, but it also applies to *physical* conditions and relations. It seeks to discover man's wants and tastes; *what* they are; *why* they exist; and having determined these points, the question immediately arises: *how* ought these wants and tastes to be gratified and managed? Hence the laws of health, wealth, pleasure, labor, production, exchange, commerce, distribution, consumption, demand, &c.

Thus arise the Arts of personal, domestic, social, and political Economy.

The limits assigned to this volume forbid the insertion of extensive observations, to show how a knowledge of Humanics would have enabled the economists Smith, Say, Ricardo, Malthus, Mill, Carey, &c., to have solved the intricate problems they studied.

It is, however, evident that as the economical arts seek to provide for man, they must provide for him according to his nature, his rational and passional constitution. His character and destiny should be a law unto their art. It should posit man as he *is*, as he ought to be, and as he is becoming singly and socially. Such is the condition to which their solutions should conform; for if they do not, the body politic will reject their doctrines, just as the stomach rejects repugnant aliments and drinks.

## III.

### SOCIETY AND GOVERNMENT.

Here again is a subject too extended for this volume; but here again let it be noted, that those who treat of the art of government, should look carefully to the Science of Society, *as based upon* HUMANICS.

Too often is government conceived as the art of coercing individuals and minorities; or as the means of enabling majorities to realize their caprices and arbitrary decisions.

It should, on the contrary, be looked upon as the refuge of individual liberty, and as the guaranty of minority rights; as a check upon the tyranny of majorities and of princes.

Hence the importance of framing bills of rights and liberties, in terms of great scientific precision, and of providing barriers against any violation of first principles.

## IV.

#### THE SOUL AND ETHICS.

It is the Science of the Soul which discloses the true principles of moral action.

It appears clearly to my mind, that none of the animal feelings are either moral or immoral, and that all our ethical ideas flow from our *thinking spirit*, which I hold to be identical with the soul.

Which one of our instincts, propensities, or sentiments, are in themselves virtues? If the reader mentions one, let him inquire if it does not involve, in some degree, the elements of thought, or some act of reason.

Are not all our feelings and emotions liable to run into excesses, vice, and crime? If there is one I have not been able to discover it; and if the reader can name one, let him see if it is not merely *one* of the terms in a scale, which, as reason increases or diminishes in force, rises or falls, from some point of indifference, to merit on the one side, or guilt on the other.

Are not our feelings and sentiments multiple, and of various tendencies? Self-love is necessary; so is social love; and between absolute misanthropy and maniacal philanthropy, there are *passional* stages and conditions, which may be the prompters of good or evil deeds; one or the other, according to folly or wisdom, use or abuse; for there is no inherent force in these numerous and diverse impulses, to make them, singly or collectively, assume the form of virtue rather than that of vice, without the tuition of reason.

In every circumstance, reason or principles, discovered by reason, must give us the right position and direction among our conflicting motives. Reason is evidently the only regulator and arbiter, and therefore reason is the true originator of Virtue. Without reason there can be no rule of conduct, no limit to any excess or furor of desire or affection, and therefore Virtue is rationalized passion.

### GOD AND RELIGION.

Before man began to study himself, when he was yet a savage or an infant, and exclusively attentive to the outward world, his mind was unconsciously directed, in its operations, by the causative force he felt as motive and volition.

This feeling was the sum of his own existence; so that when affected by natural things—fire, thunder, water, winds, earth, plants, sun, moon, stars, planets, &c.—he at once imagined them to be *voluntary* causes or powers.

He had not thought of any distinction between organic and rational action, and hence could not see wherein any active operation of things was distinguishable from the intentional acts of men.

Thus, he at once presumed all things in nature to be individual existences, having like himself the *will* to do what they did; and finding that they were stronger than he was, he yielded to their superior force. By prayers and offerings, he solicited their forbearance and favor.

Had man, from the beginning, perceived that there was a hierarchy of natural forces—original, mediate, and immediate causes—a difference between material and voluntary movement—that above the particular phenomena were others more and more abstract, and of greater and greater scope, and that we may ascend to a supreme head of universal unity—he could not have made divinities of the material bodies which affected his senses.

Had he bethought himself

— of many forces,

— of each one of these many beings absolutely distinct and special,

— of each force as possessing properties or laws of its own,

— of the imponderability of these forces,

— of their permeating one another,

— of their pervading all material things,

— of one controlling the other, term beyond term, till the final unit of eternal and infinite thought became evident;

— had man, I say, at the outset bethought himself of these possibilities, he could not have fallen into idolatry, or even into mythophilism.

But in his ignorance (though obedient to a true

principle) he could not help viewing each concrete agent of force as a *personality*, endowed with an individual volition.

The more we study all the known religions, whether we examine them through the medium of history, or observe them by means of travel, the more certain will we be that the necessary conception of causative force, or of adequate power, as producing change, is the foundation of all natural theology, and of faith in revelation.

Even Atheism sets up the necessity of causative force as the pedestal of its argument; and the only difference between materialism and theism, atheism and Christianity, is that the one denies and the other asserts, an *intelligent* cause. Both agree in the necessity of causative force. The materialist thinks the inherent properties of matter are sufficient to explain all things, even adaptation, design, and thought; but the theist is no more satisfied to stop at this physical theory, than Socrates was to content himself with the embodied gods of Greece; and so the theist goes on, obedient to the laws of mind, to seek for, till he finds, a living, intelligent, and universal cause.

Comte in his positive philosophy strives to discredit the use of the idea of cause, and would fain abolish even the words "cause" and "force." He denounces them as unphilosophical. He was conscious that his materialism could not withstand the admitted validity of their import. But he could not rid his own mind of the ideas expressed by those words. So he found it constantly and absolutely necessary to bring their *meaning* into his service. He abolished the name but smelt the rose. Hence, to gratify his whim of dislike, and yet give sense to his language, he hypocritically uses the synonyms and equivalents of the discarded words, and instead of "force," says "property," and the like; instead of "cause," says "influence," and the like. Yet such is the irresistible *influence* of the *properties* of the mind, that in several instances he unwittingly employs the very terms he condemns, so that, here and there, in his ponderous book, we find "cause" and "force," in their legitimate place, under his pen. Indeed, no man can frame and write a connected theory of natural, mental, and social philosophy, without these words, or others, expressing identical ideas.

The idea of causative force cannot be discarded, nor its positiveness denied; and the error of superstition was not in deducing religion from the fact of causation, but it was in the PERSONIFICATION of apparent causes.

Causative Force, embodied or personified, was the first deity naturally conceived by the mind of man; but the idea of the *one* supreme power was not the first to arise, and hence the beginning of natural theology was polytheism.

As the idea of causative force presents itself directly to thought in four ways, so the gods of polytheism may be distinguished into four kinds:

1°. Gods who were the *powerful Aspects of Visible and tangible Matter*, directly adored as they appeared individually, or as they were personified in imagination. Thus we have the Heavens or Jupiter, the Air or Juno, the Earth or Pan, the Fire or Vulcan, the Waters or Neptune, the Sun or Osiris, Mithra, Apollo, &c., the Moon or Isis, Diana, &c., the Morning or Aurora.

2°. Gods who were the representation or personification of the abstract and intangible *forces of Matter*. Thus we have Time or Saturn, Horus, &c., Heat or Vesta, Vegetation or Ceres, Health or Hebe, Beauty or Venus, Strength or Hercules, Death or Pluto, Serapis, &c.

3°. Gods who were the personification of the *Emotional Forces* felt in the human organism. Thus we have Courage or Mars, Love or Cupid, Revenge or Nemesis, Joy or Euphrosine, Remorse or the Fairies, Mirth or Momus; &c., &c.

4°. Gods who were the personification of the *Causative Force of* Thought. Thus we have Wisdom or Minerva, Commerce or Mercury, Justice or Themis, Medicine or Esculapius, Science or the Muses, Thought or Prometheus, the Soul or Psyche, &c.

It is not my design to offer any thorough analysis of Heathen Mythology, but merely to call attention to what I consider as the true origin of the Olympian deities. An examination of the Egyptian, Persian, Indian, and Scandinavian theogonies, would furnish abundant illustrations of the theory just stated. The abstract forces and ideas adored as deities might not appear so well conceived and personified as in the Grecian system; but they are just as palpable, though crude.

Nor need we be embarrassed by the figures of animals, or *the* chimerical shapes attributed to many deities. It is plain that when ignorance and superstition assume the Aspects and Forces of Nature, the Emotional and Thinking energies of Humanity, as personal existences or individuals, exercising their power on nature and in man, it was imagination, coincidence, accident, analogy, &c., which gave *forms* to these gods. Thus the breeding, invasion, and services of certain beasts, the characteristic qualities or appearance of certain animals, were associated by analogy with the myths, and served to represent them. In the same way even at the present day the devil is personified as a man with horns, a tail, cloven feet, fiery eyeballs, smoking nostrils, &c.

As to the histories or legends of the gods, they are evidently allegories arising very naturally out of the idea of the gods themselves, as connected with the cosmogonical notions of their votaries, the changes of seasons, periodical or extraordinary catastrophes, and the movements of the heavenly bodies with which the myths became inevitably associated, from the very nature of the case, as the gods were in fact the powers of nature, acting in nature as the object of their dominion.

Now, if we follow superstition through its successive stages, we perceive that while it constantly and indiscriminately transforms causative agents and forces into personal gods, at the same time thought gradually and progressively introduces more rational myths, a more elevated theogony.

Always obedient to the innate consciousness of causative force as the starting point, and always seeking a more perfect conception of this force, man advances from the idolatry of concrete personifications to the mythology of impersonal deities, in the following series: the Ormuzed and Ahriman of Zoroaster, the Great Totality of the Pantheists, the Soul of the World of the Grecian philosophers, the Supreme Generator of the Kabbalists, the Grand Architect of the Gnostics.

But it was only out of the Jewish faith, and finally from Jesus, that man obtained a really pure conception of the Deity. No identity with matter, no figure, no plurality, but the causative force of Thought evolving the Spirit of Wisdom, Truth, and Love, eternal and infinite.

And thus all doubt and inconsistency disappears; for we are relieved from considering God as an object posited in time and place, and we are permitted to regard him, not as distinct from, but as identical with, that universal causative force which is manifested as omnipotent *mind;* or self-subsistent reason and supreme design, of which our intellect is but a faint reflection.

I have already, through reason alone, demonstrated the positive existence of Deity as proclaimed in the Jesuic Dogma; and now I close this book by a question to the churches.

Do you fully perform your duty to God and his children? Is the world improving morally and rationally under your administration? Is not vice and sin gaining ground against you?

Few of you could truthfully give me an affirmative answer.

Then something remains to be done which you do not do, or cannot do under your present discipline.

Allow me to suggest a programme.

Introduce your congregations to the study of the Apostolic Record according to the following principles:

That whereas the *doctrines* of Jesus are addressed to man's convictions, and intended for man's observance, they are not repugnant to human REASON, and do not transcend the limits of human understanding.

That the *doctrines* of Jesus are founded upon grand

logical premises, which can be shown to be valid and true, through processes of natural and scientific reasoning.

That reason and faith do not necessarily controvert each other, and whenever they apparently do so, there is error, either in our faith or in our judgment; and the error can only be removed by discovering *the point at which* our pure, just, and enlightened reason on the one side and our religious faith on the other, may be logically reconciled, and exist in harmony and candor.

That reason must and will finally triumph over any sectarian creed which is not conformable to the laws of mind, and to the imperative fact that *every truth is consistent with all truth.*

That the Apostolic Record must be read according to the *main rational idea* of the whole book, and so that the interpretation of the texts sectarians contend about, should subserve the logical consequences of this main *rational* idea; and thus obey the warning: "the letter killeth but the spirit giveth life."

But it is not enough to point out the necessity of studying the Apostolic Record according to these principles. A *method* should be devised; and that method should be calculated to take effect among the masses, and afford its benefits to the whole people. It should admit the principle that the popular mind is anxious for such grounds of belief as will stand the scrutiny of reason, and that the church does not fear the light of science, but on the contrary submits to the precept: "*prove* all things; hold fast that which is good."

My plan would be:

1. Have preachers, of course; but let them be men of large minds, lovers of truth, fearing not argument, discussion, evidence; courteous to hear and answer; understanding philosophy; and able to expound (in popular terms and figures) the Jesuic System in its analogy and relation to the Science of Man and the process of thought: men able to start from germ-points, focal-lights, first principles, initial facts, primary ideas, standard criterions; men who know how to demonstrate supreme laws, innate properties, necessary limits, adequate force, essential design, and generative liberty.

2. But (besides the preacher, besides prayer meetings and the like) the congregation must assemble in class conferences for mutual instruction in all the subjects above mentioned; and this mutual instruction should consist in the interchange of ideas by means of addresses, lectures, poems, apologues, historical selections, scientific illustrations, logical demonstrations, originating from the members of the class, and discussed among themselves, apart from all personal or partisan interest, in a spirit of anti-dogmatic tolerance; and bringing up questions concerning the *laws* of artistic, economic, political, moral, and religious action.

3. And congenial to this, there should be a religious

press and propaganda, independent of sectarian ambition, harmonizing with human progress and sympathizing with the intellect and science of the age. The several churches should, if possible, have their respective periodicals to report or publish the sermons of the minister, the intellectual transactions of the class conference, and the select productions of the members, so that all of them might have copies to preserve and distribute.

How this would operate to awaken thought, advance true views of religion, and inspire zeal for the dissemination of enlightened opinions, I need not explain, for it is self-evident.

I say nothing of the charities of brotherhood, of active benevolence, for they necessarily appertain to a church organization. I suggest only the points essential to my idea of reform.

That a higher standard of religious education is wanting in the United States and in England, to keep pace with the state of knowledge and civilization, and to satisfy the cravings of a liberal and truthful public mind, is plainly to be seen, even in the success of empirical speculators, on the general desire to greet the new lights dawning on the religious world; and I predict that if the church does not move in that direction, she will be left behind, among those who have not yet advanced beyond the prejudices, superstition, and fanaticism of the SIXTEENTH century.

The highest *act* of religion is the study of the laws, process, and conduct of thought—the culture of mind and the development of reason ; for it is thought, reason, design, that links us to God. The wider and higher our thought extends and rises, the nearer we approach the throne of Deity. By thought I do not mean vivid imagination merely, soaring fancy and the like ; but also sure-footed wisdom whose ascent is not only *positive*, but surmounts the loftiest ideality.

Thought is the true Jacob's ladder. By it alone, by the steps it affords, we may hope to reach heaven.

Nor let any one in malice suggest that I forget the moral law ; for I have shown and will ever contend, that Faith, Hope, and Charity, (in that which makes them *more and other* than Instinct, Desire, and Sympathy,) are due to thought ; exist only through man's rational powers. Take reason away, and a brute incapable of virtue or merit remains ; while, on the other hand, it is certain that, as the light of knowledge and the power of reason prevail in society, so do peace, order, and love have sway. This is so because thought, mind, or reason alone can disclose, and hence bring us to—1°, consciously experience ; 2°, understand ; and 3°, cherish the good, truth, and beauty of social love and harmony. Without reason man is simply *gregarious*, a hating and envious, or to say the least, a careless denizen of society ; but when reason illumines the gregarious feeling, this feeling becomes, in the rational light within us, the reign of God over his children, the fraternity of immortal souls, the triumph of perfect liberty, and the empire of universal equality.

I am satisfied that religion may *safely* relieve herself of bigoted and dogmatic influences, to make emancipated and fearless reason her bosom Companion.

# RETROSPECT.

I have had my say, and have tried to present a synoptical view of the complex and intricate constitution of man. With one retrospective glance, I now bid the reader adieu.

## I.

1. Man is truly a microcosm of the Universe. He comprises the material and the ethereal; for while he asserts a spiritual essence, his body is composed of earthy materials, which are borrowed from inorganic nature, to constitute a Vital organism.

2. Man's Vitality presents the same phenomena, and fulfils the same functions, as the Vitality of Vegetation.

3. The correspondence of the functional organism of man with that of PLANTS, embraces a multitude of particulars too generally overlooked, or thoughtlessly regarded as animal.

## II.

ANIMALITY in man embraces several phases; viz.:

1. *Instinct*, which corresponds with the functional action of plants, and the mechanical movement of sympathetic nerves.

2. *Sensation*, which is the *passive* sensibility of the nerves of external sense.

3. *Emotion*, which is the direct action of *sympathetic* nerves upon internal feeling, or the reaction of the sensuous upon the motor nerves.

4. *Impressibility*, or the "concrete IMAGE," or undivided picture of entire impressions received by the cerebrum, and furnishing the knowledge of *qualities* and *facts*: the objective materials of thought apart from all quantitative ideas.

5. *Memory*, which recalls past impressions and emotions.

6. *Locomotion*, enabling animals to *obey* (in a great variety of ways) the direct *impulses* of INSTINCT, and the proximate *attractions* and *repulsions* of FEELING.

## III.

1. In the possibility of this variety of action through the passive subjection of the organism to many purely sensational and animal influences and guides, we find a sufficient explanation of the acts of brutes beyond the apparent limits of instinct; and we are enabled to

understand how the animal which receives proximate impressions and feels primitive emotions, acts *automatically*, and is always either drawn or driven by mere feeling aided by mere perception.

2. But in man, all the primary feelings and emotions are interfered with by thought or reason, which by intermixture with the animal desires and affections, converts them into the higher sentiments:—the love of Truth, Beauty, Morality, and Utility, while it imparts the boon of Liberty.

3. Up to the limit of passive faculties man is the puppet of necessity—the mere tool of sensuality and *egotism ;* but beyond the passive or animal elements of his organism, man is the ruler of his members and the fit agent of social feeling and social order.

## IV.

1. Man thus rises to Society and Freedom, because, within the world of mind, and distinct from matter, there is an ACTIVE and initial principle which acts upon the materials and contents, qualities and facts furnished by the instincts, senses, and emotions.

It is this *active* principle which Locke (after trying to prove that there were no innate ideas) finally recognizes (B. 2, C. 12, §§ 1 and 2) as a "power of the mind to make new complex ideas "—"infinitely beyond what sensation or reflection furnished it with." This is the *active* principle which Hume (while trying to reduce all mental phenomena to sensuous impressions, present or remembered) is obliged to do homage to, as "the liberty of the imagination to transpose and change its ideas." "Nothing," says he in his Inquiry, Sec. V., Part 2, "is more free than the imagination of man; and though it cannot exceed the original stock of ideas furnished by the *in*ternal and *ex*ternal senses, it has unlimited power of mixing, compounding, separating, and dividing these ideas, in all the varieties of fiction and vision." "Its effects," says he in his Treatise, Sec. IV. and VII., "are everywhere conspicuous; but as to its causes they are mostly unknown, and must be resolved into *original* qualities of human nature which I *pretend not* to explain." "It is a *magical* faculty of the soul,"—"inexplicable by the utmost efforts of the human understanding." It is this magical and active principle, which Condillac calls to his aid to animate his statue, and designates as "the mind's transformation of itself and of its own ideas;" but Condillac never stops to show the possibility of this transforming process, without an adequate and specific quality or force, to produce the effect. It is this active principle which many other philosophers have noticed; but since Locke, Hume, and Condillac are the beginning, middle, and end of modern sensationalism, I have preferred to cite them as my witnesses against their own one-legged philosophy.

2. Hence I have separated the active principle from the passive, proclaimed the non-identity of thought

and sensation, of subject and object, and have held them to be distinct things having a common focus, in consciousness.

(Without this duality and this common focus, human nature is wholly inexplicable; since nothing can feel itself, or move itself, or lift itself, or see itself, or know itself by means of itself alone; for we are all aware, that the nerves and brain do not feel themselves but feel all other things—that the body "will not go" if motive force is not supplied in food—that inertia is only overcome by the action of some distinct and other force—that the eye cannot see itself, the mirror cannot reflect itself; and finally, that consciousness does not know itself, but what it does know are the impressions of the objective world on the one side, and the dictates and movement of the thinking archeus on the other.)

3. The *procedure* of this thinking archeus I have identified with the *ideation of the* UNIT, and the *consequent* LAWS OF NUMBER; for if the process of thought cannot begin without a quantitative term of comparison, or, in other words, without the unit; and if a term of comparison, whatever it may be, must be dealt with as a unit, then number and its laws are indeed the beginning and elements of the thinking process.

## V.

1. With what success I have traced thought back to the first principle and law of number, I leave the

reader to judge; and I call upon philosophers to find, if possible, a better demonstration of the nature of the *active* principle of the human mind. This much, however, is certain, that the force of this active principle (coming from the sphere of eternal order and dwelling in man) constitutes the essential distinction between men and brutes; and sets the distinctive mark on man, as man.

2. With this active archeus or causative force of mind, Science becomes possible; and man understands Nature, Self, Society, Spirit, and God; and is capable of free artistic, economical, political, ethical, and religious action.

Freedom and inventiveness are essential marks of thought.

3. And one thing more is certain, that no bodily root or organ can be assigned to this active principle which we must recognize as the only image of God within us; for it is (as he is) spiritual and rational, and it may be denominated the finite type of the infinite and eternal archetype of wisdom and power which controls the Universe.

THE END.

## NEW PUBLICATIONS AND NEW EDITIONS

PUBLISHED BY

# D. APPLETON AND COMPANY,

### 346 and 348 Broadway.

---

The Foster Brothers : Being the HISTORY of the SCHOOL and COLLEGE LIFE of TWO YOUNG MEN. 1 vol. 12mo. $1.

"*As fresh as the morning........It abounds in fun, and in relish of the activities, competitions, and sports of boyish and adolescent life.*"—DAILY NEWS.

"*Full of life, and fun, and vigor...... These sketches of school and college life are among the happiest of their kind. Particularly well written is the account of life at Cambridge.*"—EXAMINER.

Passages from the Autobiography of SIDNEY, LADY MORGAN. 1 vol. 12mo. $1.

"*This volume brims with sense, cleverness, and humor. A lively and entertaining collection of great men's thought and quick woman's observation ; a book to be read now for amusement, and to be sought hereafter for reference.*"—LONDON ATHENÆUM.

"*A charming book. It is long since the reading public has been admitted to so great a treat as this fascinating collection of wit, anecdote and gossip. It is a delightful reminiscense of a brilliant past, told by one of the best wits still extant.*"—LONDON DAILY NEWS.

Onward ; or, The Mountain Clamberers. A Tale of Progress. By JANE ANNE WINSCOM. 1 vol. 12mo. 75 cents.

CONTENTS.—LOOKING UPWARDS; COLIN AND JEANIE; THE FAMILY AT ALLEYNE; OFF! OFF! AND AWAY; ENDEAVORING; EDWARD ARNOLD; POOR, YET NOBLE; LITTLE HARRY; POOR JAMIE CLARK; FIELDS WHITE UNTO THE HARVEST; THE SAND HUTS; THE DRUNKARD'S COTTAGE; THE INFANT'S MINISTRY; STAND STILL; OLD MOSES AND LITTLE ADAH; THE ROCKY GLEN; SALOME; WIDOW M'LEOD; STAFFA AND IONA; CLOUDS AND SUNSHINE; FAITH'S CONFLICT; FAITH'S VICTORY; REUNION; SUMMER DAYS; THE FADING FLOWER; THE UNEXPECTED ARRIVAL, A WEDDING DAY; THE MOUNTAIN-TOPS APPEARING; HASTENING ON; THE SIRE'S BIRTHDAY; THE SUMMIT GAINED.

**Shakers:** Compendium of the Origin, History, Principles, Rules and Regulations, Government and Doctrines of the United Society of Believers in Christ's Second Appearing, with Biographies of Ann Lee, William Lee, Jas. Whittaker, J. Hocknett, J. Mescham, and Lucy Wright. By F. W. EVANS. 1 vol. 12mo. 75 cents.

**Cyclopædia of Wit and Humor,** Comprising a Unique Collection of Complete Articles, and specimens of Written Humor from Celebrated Humorists of America, England, Ireland and Scotland. Illustrated with upwards of 600 Characteristic Original Designs, and 24 Portraits, from Steel Plates. Edited by WILLIAM E. BURTON, the Celebrated Comedian. Two vols., 8vo., cloth, $7. sheep, $8; half mor., $9; half calf, $10.

" *As this task is a labor of love to Mr. Burton, we are sure of its being well performed.*"—NEW YORK TIMES.
" *The editor has raked many old pieces out of the dust, while he has drawn freely from the great masters of humor in modern times.*"—N. Y. TRIBUNE.
" *We do not see how any lover of humorous literature can help buying it.*" PHILA. PENNSYLVANIAN.
" *Mr. Burton is the very man to prepare this Cyclopædia of Fun.*"—LOUIS. JOURNAL.
" *We do not know how any family fond of the ludicrous can afford to dispense with this feast of fun and humor.*"—NEW BEDFORD MERCURY.

**From New York to Delhi.** By the way of RIO DE JANEIRO, AUSTRALIA AND CHINA. By ROBERT B. MINTURN, JR. 1 vol. 12mo. With a Map. $1 25.

" *Mr. Minturn's volume is very different from an ordinary sketch of travel over a well-beaten road. He writes with singular condensation. His power of observation is of that intuitive strength which catches at a glance the salient and distinctive points of every thing he sees. He has shown rare cleverness, too, in mingling throughout the work, agreeably and unobtrusively, so much of the history of India, and yet without ever suffering it to clog the narrative.*"—CHURCHMAN.
" *This book shows how much can be accomplished by a wide-awake, thoughtful man in a six months' tour. The literary execution of Mr. Minturn's book is of a high order, and, altogether, we consider it a timely and important contribution to our stock of meritorious works.*"—BOSTON JOURNAL.

**Le Cabinet des Fées; or, Recreative Readings.** Arranged for the Express Use of Students in French. By GEORGE S. GERARD, A. M., Prof. of French and Literature. 1 vol. 12mo. $1

" *After an experience of many years in teaching, we are convinced that such works as the Adventures of Telemachus and the History of Charles XII., despite their incontestable beauty of style and richness of material, are too difficult for beginners, even of mature age. Such works, too, consisting of a continuous narrative, present to most students the discouraging prospect of a formidable undertaking, which they fear will never be completed.*"—EXTRACT FROM PREFACE.

**The History of Civilization in England.** By Henry Thos. Buckle. Vol. I. 8vo. Cloth. $2.50

*Whoever misses reading this book, will miss reading what is, in various respects, to the best of our judgment and experience, the most remarkable book of the day—one, indeed, that no thoughtful, inquiring mind would miss reading for a good deal. Let the reader be as adverse as he may to the writer's philosophy, let him be as devoted to the obstructive as Mr. Buckle is to the progress party, let him be as orthodox in church creed as the other is heterodox, as dogmatic as his author is sceptical,—let him, in short, find his prejudices shocked at every turn of the argument, and all his prepossessions whistled down the wind,—still, there is so much in this extraordinary volume to stimulate reflection, and excite to inquiry, and provoke to earnest investigation, perhaps (to this or that reader) on a track hitherto untrodden, and across the virgin soil of untilled fields, fresh woods and pastures new,—that we may fairly defy the most hostile spirit, the most mistrustful and least sympathetic, to read it through without being glad of having done so, or, having begun it, or even glanced at almost any one of its 854 pages, to pass it away unread.*—New Monthly (London) Magazine.

**Legends and Lyrics.** By Anne Adelaide Proctor, (Daughter of the Poet, Barry Cornwall.) One very neat volume, 12mo. Second edition. 75 cents.

*This is the charming volume of fresh and tender poems, by the daughter of one of England's most honored and popular poets, which has lately been received with so hearty a welcome in England and America. Choice portions of it, copied by the press with lively praises, have found their way to the firesides.*

**The Household Book of Poetry.** Collected and Edited by Charles A. Dana. 1 vol. 8vo. 793 pages. Third edition. In half morocco. Gilt top. $3.50

*As the New-York correspondent of The Boston Transcript enthusiastically writes, 'The elegiac composition, the exquisite sonnet, the genuine pastoral, the war-song and rural hymn, whose cadences are as remembered music, and the couplets whose chime rings out from the depths of the heart; whatever the old English dramatists, the ode writers of the reign of Anne and Charles, the purest disciples of heroic verse, the Lakists, the Byronic school—Wordsworth and Dryden, Mrs. Hemans and Scott, Shakspeare and Hartley Coleridge have made precious to soul and sense, are herein brought together; and more than this—the many isolated single notes, whose lingering harmony embalms their author's name, with the numerous fugitive "brilliants," heretofore of unknown parentage, cut from newspapers for the last half century—the deep, soulfull utterances of heroes and mourners, lovers and exiles, devotees of nature and worshippers of art—are here elegantly garnered and chronicled.'*

*"It is just such a volume as a man may give to a woman, albeit that woman is his mother, his sister, or his wife, and is richly worth the place it claims on a lower shelf within arm's length, in the most select library."*—Chicago Journal.

## The Coopers; or, Getting Under Way.

By ALICE B. HAVEN, Author of "No Such Word as Fail," "All's Not Gold that Glitters," etc., etc. 1 vol. 12mo. 336 pages. 75 cents.

"*To grace and freshness of style, Mrs. Haven adds a genial, cheerful philosophy of Life, and Naturalness of Character and Incident, in the History of the Cooper Family.*"

## A Text Book of Vegetable and Animal Physiology

Designed for the use of Schools, Seminaries and Colleges in the United States. By HENRY GOADBY, M. D., Professor of Vegetable and Animal Physiology and Entomology, in the State Agricultural College of Michigan, &c. A new edition. One handsome vol., 8vo., embellished with upwards of 450 wood engravings (many of them colored,) Price, $2

"*The attempt to teach only Human Physiology, like a similar proceeding in regard to Anatomy, can only end in failure; whereas, if the origin (so to speak) of the organic structures in the animal kingdom, be sought for and steadily pursued through all the classes, showing their gradual complication, and the necessity for the addition of accessory organs, till they reach their utmost development and culminate in man, the study may be rendered an agreeable and interesting one, and be fruitful in profitable results.*

"*Throughout the accompanying pages, this principle has been kept steadily in view, and it has been deemed of more importance to impart solid and thorough instruction on the subjects discussed, rather than embrace the whole field of physiology, and, for want of space, fail to do justice to any part of it.*"—EXTRACT FROM PREFACE.

## The Physiology of Common Life.

By GEORGE HENRY LEWES, Author of "Seaside Studies," "Life of Goethe," etc. Vol. 1. Just Ready. Price $1.

### EXTRACT FROM PROSPECTUS.

*No scientific subject can be so important to Man as that of his own Life. No knowledge can be so incessantly appealed to by the incidents of every day, as the knowledge of the processes by which he lives and acts. At every moment he is in danger of disobeying laws which, when disobeyed, may bring years of suffering, decline of powers, premature decay. Sanitary reformers preach in vain, because they preach to a public which does not understand the laws of life—laws as rigorous as those of Gravitation or Motion. Even the sad experience of others yields us no lessons, unless we understand the principles involved. If one Man is seen to suffer from vitiated air, another is seen to endure it without apparent harm; a third concludes that "it is all chance," and trusts to that chance. Had he understood the principle involved, he would not have been left to chance—his first lesson in swimming would not have been a shipwreck.*

*The work will be illustrated with from 20 to 25 woodcuts, to assist the exposition. It will be published in two volumes, uniform with Johnston's 'Chemistry of Common Life.'*

**The Banks of New York; Their Dealers; The Clearing-House;** and the Panic of 1857. With a Financial Chart. By J. S. Gibbons. With Thirty Illustrations, by Herrick. 1 vol 12mo. 400 pages. Cloth, $1.50.

*A book for every Man of Business, for the Bank Officer and Clerk; for the Bank Stockholder and Depositor; and especially for the Merchant and his Cash Manager; also for the Lawyer, who will here find the exact Responsibilities that exist between the different officers of Banks and the Clerks, and between them and the Dealers.*

*The operations of the Clearing-House are described in detail, and illustrated by a financial Chart, which exhibits, in an interesting manner, the Fluctuations of the Bank Loans.*

*The immediate and exact cause of the Panic of 1857 is clearly demonstrated by the records of the Clearing-House, and a scale is presented by which the deviation of the volume of Bank Loans from an average standard of safety can be ascertained at a single glance.*

**History of the State of Rhode Island and Providence** Plantations. By SAMUEL GREENE ARNOLD Vol. I. 1636–1700. 1 vol. 8vo. 574 pages. $2.50.

*To trace the rise and progress of a State, the offspring of ideas that were novel and startling, even amid the philosophical speculations of the Seventeenth Century; whose birth was a protest against, whose infancy was a struggle with, and whose maturity was a triumph over, the retrograde tendency of established Puritanism; a State that was the second-born of persecution, whose founders had been doubly tried in the purifying fire; a State which, more than any other, has exerted, by the weight of its example, an influence to shape the political ideas of the present day, whose moral power has been in the inverse ratio with its material importance; of which an eminent Historian of the United States has said that, had its territory "corresponded to the importance and singularity of the principles of its early existence, the world would have been filled with wonder at the phenomena of its history," is a task not to be lightly attempted or hastily performed."* —EXTRACT FROM PREFACE.

**The Ministry of Life.** By MARIA LOUISA CHARLESWORTH, Author of "Ministering Children." 1 vol., 12mo., with Two Eng's., $1. Of the "Ministering Children," (the author's previous work,) 50,000 copies have been sold.

*" The higher walks of life, the blessedness of doing good, and the paths of usefulness and enjoyment, are drawn out with beautiful simplicity, and made attractive and easy in the attractive pages of this author. To do good, to teach others how to do good, to render the home circle and the neighborhood glad with the voice and hand of Christian charity, is the aim of the author, who has great power of description, a genuine love for evangelical religion, and blends instruction with the story, so as to give charm to all her books."*— N. Y. OBSERVER.

# D. APPLETON & CO.'S PUBLICATIONS.

**The Handy-Book on Property Law, in a series of Letters.** By Lord St. Leonards, (Sir Edward Sugden.) 1 vol., 16mo., Cloth, 75 cents.

"*This excellent little work gives the plainest instructions in all matters connected with selling, buying, mortgaging, leasing, settling and devising estates; and informs us of our relations to our properties, our wives, our children, and our liabilities as trustees, executors, &c., &c.*"—TRIBUNE.

**The Manual of Chess;** Containing the Elementary Principles of the Game. Illustrated with numerous Diagrams, recent Games and Original Problems. By CHARLES KENNY. 1 vol. 12mo. Price 50 cents.

"*Within the compass of this work I have included all that is necessary for the beginner to learn. In recommendation of this Manual, I can safely assert that it contains more than any publication of the same dimensions. The Problems contained herein, as also one of the 'Games actually played,' are original, and have never been published.*"

**The Book of Chess;** Containing the Rudiments of the Game, and Elementary Analysis of the most Popular Openings, exemplified in games actually played by the great masters, including Staunton's Analysis of the Kings and Queens, Gambits, numerous Positions and Problems on Diagrams, both original and selected; also, a series of Chess Tales, with illustrations from original designs. The whole extracted and translated from the best sources. New Edition. By H. R. Agnel. $1.25.

**Sixty Years' Gleanings from Life's Harvest.** A Genuine Autobiography. By JOHN BROWN. 1 vol. 12mo. Cloth, $1.

"*A remarkable book in every respect, and curiously interesting from beginning to end. John Brown lived with 'all his might,' and the 'Life' he writes is, in its abundance and variety of tragic and comic ups-and-downs, as good as a play. His experiences partook of all the quick changes and boisterous bustle, and rude humor of an old English fair; and as they are presented in this volume they afford a picture of the times he lived and incessantly moved in, which, in much of its bold handling, is not to be surpassed by less spirited pencils than those of Fielding and De Foe. The moral, even as you trace it through the bustling table of contents, is of unmistakable application for every fine young fellow of sound natural principles who has to shoulder his own way to good citizenship and a share of social influence.*

"*As a neglected child, a 'juvenile offender,' an ingenious vagabond, a shoemaker, a soldier, an actor, a sailor, a publican, a billiard-room keeper, a Town Councillor, and an author, Mr. Brown has seen the world for sixty years, and he unhesitatingly describes all that he has seen, with fidelity of memory and straightforward simplicity of style.*"

www.ingramcontent.com/pod-product-compliance
Lightning Source LLC
Chambersburg PA
CBHW020309240426
43673CB00039B/753